WILD
guide

Central England
Hidden Places, Great Adventures
and the Good Life

Nikki Squires, Richard Clifford & John Webster

WILD
THINGS
PUBLISHING

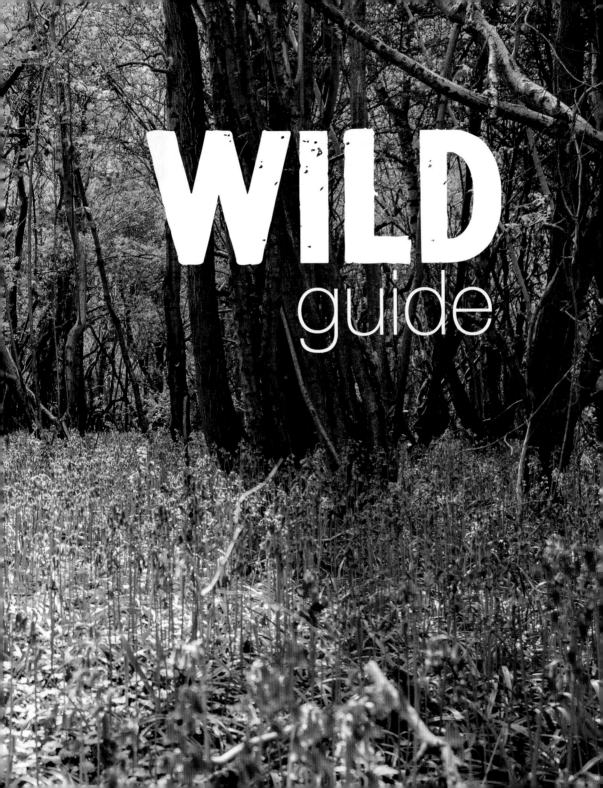

WILD
guide

Dragon Cruck, p118

Contents

Regional Overview

The Windpump, Cottingham p145

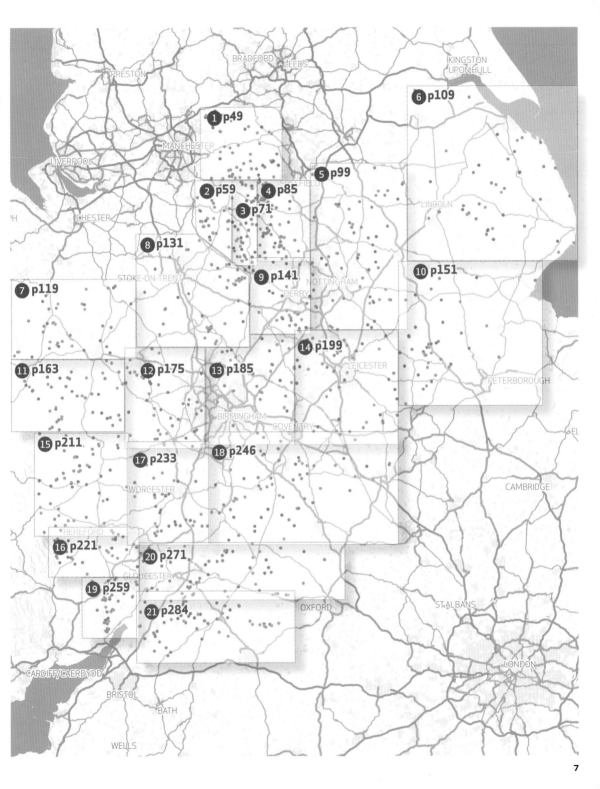

1 p49
2 p59
3 p71
4 p85
5 p99
6 p109
7 p119
8 p131
9 p141
10 p151
11 p163
12 p175
13 p185
14 p199
15 p211
16 p221
17 p233
18 p246
19 p259
20 p271
21 p284

PRESTON
BRADFORD
LEEDS
KINGSTON UPON HULL
MANCHESTER
LIVERPOOL
CHESTER
LINCOLN
STOKE-ON-TRENT
NOTTINGHAM
DERBY
LEICESTER
PETERBOROUGH
BIRMINGHAM
COVENTRY
CAMBRIDGE
WORCESTER
HEREFORD
ST.ALBANS
GLOUCESTER
OXFORD
LONDON
CARDIFF/CAERDYDD
BRISTOL
BATH
WELLS

The Brand Folly p195

Introduction

Central England has its fair share of urban conurbations, but it is also a beautiful, rural palimpsest. Here is a page upon which we can still read the traces of past human development, as its unique history is written and rewritten over time on the landscape itself. And even here, there are those special, magical places that have remained untouched for millennia, as if frozen in time.

High hills to fertile floodplains

The topography here is as diverse as you will find anywhere in Britain. Within a couple of hours you can go from climbing the rocky crags of the Peak District to picnicking in the lush, wild flower-strewn meadows of South Warwickshire. From east to west you can pass from exploring the old, marshy waterways of the flat Lincolnshire Fens to scrambling up the moody ruin of a Norman castle in the Welsh Marches or kayaking down the ancient gorges of the verdant Wye Valley.

This rich variety of landscapes is the result of vast tectonic shifts over thousands of millions of years, since Britain lay on the Equator under the warm Rheic Ocean. The millions of tiny sea creatures deposited then calcified to form the limestone bedrock of the Peaks and the classic golden stone of the Cotswolds, while the valuable coal deposits that shaped the human history of the Midlands came from swamps and rainforests in Triassic river deltas.

Historic remains

The Romans conquered a rich, fertile, forested land and made it their home for nearly 400 years. They brought with them an infrastructure that is still in evidence today: the straight roads, the legal system and the solar calendar of 365 days. They also left us the outlines of forts and remains

Pagan Oak p228

of beautifully tiled villas and baths, seen in their biggest concentrations in the Cotswolds and Herefordshire.

The Anglo-Saxon era saw tremendous growth here, and many of the pretty villages, such as Southwell in North Nottinghamshire, grew and prospered. The Normans built castles, monasteries and fortifications, most evident along the turbulent Shropshire and Herefordshire borders, their brooding presence a reminder of more troubled times. Things were more peaceful in Lincolnshire, which has few castles but the highest concentration of abbeys in England.

The 14th-century wool trade created a boom for the rural economy of Central England. Some villages disappeared as the shift to livestock farming reduced the need for labour, leaving only bumpy outlines and lonely, ruined churches, while others expanded into market towns. Trade routes were established and packhorse bridges were built, such as the pretty Goyt Valley in the Peak District and the graceful Essex Bridge in Derbyshire. The increase in movement around Central England created a need for coaching inns, many of which still exist today, and names such as The Woolpack in Slad or The Nag's Head in Malvern hark back to roots in the time of packhorse trails.

In the early 1500s, Henry VIII 'dissolved' many of the beautiful monasteries and priories, disbanding their religious orders, seizing their wealth, and selling off their buildings. Astonishingly, many remains survived this transition fairly intact, and those in Lincolnshire and North Nottinghamshire are very good examples, an impressive reminder of the importance they played in our history.

The Industrial Revolution had a huge significance in this region – in fact its epicentre was the heart of Derbyshire. Coal and iron transformed the landscape. Mines and mills sprang up, rivers were harnessed for their power, valleys rang to the sound of hammers on metal and mill wheels turning, and a layer of black soot muffled much of the once-green countryside. The soot and noise are long gone, and the canals and train lines that were built to transport goods are now disused, instead offering delightful walks and cycle routes. Sapperton Tunnel in the Cotswolds, the Monsal Trail in White Peak, and the Water Rail

Bamford Edge p77

Way in Lincolnshire are all easy to explore. Old pits from which coal, limestone or gravel were taken have been released back to nature as havens for wildlife and can be perfect for a cooling dip after a picnic on a hot summer's day.

Since ancient times humans have looked to nature, and to high places in particular, for sanctuary and peace in both life and death. The awe-inspiring tiered earthworks of Iron Age hillforts, such as British Camp in the Malverns, are testament to the power of high ground, while Neolithic tombs and barrows with celestial alignments atop stunning vistas, like Minning Low in the Dark Peak, show just how spiritually important these places were. It is incredible to think, when sitting atop the Long Mynd in Shropshire or The Roaches in the South West Peaks, that we are moved in the same way by the same enchanting panoramas over 2,000 years later.

The joy of exploring our wild places

Many of us feel that we have the wrong balance in our lives, that the pace of life is too quick, that technology leads us, and especially our children, to spend too many hours staring at a screen rather than at the real world. Maybe it is time to realign ourselves with the beauty of a sunset seen from the top of a hill that we have climbed ourselves, or a wild flower-filled meadow that we can brush with our hands while we picnic. Some things have to be felt directly: the serenity of paddling down a beautifully tranquil river, the freshness of a plunge under an ice-cold waterfall, and the deep content of sitting around a campfire, toasting marshmallows with friends and exchanging stories with our children of that time when....

We wish you many wonderful adventures!

Nikki, Richard and John

Finding your way

An overview map and directions are provided, but the latitude, longitude for each location, provided in WGS84 decimal degrees, is the definitive reference and can be entered into any online map site, such as Google, Bing or Streetmap. The latter two provide Ordnance Survey mapping overlays, which show footpaths. OpenStreetMap increasingly shows paths, too. Print out the map before you go, or save a 'screen grab'. Map apps such as ViewRanger or Memory-Map are useful, and you can also enter the co-ordinates into your smartphone GPS or car sat nav (enable 'decimal degrees'). Postcodes are provided for convenience, but only provide a rough location. If you have paper maps, look up the equivalent National Grid reference in the conversion table at the back of the book. If a parking place is mentioned, always make your own judgment and be considerate. Most places listed are on a public right of way, or on open-access land. However, some places, usually marked ⁉️, may not be. They may be private and you will need to make your own judgment about whether to proceed or seek permission from the landowner.

Where two places are named in the title, the focus of the text is always the first. Walk-in times given are one way only, allowing 15 mins per km, which is quite brisk. Abbreviations in the directions refer to left and right (L, R); north, east, south and west (N, E, S, W) and direction (dir). There are also: National Trust (NT), English Heritage (HR), Royal Society for the Protection of Birds (RSPB), National Nature Reserve (NNR), Youth Hostel Association (YHA), National Cycle Network (NCN) and Camping and Caravanning Club (CCC).

Wild & responsible

1. Fasten all gates and only climb them at the hinges.
2. Keep your dogs under close control, especially around livestock and in nature reserves.
3. Take your litter home, and gain good karma by collecting other people's.
4. If you wash in streams or rivers, use only biodegradable soap, or none at all.
5. Take special care on country roads and park considerately, to allow room for a tractor or truck.
6. Take map, compass, whistle and waterproof clothing when venturing into remote or high areas.
7. Always tell someone where you are going, and do not rely on your mobile phone.

Stiperstones p157

Best for
Wild swimming & canoeing

With water quality never better, and many inflatable crafts now available, it's a perfect time to try wild swimming, canoeing or paddleboarding. Float downstream and view the landscape at an aquatic pace.

Just because a river or lake is on a footpath or open-access land, however, doesn't mean there is a legal right to swim or canoe. Places marked with ⛱ may be used by swimmers, but there may be no official right to swim, or rights may be contested and discouraged (especially if also marked ❓). No Swimming signs are proliferating and it is for the reader to make an assessment about what is appropriate. Always be discreet, and choose a spot away from anglers, birdwatchers and boaters. If asked to leave, do so politely.

We have swum in all of the rivers and lakes in this book but it is also important to make your own safety assessment on arrival. Heavy rainfall, localised pollution and the weather can affect water quality and the risks. Above all be respectful of these delicate ecosystems and the wildlife living in them.

Be safe

1 Never swim alone, and keep a constant watch on weak swimmers.

2 Cold water can dramatically decrease swimming ability, create cold shock and cause drowning through panic. Know your limits, enter slowly and stay close to the shoreline.

3 Never jump into water unless you have thoroughly checked for depth and obstructions.

4 Avoid strong currents, such as those directly under large waterfalls or weirs, or those found in river rapids during floods: they can drag you under.

5 Always make sure you know how you will get out before you get in.

6 Wear footwear if you can.

7 Never swallow the water and avoid front crawl. Avoid direct contact with blue-green algae, and be wary of water quality in lowland areas during droughts and heavy rain. Cover cuts with plasters if worried, and if you develop flu-like symptoms tell your doctor you have been in a river.

Best for
River walks & waterfalls

As a child, I distinctly remember an outward-bound residential school trip to the Peak District. There was an exciting, hour-long river hike within a damp, mossy dale, and I was totally absorbed in the physical challenge, the adventure and the feeling of accomplishment having completed it. Most of us will have some such memory, and the feeling doesn't have to stay in your childhood.

There are numerous beautiful springs which emanate from the steep-sided valleys of Central England. There are beautiful streams and gorges to explore and scramble along. But the real jewels in the crown are the stunning waterfalls with chilling plunge pools that awaken the senses after an arduous climb up winding paths or across great river boulders. The child in everyone wonders what lies behind a waterfall, and I'd be loath to ruin the secret for those who have never found out.

Best for
Ancient & Sacred

Religion was once integral to the lives of the whole population, the length and breadth of the country. Devotion, tithes, and benefactors led to the creation of many stunning, elaborate and often quirky structures, from graceful abbeys to hidden hermitages. Centuries ago, people dedicated their lives to the pursuit of aesthetic beauty in their creations and buildings, and left a wealth of places for others to appreciate for centuries to come.

Crosses, wells, sacred stone circles, enigmatic burial mounds and hermitages ✝ carved out of the rock by hand have provided places of meeting or retreat for millennia. These can be found from the most obvious of places to the most unusual and remote, from village churches still in use to ancient refuges deep in chasms and lonely monuments high on hilltops.

Even if we personally no longer share the same beliefs as their creators, we cannot help but be moved by a moment's quiet contemplation in some of the most beautiful and sacrosanct places on earth.

Best for
Easy peaks & scrambles

Humans have always had the innate urge to climb hills and mountains. To reach the top, to conquer a summit, to feel lords of all we survey. The reward for the energetic walk up is the wonderful vantage point and perhaps the chance to enjoy a spectacular sunset ▢. Many summits have been marked over the centuries with beacons, monuments, towers and memorials, and others have dramatic natural rock formations that provide a further source of interest and adventure (e.g. The Trinnacle), or perhaps even some easy scrambling ▢.

We should remember that it was Kinder Scout, a hill in the Peaks, which was the destination for one of most successful cases of civil disobedience this century, an act of trespass by ramblers in 1932 that led to the designation of the UK's first National Park across the Peak District. The desire to climb a hill is at the heart of the access we enjoy to our open countryside in England today.

Be safe

1 On high ground be prepared for the weather to deteriorate faster than you can retreat.

2 On high ground be prepared with waterproofs, warm clothes, whistle, compass, map, torch, snacks and water. A 'group shelter' and GPS are also useful.

3 Always be prepared to turn back if you don't feel confident on a scramble or climb.

4 Many scrambles are in high and remote locations; be especially cautious on wet and windy days, when some scrambles will feel even more exposed.

5 Research the scramble route thoroughly before you leave – there is much information online.

Best for
Woods, meadows & wildlife

Our country is, perhaps surprisingly, home to 80 percent of Europe's ancient oak trees, many of them found in churchyards and around quaint, old villages. Our pockets of ancient woodland  are a living connection to bygone eras, and a stroll amongst grand, twisted oaks, magnificent beeches and stunning sweet chestnuts never fails to relieve the stresses of modern life.

They are also vital for the rich diversity of wildlife they support. Whatever we plant today will take centuries to knit up the complex, interconnected webs of life found in an ancient wood. Woodland mosaics, fields and meadows managed in a traditional, organic way all allow for wild flowers, with thriving seas of daffodils, bluebells, snowdrops, primroses, orchids, ramsons and buttercups.

These wondrous, wild habitats where nature can thrive once more are in turn places for stunning birdlife, butterflies and mammals to belong, to be appreciated, without competition from our demands. They are magical places to explore, to build dens, to climb trees, to have picnics and to reconnect with nature.

Best for
Ruins & Follies

As a nation we are spoilt for choice in the sheer number and quality of amazing buildings scattered around the country. From serious fortifications, castles and spiritual centres of worship, to works of aristocratic whimsy, there is something to see around every corner ▣.

When we first started to learn our history as children, the evocative stories of our ancestors engaged in battle over fortified lands created romantic notions of knights and heroes, further fuelled by the legends of less strictly historical figures like King Arthur and Robin Hood. Later, when we come to own homes of our own, there is perhaps a touch of envy in seeing how the other half once lived – and perhaps an intrigue into how quickly it can all slip away into ruins.

English Heritage ▣ and the National Trust ▣ do a fine job of preserving many sites, but we think the greatest joy is finding some almost-forgotten, hidden-away remnant of our past, nestled in an overgrown corner of a field or wood.

Best for
Industrial Heritage

Victorian engineering left us some of the finest structures in our architectural history. Commodities that were first exploited by the Romans were quarried, mined, processed and transported in staggering quantities, demanding a massive new infrastructure. Canals and railways, now often redundant, provide safe and interesting places to walk and cycle, keeping us attuned to this vibrant period in our history.

Many places in Central England reflect how the landscape changed when the textile and mining industries exploded into life. Places like Titterstone Clee Hill in North Herefordshire, mined since medieval times for basalt, ironstone and latterly coal, were reshaped for ever. And the modern, mill-powered factory system pioneered by Richard Arkwright in Derbyshire was copied nationally, most significantly in Shropshire, Staffordshire and Warwickshire.

With modern technology having moved on, both to new methods and to new places, many of these Industrial Revolution structures have been left dotted around our landscapes just waiting to be discovered – a mill at the side of a meandering river, a limekiln in a rugged ravine, or a crushing wheel on the quarried side of a hill that was once the site of rich seams of metal.

Be safe ▼

1 Always carry backup torches.

2 Always tell someone where you are going.

3 Always wear a helmet — a single small rockfall can kill.

4 It is dangerous to enter any mine tunnel without an experienced guide. Peer in from the outside.

5 Mine tunnels that are propped up with wood are more risky than tunnels hewn through sheer rock.

6 Rotten false floors may be concealing deep voids, which could give way at any moment. Partially flooded tunnels, with water underfoot, are somewhat safer as the void is already filled.

Best for
Picnics

We often look back on our childhoods through a very personal shade of rose-tinted spectacles, yet I'm sure most of us can recall a family picnic with relish. Food of course tastes better in beautiful surroundings, but deep down the true value at the heart of even the finest selection of savoury and sugary treats is the way that it brings a family or a group of friends to spend some slow, quality time with each other. In today's fragmented, rushed, and too-often-online world, this is ever-more paramount.

There remains, and always will do, something truly magical about sharing a feast bathed in sunshine, with the people you love, sequestered away in a secluded place, along a lush riverbank or inside an atmospheric ruin ⛩.

We visit these places because we recognise their beauty, so please, always take your rubbish home with you. If others have been less careful, gain some good karma and take theirs, too.

Best for
Slow food & drink

From the Vale of Belvoir and its world-renowned, pungent, blue cheeses to ancient Herefordshire cider orchards, travelling in Central England today offers an incredible adventure in both food 🍴 and drink 🍷. Whether you fancy a well-hung, rare-breed, grass-fed steak treat, an organic sourdough loaf or some freshly-picked strawberries for your picnic feast, you'll find a delightful array of farm shops, micro-breweries, delis and village shops waiting to tempt you away from the supermarkets.

Eating locally and seasonally not only gives us a real taste of the local culture and traditions of the region, but also supports the craft producers and farmers, and their heritage breeds – both animal and vegetable. The farm shops and village shops and their cafés are now important hubs for many rural communities and offer a warm welcome to visitors.

For something more indulgent head to one of the many fantastic gastropubs, where you can feast on the best local produce cooked to perfection by renowned chefs.

Our food choices have a huge consequence on our environment, so choose your fare thoughtfully and the rewards will be manifold.

...S TO THE KINGS ARMS

...GILL
...N FARM (8M)
LONGHORN BEEF
...SHLEY TUPP LAMB

GWILYM & ALEX (12M)
ROSE VEAL
MUTTON
LAMB

... HONEY (9M)

HECKINGTON

To CRAIG... G...

PARKS FARM
ASPARAGUS (42M)

• STAMFORD ORGANIC APPLE JUICE
• JOLLY DALE CIDER

BOURNE

PETERBOROUGH GAME 26M

A1

...NE

...HAMBLE

EMPINGHAM

MARKET DEEPING

To THORNHAM
THORNHAM
& LANCASHIRE MUSSE...
(75...

STAMFORD

...KHAM
...GLEFON
HAMBLETON
RUTLAND WATER
MANTON

...NGHAM
WING
...PXTON

...NGHAM

T&J FINE FOODS
DRY STORES
(13M)

GRASMERE FARMS
PORK (21M)

...GLOUCESTER

ROCKINGHAM

MANTON P.Y.O
BERRIES / ASPARAGUS (2M)

PILTON
LESLEY & MALCOLM AT FOX COVERT FARM (1 MILE)
MANGALITSA PIGS

OAKHAM - GRAINSTORE BREWERY (5M)
     - STEVE BYRNE - FRESH VEGETABLES (6M)
     - GRAHAM - RUTLAND CATERING
     - ROB & ADRIAN SALT - G.S WELDING - METAL WORK

GS - BOB & JOY JEXNES

Best for
Cosy pubs

After a morning spent adventuring in secluded woodlands or an afternoon jumping into a remote river, there is nothing that quite beats a locally brewed pint in friendly and relaxed surroundings. And some of our favourites are the ones that have stood the test of a very long time ◘.

All a pub really needs, apart from what is in your glass, is a table around which people sit and talk, sharing stories and perhaps some food. It is one of the very few places where people from all walks of life sit on the same, equal terms. It is not about the decor, the food or Michelin star ratings. It is about people.

Many pubs have become soulless, formulaic and corporately whitewashed over the decades, and between taxes, drink-driving, the smoking ban and supermarket deals, recent years have been particularly difficult. But if you know where to look, some old gems still remain – cider houses, parlour pubs and unspoilt historic inns all bound by the same welcoming, unfussy charm that makes every visitor's heart glow.

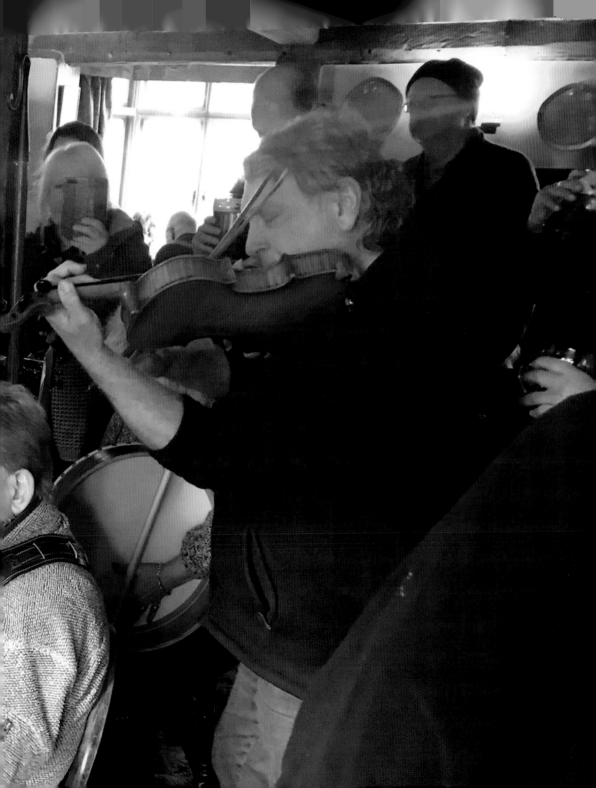

Best for
Camp & sleep

There is a certain triumph in finding a place to rest your head at the end of the day, without neighbours or a bill to pay in the morning, and it is always exciting to find a place to wild camp responsibly (■ marks places we have bivouacked, though you will need to make your own judgements). However, wild camping is not always legal or practical, and the next best thing is a back-to-basics camping field with a super ▲ location, campfires ◢ and perhaps even a wood-fired pizza oven .

For special occasions, or when the weather makes pitching your tent seem purgatorial, rent a wriggly tin chapel in the woods in the Shropshire Hills, try 'champing', camping in a church, or snuggle down in a real gypsy caravan, shepherds' hut, tree house or even a converted helicopter ◿. For more luxury and space there are castles, handmade oak cabins and idyllic cottages to rent – each of them charming, full of character and still giving a sense of sleeping close to the wild.

Wild camping

1 Camp above the highest fell wall, well away from towns and villages.

2 Leave no litter, remove other people's, and don't bury litter.

3 Do not light any fires, even if there's evidence that fires may have been lit by others.

4 Stay for only one night.

5 Keep groups very small – only one or two tents.

6 Camp as unobtrusively as possible, with inconspicuous tents that blend into the landscape.

7 Take away tampons and sanitary towels; burying them doesn't work, as animals dig them up again.

8 Perform toilet duties at least 30m (100ft) from water, and bury the results with a trowel.

HIGH PEAK

Our perfect weekend

→ **Take** a stroll across Torrs Gorge on the dramatic Millennium Walkway and then relax with an ice cream at Grandpa Greene's.

→ **Cool** off under cascades of water as you ascend the valley to Kinder Downfall, then take a walk to the Woolpacks on Kinder Scout plateau and view the falls from above.

→ **Trek** to the tragic aircraft remnants and strange Kissing Stones atop Bleaklow to work up an appetite for local ales and hearty fare at The Beehive in Glossop.

→ **Feel** like you're on top of the world on the Trinnacle pillar before descending the delightful series of falls in the Greenfield Brook Valley.

→ **Marvel** at the works of nature and industry at Pule Hill Arch, then quench your thirst at Riverhead Brewery Tap in Marsden.

→ **Refresh** your tired limbs in the natural spring of Fair Nook and buy dry-aged beef from J Brindon Addy's for a campsite BBQ at Uppergate Farm.

→ **Jump** into the Derwent with the family at Slippery Stones after seeking out the natural 'fortresses' of Alport Castles.

High Peak conjures up a rugged, uninhabited, windswept moorland, a wild and sometimes bleak landscape befitting of a brooding Byronic hero on horseback. But on a sunny day, this high-plateau area of the wider Dark Peak region offers breathtaking views from the summit of many 'lows', from the Old English hlaw, meaning hill.

Bleaklow is the second-highest hill in the Peaks, marked at its summit with a stone cairn, but more interesting are the wind-whipped Wain or Kissing Stones nearby. The remains of a reconnaissance plane are also strewn quite close, from a crash in 1948. You will need a sturdy pair of walking boots and an OS map for many of these places, as they are remote and the weather can change within minutes.

Joined by a neck of gritstone is Bleaklow's sister, Kinder Scout, site of a mass trespass in 1932, campaigning for access to the countryside for ordinary people. The famous Kinder Downfall is the highest waterfall in the Peaks – on a windy day the water appears to flow back up, and it is known to freeze during particularly harsh winters. For a different perspective, try walking up the Kinder River from the reservoir and enjoy a pretty valley walk with pools and mini-waterfalls. Atop the plateau are the beautiful, wind-carved Woolpacks, huge gritstone boulders offering the perfect refuge for a picnic or a bit of bouldering with older kids.

Further north are a number of stunning waterfalls, some of which are easily accessible. Wildboar Crux is quite a scramble up the often dry lower section, but rewards your efforts with a secluded cascade of refreshing and beautiful plunge pools. For children, Middle Black Clough is a glorious walk up the river, with various points along the way to paddle and enjoy the water. Further up is a ledge to stand on under the tumbling water. Wessenden Falls is a secret, hidden away behind a mass of rhododendron bushes: secluded, cold, perfect.

Over to the east, the Derwent Valley houses the triple reservoirs of Howden, Upper Derwent and Ladybower. The young Derwent River that feeds these is a playful, bubbling brook at the Slippery Stones, once a treacherous packhorse crossing. It now offers hours of fun as a great spot to jump into one of the many deep, peaty pools.

The lack of light pollution in these areas means stargazing here is easy, under canvas at Orchard Camping or Fieldhead Campsite in Edale. Alternatively, sling up a hammock between two trees, listen to the skylarks spiralling their song down from up high, and watch the stars start to twinkle as the sun goes down.

PLUNGE POOLS

1 FAIR NOOK SPRING

A sliver of aquamarine, crystal-clear, refreshing water awaits visitors to this spring-filled quarry. Leave it tidier than you find it, to help others enjoy it.

→ Take Wessenden Head Rd SW out of Meltham for 1½ miles, past HD9 4HW. Pull off near gate of old quarry road at 53.5795, -1.8747. Follow road for 300m to disused building and turn L onto track before it. Follow 400m looking out for a trail on L through bushes down to water. Alternative scenic walk 1 mile along Royd Edge ridge from end of Calmlands Rd in Meltham (HD9 4HQ).

20 mins, 53.5800, -1.8706 🏊🚙❓🏕🚗🚐🔆

2 SLIPPERY STONES

A pretty stretch of the young Derwent River with grassy banks and a deep pool, perfect for jumps, leaps and somersaults. Water crystal clear, but tinted brown from the peat, and some claim it's fizzy like Cola.

→ From A57 8 miles W of Sheffield take road signed Derwent Valley Dams. If possible, follow 7½ miles to head of Howden Reservoir (past S33 0BB) and park at end. Walk about a mile upstream to pool 300m above footbridge. At weekends, car access restricted to Fairholmes car park after 2½ miles – bring a bike for the rest!

25 mins, 53.4546, -1.7470 🏊🚙🚶🚐🚗

3 MERMAID'S POOL, KINDER SCOUT

If you're here early enough to look into the water at sunrise on Easter Sunday you may see the mermaid who promises immortality. Otherwise, just jump in and have a swim!

→ Park and walk around Kinder Reservoir and up the river as for Kinder Downfall waterfall (see entry). Immediately after the woods on N bank (around 53.3925, -1.8909) look for a path L up hill to the pool. OS map and walking boots essential.

90 mins, 53.3948, -1.8895 🏊🏔🚶🚗🔆

FABULOUS FALLS

4 KINDER DOWNFALL

The tallest waterfall in the Peak District, this can be a tiny trickle in summer, while in wet and windy conditions the water is often blown back up to create an impressive spray, visible for miles around. Walk up from the reservoir to enjoy pools and falls along the way, and for a longer walk take in the Mermaid's Pool (see entry).

→ Park at Bowden Bridge car park E of Hayfield on Kinder Rd (SK22 2LH). Follow Kinder Rd on to reservoir, straight ahead through gate at entrance, keeping reservoir to your R until you reach bridge over Kinder River at far end. Follow the riverside path – under 2 miles, but uphill. OS map and walking boots recommended.

90 mins, 53.3970, -1.8771 🏊🚙🚶🏔🚗🔆

5 BLACKDEN BROOK WATERFALL

Walk beside, or if you are more adventurous scramble up, a series of small waterfalls that make up the infinitely pretty Blackden Brook. Shallows for paddling and deep pools for plunging provide something for everyone in this tranquil location.

→ Take A57 E out of Glossop for 7¼ miles after passing Royal Oak pub (SK13 8QY) and park in large lay-by R (53.4022, -1.8050). Take signed path S 500m, over river to wall corner. Follow wall for ½ mile until it ends, then take path W down to brook, and 200m S to find larger falls.

30 mins, 53.3958, -1.8103 🏊🚙

6 THE CRUX, WILDBOAR CLOUGH

Take the meandering path through twisted trees and then scramble up to the seclusion of this waterfall and plunge pool.

→ Take Woodhead Rd/B6105 N out of Glossop about 3½ miles, to park after SK13 1JF at Torside pay car park by reservoir. Walk up to cycle path and follow L 300m, then take signed path for Wildboar Clough R. Follow footpath about 1 mile through woods and up rocky gorge to waterfall.

60 mins, 53.4785, -1.8809

7 FAIRBROOK WATERFALL

Small meadows, purple heather, shady trees, and cascading small waterfalls on a remote but easy walk, ideal for families.

→ Take A57 E out of Glossop for 7 miles after passing Royal Oak pub (SK13 8QY) and park in lay-by (53.4098, -1.8295). Follow road on S 400m taking path R down and over stream via stepping stones. Continue W for 500m to falls.

20 mins, 53.4059, -1.8368

8 WESSENDEN FALLS

Truly magical, secret waterfall hidden behind a sea of rhododendrons. Picnic, then skinny-dip in the plunge pool. Blake Clough waterfall nearby is also worth a look.

→ Head S out of Marsden along Binn Rd just past HD7 6HQ and park in lay-by R at head of track to reservoirs. Walk down track 1½ miles to lay-by on R opposite farmhouse (53.5758,

-1.9176). Head down hill from lay-by to R, across stream, under the rhododendrons to pool. Blake Clough waterfall at 53.5728, -1.9252.

45 mins, 53.5751, -1.9181

9 GREENFIELD WATERFALL

Delightful cascades and natural infinity pools make this an unforgettable walk. Plenty of secluded spots for the adventurous – you can continue up for the most limber to climb the Trinnacle rock (see entry).

→ Take A635 E out of Greenfield 1¼ miles to Binn Green RSPB car park at OL3 7NN. Follow track down to dam and turn L onto main footpath. Walk for 1½ miles past 2 reservoirs and turn R up Greenfield Brook gorge at weir. Continue up and cross river for Trinnacle.

45 mins, 53.5394, -1.9431

10 MIDDLE BLACK CLOUGH

A beautiful scramble up the side of a waterfall suitable for all the family, with dipping pools and paddling all the way up. Take a picnic and make a day of it.

→ On A628 NE of Glossop, 2 miles E of junction with A6024, turn down slip road opp lay-by to car park for Three Black Cloughs (SK13 1JE). Follow path ⅛ mile with Etherow River on your L. Just after steep path to R, and

small clearing in trees, the path crosses the river. Keep following with river now to R as you head uphill to falls.

60 mins, 53.4876, -1.8263 ⛴🥾🚶🏕🏞🚲

LAKES & RESERVOIRS

11 HOWDEN DAM

Impressive dam designed for the water to cascade over the top. Famous as the site where the RAF Dambusters practised before heading to Germany. Continue upriver to swim at the Slippery Stones (see entry).

→ From A57 8 miles W of Sheffield take turning signed Derwent Valley Dams (dir S33 0BB). Park at Fairholmes car park and walk or cycle on 2½ miles.

50 mins, 53.4285, -1.7470 🚶🚲

12 TORSIDE RESERVOIR OVERSPILL

Visit this uniquely curved piece of Victorian engineering after heavy rainfall to see the full majesty of the water cascading over the top into the channel.

→ Take Woodhead Rd/B6105 N out of Glossop about 3½ miles, to park after SK13 1JF at Torside pay car park by reservoir. Footpath around reservoir.

2 mins, 53.4827, -1.9169 🚶

13 LANGSETT RESERVOIR

A beautifully peaceful, wooded reservoir with many paths for gentle strolls and peaty but clear water. No Swimming signs. Red grouse nest up on the moor, where there are longer walks.

→ From A616 at Langsett (S36 4GY) turn signed Strines and Derwent Valley and follow 1 mile, bending R at Midhope Lane, to park at end of barred track/road on sharp L bend. Walk down track and head R at water.

15 mins, 53.4931, -1.6859 ⛴❓🚶➕

14 AGDEN RESERVOIR

A beautiful, tree-lined reservoir with crystal-clear water and various walks around it. No swimming signs.

→ Head W out of Low Bradfield (S6 6LB) from cricket club and take first R signed Strines. Follow ½ mile to park on R in lay-by after bend. Path around water just over wall.

5 mins, 53.4297, -1.6144 ⛴❓🚶

15 DARK PEAK THREE RESERVOIRS CYCLE

Fantastic opportunity to see all three reservoirs and cycle as a family through beautiful surroundings. National Trust website has details and maps; cycle hire at Fairholmes Visitor Centre.

→ Follow signs to Fairholmes car park as for Howden Dam (see entry). Derwent Cycle Hire 01433 651261.
1 min 53.4002 -1.7412

ANCIENT & SACRED

16 JACOB'S LADDER

Just beside a beautiful little packhorse bridge, the Pennine Way splits into the famously steep Jacob's Ladder and a longer, shallower path. A substantial cairn marks where they rejoin at the top of the rise. Walk on to the Edale Cross (see entry).

→ From Barber Booth (S33 7ZL) head W ½ mile to parking area L. Walk back and take path by railway bridge L to join Pennine Way. Follow 2 miles, past Highfield Farm Campsite and Upper Booth Farm. OS map recommended.
40 mins, 53.3722, -1.8688

17 EDALE CROSS

A medieval wayside cross made of local gritstone marking a parish boundary. Found in the peat by farmers in 1810 and re-erected, though without the base it probably once had.

→ Park and walk to the cairn atop Jacob's Ladder (see entry). Walk on ⅔ mile to find the cross resting against the wall on the R.
60 mins, 53.3716, -1.8853

RUINS & FOLLIES

18 TORRS GORGE, MILLENNIUM WALKWAY

A fascinating marriage of heritage and geology at the point where the power of the Goyt and Sett rivers has been harnessed for over 200 years. Old cobbled paths, mill ruins, weirs and imposing bridges are all found along this part of the Midshires Way.

→ Park in Rock Mill Lane (53.3654, -2.0024) in New Mills, follow steps down to river. Other access points along the Way for longer walks.
5 mins, 53.3646, -2.0021

19 BOOT'S FOLLY

Constructed in the 1920s so that Charles Boot could see the graveyard at High Bradfield, where his wife was buried. Now derelict; the spiral staircase was taken out after a cow got stuck halfway up it.

→ To walk from Strines Reservoir, park in small pull-off by signed bridleway on road from Low Bradfield along the N side (53.4143, -1.6598). Walk down and around L to join Sheffield Country Walk heading S.
20 mins, 53.4055, -1.6549

ROCK FORMATIONS

20 ALPORT CASTLES

Considered to be the result of the largest landslide in the UK, these natural 'castles' are stacks of gritstone rock that take on the appearance of motte and bailey forts. Delightful.

→ Follow A57 for 8 miles E from Glossop dir S33 0BJ. There is room for one car beside NT Hayridge Farm sign on A57, one more in turning R 350m further just before bridge. Take marked path N from bridge to Alport Castles Farm, then footpath to R uphill to the castles.
40 mins, 53.4196, -1.7892 🖼️

21 PULE HILL ARCH, MARSDEN

Formed by natural weathering, this archway is a fascinating reward for a climb up Pule Hill, past ventilation shafts for the railway tunnel below and remains of quarry workings. Seek out the poem carved here, part of the Stanza Stones project.

→ Take A62 E out of Marsden for 2 miles, to HD7 6NL, and park in lay-by L shortly after (53.5945, -1.9573). Climb over stile and up to disused incline. At summit turn R and carefully drop down to the arch.
20 mins, 53.5939, -1.9535 🖼️🚶🏻🏞️

22 THE WOOLPACKS, KINDER SCOUT

At the top of Kinder Scout, these gritstone boulders have been sculpted by the wind and rain into fantastical shapes. Stunning views over the Edale Valley, the perfect place to rest, picnic and have a bit of bouldering fun.

→ From Edale pay car park (S33 7ZQ), walk N through village to start of Pennine Way. L opp school. Keep R signed Grindslow Knoll after 400m for summit and along brow to rocks, 2⅓ miles. OS map and walking boots essential. An alternative route up Crowden Brook from Upper Booth Farm makes an interesting scramble. Other routes via the venerable Jacob's Ladder staircase (see entry) on OS map.
90 mins, 53.3795, -1.8643 🖼️🍴🏕️🚴

23 SALT CELLAR, DERWENT EDGE

A collection of wind-sculpted gritstone tors accompanies the outstanding vista here, including the Cakes of Bread and Coach and Horses, but most prominent is the Salt Cellar.

→ Follow footpath behind Ladybower Inn (S33 0AX, see listing) W 300m and take R fork. Continue for 2¼ miles, going straight over two crossings along the way and passing Coach and Horses. Cakes of Bread are ½ mile further.
50 mins, 53.3996, -1.7067 🚴🚶🏻🏕️

24 THE TRINNACLE, SADDLEWORTH MOOR

Stand bravely atop this dramatic triple pillar and survey the stunning valley and reservoirs. Can be combined with Greenfield waterfall (see entry) in a circular walk.

➔ Park and start walk as for Greenfield Waterfall, but take track R across Yeoman Hey Reservoir dam and then path up hill L after cattle grid. At top turn L past memorial cross and along brow ridge (1 mile) or across plateau (¾ mile) to Trinnacle. Use GPS for exact location. Can continue on to river and descend past waterfall.

60 mins, 53.5399, -1.9460 📷🚶

25 KISSING STONES, BLEAKLOW

Bleaklow is a stunning gritstone moorland, situated 600m above sea level and the source of the Derwent River. This strangely profiled pair of stones, which are best viewed from their western side, are marked Wain Stones on OS maps. Nearby you will find the haunting site of a Superfortress aircraft crash that occurred in 1948.

➔ Take the A57 E of Glossop for 3½ miles after passing Royal Oak pub (SK13 8QY) and park in long lay-by L where Pennine Way crosses. Take the Pennine Way N and follow it uphill for 1¾ miles, look for paths L to the stones. The crash site is at 53.4509, -1.8647. OS map, walking boots and all-weather clothing essential.

90 mins, 53.4597, -1.8644 📷➕🚶

26 BUCKSTONES, MARSDEN MOOR

Superb panoramic views from this vast and rolling moor across the Upper Colne Valley, once a hive of activity during the Industrial Revolution.

➔ Follow the A640 out of Huddersfield (HD3 3FT) for 6 miles to Marsden View car park L opp junction with B6114. Walk S to Buckstones; can continue down to March Haigh Reservoir.

5 mins, 53.6174, -1.9760 🚶📷

MAGICAL MEADOWS

27 CARR HOUSE MEADOWS

Overlooking the Ewden Valley, this delightful wild flower-laden hillside is a perfect romantic picnic location along a narrow, stone-walled country lane.

➔ Park in Wharncliffe Side (SE5 0DD) and walk W on Brightholmlee Road for 1 mile to stile L into reserve.

20 mins, 53.4541, -1.5760 🌼🐕🏕🚶

SLOW FOOD

28 THE STRINES INN

Traditional country pub serving hearty food, including their famous home-made pies. Incredible views from the garden.

→ Mortimer Road, Bradfield Dale, S6 6JE, 0114 2851247.
53.4118, -1.6667

29 J BRINDON ADDY

This excellent food hall was built up from a stall beside the road, and master butcher Brindon speaks with passion about the local livestock farms where he sources his meat. The dry-aged beef is simply sublime.

→ Penistone Road, Hade Edge, HD9 2JG, 01484 682897.
53.5475, -1.7790

30 GRANDPA GREENE'S LUXURY ICE CREAM

Fabulous, creamy ice creams in a gorgeous canalside setting. Breakfast, brunch, lunch and coffee and cakes all made using local produce also served

→ Ward Lane, Diggle, OL3 5JT, 01457 872547.
53.5647, -1.9969

31 BRADFIELD BREWERY

Family-run brewery and onsite shop on a working farm with tremendous views. Traditional hops and malts produce a range of award-winning craft ales.

→ Watt House Farm, High Bradfield, S6 6LG, 0114 2851118.
53.4268, -1.5957

32 YUMMY YORKSHIRE/HIDE & HOOF

An ice cream parlour with a farm restaurant upstairs: the names say it all. Heart-warming local producer bringing people together.

→ Delph House Farm, Denby Dale, HD8 8XY, 01226 762551.
53.5554, -1.6727

33 THE SCHOOLROOMS, LOW BRADFIELD

Quaint tearooms with deli and gift shop, situated opposite the local cricket pitch. Serves fabulous cream teas and Sheffield vodka.

→ Mill Lee Road, Low Bradfield, S6 6LB, 0114 2851920.
53.4229, -1.6068

34 LADYBOWER INN, HOPE VALLEY

18th-century coaching inn that once served as a morgue and was the local for the Dambusters practising on the reservoir next door. Cosy booths, open fires, and locally sourced food – trout comes from the reservoir.

→ Ladybower, Bamford, S33 0AX, 01433 651241.
53.3750, -1.6942 ▣▣▣

35 RIVERHEAD BREWERY TAP, MARSDEN

Characterful pub with onsite brewery in a charming village. Ten hand-drawn ales to try.

→ 2 Peel St, Marsden, HD7 6BR, 01484 844324.
53.6013, -1.9274 ▣▣

36 THE BEEHIVE, GLOSSOP

Quaint, little backstreet village pub serving fine local ales alongside highly praised English, Thai, and vegan food.

→ 35 Hague Street, Glossop, SK13 8NR, 01457 858230.
53.4364, -1.9456 ▣▣

37 THE JUNCTION INN, DENSHAW

Lovely example of an old 'posting' or coaching inn at the point where five roads meet. Excellent Manchester ales and home-cooked food.

→ 2 Rochdale Road, Denshaw, OL3 5SE, 01457 874265.
53.5922, -2.0401 ▣▣

38 NAG'S HEAD INN, LOXLEY

Recently refurbished pub, the flagship establishment of the local Bradfield Brewery (see listing).

→ Stacey Bank, Loxley, S6 6SJ, 0114 2851202.
53.4116, -1.5669 ▣▣

39 THE CHURCH INN, UPPERMILL

Home to Saddleworth Brewery and with a Georgian church next door, this historic hostelry has charms to tempt most travellers.

→ Running Hill Gate, Uppermill, OL3 6LW, 01457 820902.
53.5537, -1.9901 ▣▣

40 OLD HORNS INN, HIGH BRADFIELD

Glorious views over the valley from the garden. Good quality, home-cooked food; try the burgers for a real treat.

→ Town Gate, High Bradfield, S6 6LG, 0114 2851207.
53.4286, -1.5980 ▣

41 HAYFIELD VIEW, CAMPING BARN

Beautifully restored little barn for 2–4, with stunning views over the Peaks.

→ Chinley Moor House, Chapel Road, Hayfield, SK22 2JS, 01663 744291.
53.3632, -1.9286 ▣▣

42 PEAK VIEW SHEPHERD HUTS

Four luxury shepherds' huts, with wood-fired hot tubs.

→ Woodhead Road, Glossop, SK13 7QE, 07508 363918.
53.4621, -1.9439 ▣

43 HADDY'S HUT, OAKER FARM

Spacious, handcrafted shepherds' hut nestled into the corner of a farm in the Hope Valley

→ Lose Hill Lane, off Edale Road, Hope, S33 6AF, 01433 621955.
53.3659, -1.7564 ▣

44 UPPERGATE FARM

Luxurious yurts and cottages located on the village edge in the stunning Pennines.

→ Upper Gate, Hepworth, HD9 1TG, 01484 681369.
53.5574, -1.7569 ▣▣

45 ORCHARD CAMPING, PENISTONE

Small, family-run campsite with just six pitches and space for one camper van, in open country on edge of Pennines.

→ Halifax Road, Penistone, S36 7EY, 01226 762889.
53.5367, -1.6224 ▣

46 HIGH LEA FARM CAMPING

Basic, family-run campsite close to the Trans Pennine Trail.

→ Steep Lane, Hoylandswaine, S36 8JQ, 01226 762531.
53.5297, -1.6092 ▣▣

47 FIELDHEAD CAMPSITE

A small, quiet campsite within walking distance of Edale station. The perfect base for walking the area.

→ Edale, S33 7ZA, 01433 670386.
53.3672, -1.8149 ▣▣▣

48 THE MOORLANDS, SADDLEWORTH

Glamping pods with stunning views over the moors and reservoirs.

→ Ripponden Road, Denshaw, OL3 5UN, 01457 874348.
53.5988, -2.0366 🏕🔥

49 THE HOLIDAY POD, PENISTONE
Delightful camping pod with BBQ and hot tub perched atop a hill overlooking the moors.
→ Middlecliffe Lane, Millhouse Green, S36 9NT, 07486 915356.
53.5328, -1.7004 🏕☢🎯

50 UPPER BOOTH CAMPING
Campsite and camping barn on award-winning working farm, with limited wifi and phone signal. A real getaway site, perfect for Pennine Way adventures. Glorious views in every direction. Closed in winter.
→ Edale, S33 7ZJ, 01422 670250.
53.3647, -1.8470 ⛺

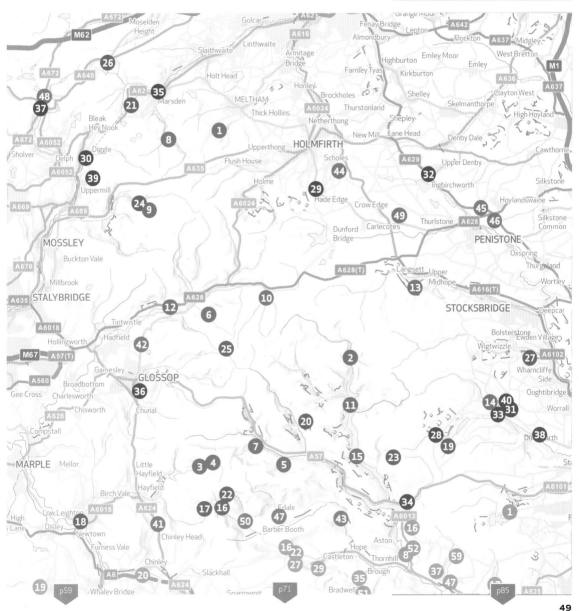

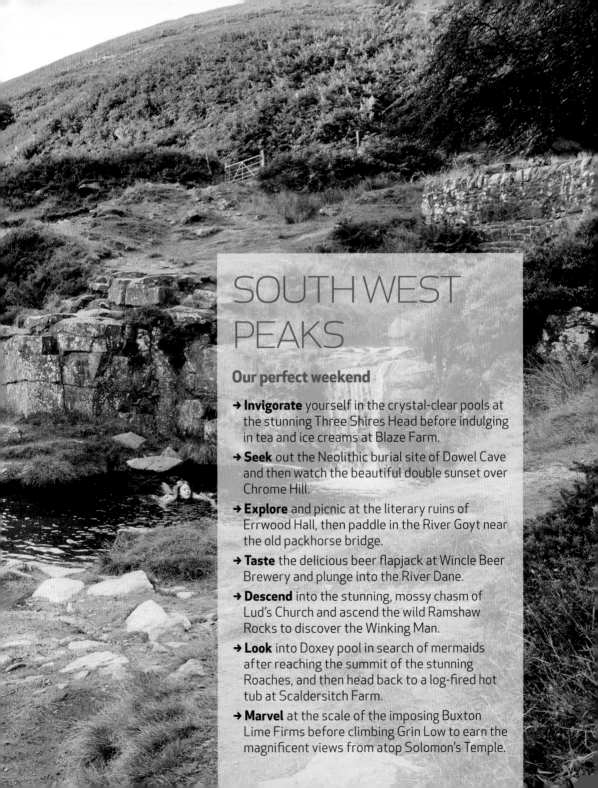

SOUTH WEST PEAKS

Our perfect weekend

→ **Invigorate** yourself in the crystal-clear pools at the stunning Three Shires Head before indulging in tea and ice creams at Blaze Farm.

→ **Seek** out the Neolithic burial site of Dowel Cave and then watch the beautiful double sunset over Chrome Hill.

→ **Explore** and picnic at the literary ruins of Errwood Hall, then paddle in the River Goyt near the old packhorse bridge.

→ **Taste** the delicious beer flapjack at Wincle Beer Brewery and plunge into the River Dane.

→ **Descend** into the stunning, mossy chasm of Lud's Church and ascend the wild Ramshaw Rocks to discover the Winking Man.

→ **Look** into Doxey pool in search of mermaids after reaching the summit of the stunning Roaches, and then head back to a log-fired hot tub at Scaldersitch Farm.

→ **Marvel** at the scale of the imposing Buxton Lime Firms before climbing Grin Low to earn the magnificent views from atop Solomon's Temple.

The South West Peaks are a breathtaking combination of rocky ridges, ancient, weather-worn crags and undulating pastures. Ideal landscapes for walking, cycling, trekking and climbing, they are full of character, stunning vistas, and charming villages.

The heather-covered hills of the Staffordshire Moorlands dominate the area to the south. They are a place of myths, legends and awe-inspiring panoramas. The Roaches and the Ramshaw Rocks, just to the north of Tittesworth Reservoir, are a wind-carved gritstone ridge line, formed by an inland lake 300 million years ago. Winking Man Rock, which appears to wink as you pass below it, is a short scramble from the main path along the Ramshaws, while the Roaches, loved by walkers and climbers alike, afford glorious views from above over the Tittesworth Valley, and are home to peregrines and red grouse. A night spent in the Don Whillans Memorial Hut, partly hewn out of the rock, is an amazing finale to a day out exploring for signed-up climbers.

Atop The Roaches, Doxey Pool is rumoured to house Jenny Greenteeth, a mermaid who tempts passers-by to a watery death. Further north is the magnificent Lud's Church, a moss-clad gritstone chasm formed by a huge landslip many years ago, into which the sun shines directly on Midsummer's Day. Among the legends that are attached to this place is one that the Lollards, followers of the Bible translator John Wycliffe, worshipped here in secret. It has also been suggested as the Green Chapel setting of the medieval poem 'Sir Gawain and the Green Knight'. These stories only add to the mystery and atmosphere of the beautiful, fern-clad fissure.

The Industrial Revolution played its role in this area, which has been mined since the Bronze Age, with extensive extraction of lead, zinc and copper. The deepest mine in Britain was once here, at the rugged Ecton Hill, but a more visible and fascinating remnant from this era is the workings of the Buxton Lime Firms. These surprisingly grand architectural structures lie at the end of an unassuming track.

Watery delights of various kinds can be found in the area. The most stunning of these is at Three Shires Head, the meeting point of three counties on the River Dane. Against the backdrop of a beautiful, 18th-century packhorse bridge are the bracing Panniers Pool, waterfalls, and heathery purple banks, perfect for a picnic. Downstream at Wincle, the Dane winds a wider path through the valley under the dappled shade of trees. There are secluded beaches with easy access to the water, perfect for all the family.

RIVER ADVENTURES

1 PANNIERS POOL, THREE SHIRE HEADS

Situated at the point on Axe Edge Moor where the counties of Cheshire, Derbyshire and Staffordshire meet, a picture-perfect pair of packhorse bridges are the backdrop for a series of delightful pools and waterfalls. Ideal for a cooling dip after a warming walk.

→ Head NE on A54 from Allgreave (SK11 0BJ) for 2½ mile and park in lay-by L. Walk on 200m to signed footpath over stile R and follow path SE to water and then downstream to bridges. ¾ mile in all.

30 mins, 53.2137, -1.9874 🏊🚶🏕🚶🏔🏕🏕

2 WINCLE, RIVER DANE

Enjoy a swim against the current in one of the deeper pools at the bend of this picturesque section of the River Dane. After your dip reward yourself with a visit to the nearby Wincle Brewery (see listing).

→ In Wincle village (SK11 0QE) follow road E and park on L just before bridge. Walk over bridge and follow footpath to L. Path down to river after 200m.

5 mins, 53.1841, -2.0525 🏊🏕🍴

3 WILDBOARCLOUGH, CLOUGH BROOK

Picnic, plunge and paddle amongst the flat rocks in this delightful stretch of the dappled Clough Brook.

→ Head N into Wildboarclough on Nabbs Rd, SK11 0BD, past the Crag Inn (01260 227239) and park 150m further up in lay-by on L opposite bridge. Walk back down to the little wooden bridge on L just before the pub.

1 min, 53.2141, -2.0276 🏊🏕🚶🍴

4 PACKHORSE BRIDGE, RIVER GOYT

Take a river walk in this impossibly beautiful valley, maybe with a stop at Errwood Hall ruins (see entry). Start at the delightful packhorse bridge and follow the bubbling, rocky stream downhill to find many picnic and plunge spots.

→ On A5004 N out of Buxton, take unsigned L to Goyt Valley after 1½ miles, follow 1½ miles and cross Errwood Reservoir dam (SK17 6GJ). Turn L and follow 1½ miles to second parking L (stop at first parking to visit ruins), beyond reservoir. Follow path down into valley to bridge. One way road: drive out to S.

15 mins, 53.2563, -1.9820 🏊🚶🏕🍴

LAKES & RESERVOIRS

5 TEGG'S NOSE COUNTRY PARK

Stunning parkland featuring beautiful green rolling hills on one side and a view across the Cheshire Plain with Jodrell Bank radio telescope on the other. There are four reservoirs to explore in this area. No Swimming signs, and anglers.

→ From A537 E out of Macclesfield turn R after 2 miles, signed Tegg's Nose (dir SK11 0AP). Pay car park L after ½ mile. Follow the Saddler's Way down to reservoirs. Alternatively avoid hills by starting at the Leather's Smithy pub (SK11 0NE, see listing).

30 mins, 53.2442, -2.0791 🏕🚶

6 TITTESWORTH RESERVOIR

A popular place for walkers, cyclists and birdwatchers. Numerous beach-like areas ideal for a paddle, but No Swimming signs. Exercise discretion.

→ Head E from The Lazy Trout in Meerbrook (ST13 8SN, see listing) and turn R into entrance just after dam to pay car park. Follow footpath around woodland area and past the second inlet to quieter areas.

15 mins, 53.1333, -2.0108 🏊🚴🏕❓🚶

ROCKS & CAVES

7 THE ROACHES
Delightful gritstone ridge popular with walkers and climbers alike. Scale the ridge to dip into the peat-dark pool known as Doxey Pool, which legend says is home to a murderous mermaid.

→ From Upper Hulme follow Roach Rd NW to lay-by R after 1 mile (after ST13 8UA). Follow track and footpath up to the L.

20 mins, 53.1596, -1.9931 🔳🏊🔻🐾🐕🔳🧗

8 WINKING MAN, RAMSHAW ROCKS
Fascinating holed rock formation 'winks' at passing drivers heading north on a fast stretch of road – worth seeing close up.

→ The rocks are to L of A53 heading N from Leek, after 3½ miles. Take L at house just before them and park in lay-by L around bend. Walk across the heath under the rocks parallel with the A53; also path along tops.

15 mins, 53.1583, -1.9712 🔳🧗🏔

9 WINDGATHER ROCKS, KETTLESHULME
Formed 360 million years ago in a river delta that lay over the Equator, this crag has vertical fault lines and horizontal strata that make it both visually striking and popular for climbing.

→ Heading S on B5470 in Kettleshulme (SK23 7QU) take L fork just after school. Follow 1 mile and park in lay-by L by wooden stile. Follow path to rocks.

5 mins, 53.3008, -2.0082 🔻🧗🔳🏔

10 CHROME HILL, LONGNOR
Walkers who scale this peak, part of the famous Dragon's Back, may be rewarded by finding brachiopod fossils (do not remove any). Around the Summer Solstice a rare 'double sunset' can be seen across its peak from Glutton Bridge. Nearby is the ancient Dowel Cave (see entry).

→ Follow the B5053 N from Longnor for 1 mile to SK17 0EN. Park on L by grey phone box just after crossing the river and follow the lane to L ½ mile, keeping R at fork. Follow the footpath uphill to L by 2nd cattle grid. Sunset from 53.1967, -1.8756.

90 mins, 53.2027, -1.8968 🔳🧗🏔

11 DOWEL CAVE, LONGNOR
Rare cave with evidence of human habitation from the Palaeolithic continuing right through Mesolithic, Neolithic, Beaker, Bronze Age, Iron Age and Roman periods. Open access for visitors but bring a torch, and please remove nothing.

13

→ From cattle grid at Chrome Hill (see entry) continue N ¼ mile and park just before farm. Find the cave up in the trees L just beyond the farm, through metal gate.

2 mins, 53.2053, -1.8882 🏞️🐾

RUINS & FOLLIES

12 WHITE NANCY, BOLLINGTON

Take a kite to fly by this curious folly overlooking the village of Kerridge, built to commemorate the Battle of Waterloo in 1817.

→ To S of Bollington in Kerridge, park near The Bull's Head (SK10 5BD). Walk up Redway Lane and follow signed footpath on hairpin bend 170m, turn R up to the folly.

10 mins, 53.2909, -2.0924 🏞️📷🍴

13 ERRWOOD HALL RUINS

The once-striking Grimshaw family mansion is a perfect summer picnic spot. Follow the path to the often missed private graveyard, with peaceful and splendid views over the valley. Continue S to swim at the packhorse bridge on the River Goyt (see entry), and visit the family's St Joseph's Shrine (see entry).

→ Start as for the packhorse bridge (see listing 4), but park at Errwood Hall car park on R by reservoir and follow signed path to house.

Graveyard to W at 53.2698, -1.9919.

8 mins, 53.2697, -1.9890 🏊🍴🚶✝️📷

14 SOLOMON'S TEMPLE, BUXTON

This folly, financed by Victorian crowdfunding, is perched atop a Bronze Age barrow on Grin Low, and affords glorious views across to Mam Tor and Kinder Scout on a clear day.

→ From A53 S out of Buxton, take L at Ladmanlow past SK17 6UJ. For walks through country park, turn L at entrance after 300m and follow to pay car park at end. Alternatively continue ¾ mile to park in small lay-by to L. Walk back 40m to gate and follow footpath up hill to tower.

15 mins, 53.2427, -1.9205 🍴📷📷

15 BUXTON LIME FIRMS

Surprisingly grand architectural limeworks, testament to the scale of the industry at the turn of the 20th century.

→ Head E out of Buxton on A6. After ¾ mile park in long lay-by R. Walk on 150m to quarry gate. Follow path past first two old buildings to kilns.

8 mins, 53.2498, -1.8856 📷🦋

14

15

16 ST JOSEPH'S SHRINE

Conical shrine to Dona Maria Dolores de Ybarguen, the Spanish governess to the children at Errwood Hall (see entry). You'll find the door unlocked and it is still visited as a memorial today.

→ Head S from of Kettleshulme (SK23 7QU) taking L fork just after school for 2 miles, past Windgather Rocks (see entry). Turn L, over cattle grid, park in lay-by R after ½ mile and follow path to shrine, keeping R.
15 mins, 53.2805, -1.9992 ✝ ✿ ⛰

17 CLEULOW CROSS, WINCLE

Hidden amongst a small copse of beech trees on a grassy tumulus stands the carved stone shaft of an Anglo-Saxon boundary cross. It featured in the climax of Alan Garner's novel 'The Weirdstone of Brisingamen'.

→ Travel W on the A54 from Allgreave (SK11 0BJ) 1½ miles to crossroads. Turn R dir Langley and park in lay-by R after 500m. Cross road and walk through gate, follow path down hill to the copse.
10 mins, 53.2036, -2.0733 ✝ ✿

18 LUD'S CHURCH, ALLGREAVE

The fern-clad, cathedral-like chasm, 80m deep, is damp and mossy even on the hottest of days. Created by a massive landslip, it was reputedly used as a secret place of worship in the 15th century.

→ From Allgreave (SK11 0BJ) take the road S dir Quarnford for 2 miles, take the hairpin R by the noticeboard to Lud's Church car park R, after SK17 0SU. Follow the road further to the footpath and follow signs.
30 mins, 53.1877, -2.0208 🚶 ➰ ✝ ✿

19 THE BOWSTONES, DISLEY

Legend says that Robin Hood and his men used these 9th-century cross shafts on the Gritstone Trail to help string their bows. Their original location is not known, but they have stood here for centuries now.

→ On Buxton Old Rd SE out of Disley turn R onto Mudhurst Lane dir Kettleshulme at SK12 2AY. At junction with Higher Lane and High Peak School after 1 mile the stones are signed R down a no through road. The stones sit at the end of the lane after ¾ mile.
1 min, 53.3286, -2.0406 ✿ ⛰

18

SLOW FOOD

20 OLD HALL INN, WHITEHOUGH

Award-winning pub with Tudor-style dining area. Fine real ales, friendly service and interesting menu with a great cheese board.

→ Whitehough, Chinley, SK23 6EJ, 01663 750529.

53.3352, -1.9430

21 WINCLE BEER COMPANY

Farmhouse-based brewery, successfully producing craft ale out of a redundant milking parlour for 10 years. Tours and tap room – don't leave without a slice of beer flapjack.

→ Tolls Farm Barn, Dane Bridge, Wincle, SK11 0QE, 01260 227777.

53.1838, -2.0550

22 THE LAZY TROUT, MEERBROOK

Friendly dining pub serving great food with fantastic views over The Roaches.

→ Meerbrook, Leek, ST13 8SN, 01538 300385.

53.1440, -2.0160

23 HILLY BILLY, BLAZE FARM

Sumptuous selection of Hilly Billy home-made ice creams in a charming tearoom, with a chance to see the farm. Closed Mondays, no card payments.

→ Wildboarclough, Macclesfield, SK11 0BL, 01260 227229.

53.2048, -2.0388

COSY PUBS

24 THE SWAN INN, KETTLESHULME

Traditional beamed inn with tasteful, modern restaurant annexe. Welcomes diners and drinkers alike.

→ Macclesfield Road, Kettleshulme, SK23 7QU, 01663 732943.

53.3153, -2.0180

25 THE CRAG INN, WILDBOARCLOUGH

Charming, traditional alehouse with warming fires and welcomes. Great base to start and end excellent walks. Closed Mon–Tues.

→ Wildboarclough, Macclesfield, SK11 0BD, 01260 227239.

53.2138, -2.0285

26 THE LEATHER'S SMITHY, LANGLEY

Walker- and cyclist-friendly traditional pub serving real ales – including their own named

– and locally sourced produce, and vegan options they are proud of.

→ Clarke Lane, Langley, SK11 0NE, 01260 252313.
53.2411, -2.0727

CAMP & SLEEP

27 SCALDERSITCH FARM, SHEEN

Tipis and yurts all with log-burners and wood-fired hot tubs. Delicious local food can be delivered to your tent door. Sorry, no pets, as this is a working farm.

→ Sheen, near Hartington, SK17 0HN, 01298 687036.
53.1361, -1.8327

28 MEG'S COTTAGE, BUTTERTON

Nestled into the corner of a conservation village, high on the moors, this cottage is the perfect retreat for a family.

→ Stoop House Farm, Butterton, Leek, ST13 7SY, 01538 304486.
53.1056, -1.8910

29 WILD BOAR, WINCLE

Delightful camping ground at the Wild Boar Inn offering amazing views and a warm

welcome. Sorry, no children.

→ Wincle, SK11 0QL, 01260 227219.
53.2018, -2.0616

30 LONGNOR WOOD CAMPSITE

Small, adults-only campsite with holiday lodges and pods available, along with a camping field.

→ Longnor, Buxton, SK17 0NG, 01298 83648.
53.1727, -1.8955

31 DON WHILLANS MEMORIAL HUT

A magical, old, rock-sheltered house, once the home of the legendary mountaineer, now hostel-style accommodation available to British Mountaineering Council members.

→ The Roaches, Upper Hulme, ST13 8UB (farm below), donwhillanshut.co.uk.
53.1567, -1.9924

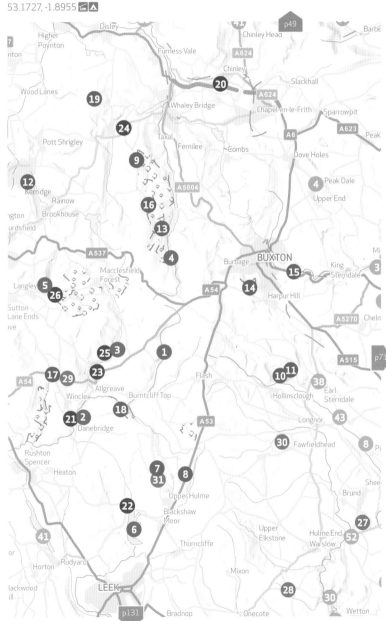

WHITE PEAK

Our perfect weekend

→ **Clamber** over the stepping stones in Dovedale to find the perfect place to dip a toe then wander along to the spectacular Renard's Arch and Ilam Rock.

→ **Scramble** up the hill to admire the views from the ancient Thor's Cave before stargazing at Alstonefield Camping Barn.

→ **Feast** on a picnic from The Old Cheese Shop at Hartington in Frank i' th' Rocks Cave and plunge into the depths of the bracing Pike Pool.

→ **Marvel** at the magnificent stones of Arbor Low then sup a traditional pint at The Quiet Woman.

→ **Fragment** the beautiful reflection of the cliffs as you dive into Water-cum-Jolly, then follow the Monsal Trail to nap amongst the wild flowers at Priestcliffe Lees.

→ **Discover** the Secret Valley of Cave Dale then wind your way through Winnats Pass to scale the heights of Mam Tor and watch the sunset.

→ **Run** around the curious lumps and bumps of Tideslow Rake before seeking out the crystal-clear waters of Cheedale.

The diverse landscape of White Peak has been inhabited since prehistoric times. People have always been drawn to its lush green valleys, where they created rolling pastures criss-crossed with an ancient pattern of drystone walls. But turn a corner and these beautiful dales throw up a huge, rocky outcrop or a wild, wooded gorge with a sliver of silver river running through it.

Many places are considered magical, and sacred burial mounds and hillforts are dotted atop escarpments and hills. At Arbor Low the enigmatic circle of 40 stones sheltered inside a huge henge exudes a mystical air, while at Five Wells on Taddington Moor you will find the highest megalithic tomb in the country, with glorious views across the valley and beyond.

Mam Tor is the crowning beauty of the area, named Shivering Mountain by locals because the rock face often glistens with water and there are frequent landslips. It is a stunning vantage point, especially as the sun sets over the hills; little wonder it was claimed as a hillfort and burial ground in the Bronze Age.

The Romans saw an opportunity to exploit the thermal springs and the lead ore, which would eventually bring booming prosperity to the area during the 18th century. Then rivers such as the Lathkill were harnessed to power mills, and galena was the local currency. Take a walk through the verdant Lathkill Dale to discover hidden remains of this era strewn along riverbanks. Bateman's House was built over a mine shaft, still accessible down a ladder today to see the water pump. Further along is the old packhorse bridge and the engine house of Mandale Mine. Another remnant of industry, the Monsal Trail is a disused railway route that links swimming spots and nature reserves.

The rivers Wye and Dove also carve gentle paths through this 300- million-year-old limestone plateau, full of fossilised creatures from a warm, tropical sea. Pike Pool in Beresford Dale offers a bracing swim in the almost azure water of the Dove; alternatively, follow the stepping stones around the rock face at Cheedale to find crystal-clear swim spots in the Wye.

Here is a landscape to awaken all your senses, from the beautiful aroma of wild spring flowers at Priestcliffe Lees to the delicious taste of summer strawberries in Millers Dale, the bracing winds of the peaks and the sounds of water over weirs in Lathkill Dale, to the blaze of autumnal fire as you clamber up to Reynard's Arch in the iconic Dovedale.

RIVERS & POOLS

1 WATER-CUM-JOLLY DALE

Wonderfully named dale with a wide expanse of river making beautiful reflections of cliffs above an old mill weir. Head upstream for clear water and a deeper swim.

→ From Monsal Head (DE45 1NL), head NE signed Cressbrook between hotel and car park. Follow 1 mile and park R by road near Cressbrook Mill. Follow signed concessionary footpath through holiday rentals to river.
10 mins, 53.2524, -1.7446 🏊🚶

2 MONSAL DALE, RIVER WYE

Well-loved verdant valley overlooked by the iconic Headstone Viaduct, with many swimming opportunities along the River Wye at the end of the Monsal Trail Tunnels (see entry).

→ In Monsal Head (DE45 1NL) drop down from bridge viewpoint by woodland path and head ½ mile L on bank to swimming above or below weir. Cross on footbridge to return by a circular loop.
15 mins, 53.2395, -1.7353 🏊🌲🚶🛶

3 CHEE DALE

This is one of the finest dales in this area, abundant with wild flora and limestone crags and worth exploring. Follow the footpaths below the cliffs along the River Wye to the stepping stones.

→ Park at Topley Head lay-by, 3½ miles E of Buxton (⅓ mile NW of turning to SK17 9TG). Follow footpath from E end down, across the Monsal Trail (see entry, with alternative paid parking), and head through Blackwell Mill Cycles. Cross bridge and follow footpath to R along river for 20 mins. Path can be muddy and floods after heavy rain.
30 mins, 53.2516, -1.8208 🏊🚶❓

4 WAINWRIGHTS QUARRY

Two quarries with clear aquamarine water and lots of ledges giving opportunities for the adventurous locals who visit. Working quarry next door, and you may be told to leave. Private but popular.

→ Take A6 N from Buxton and turn R after 1⅓ miles signed Batham Gate. Follow through Peak Dale dir SK17 8BD and park in gateway R (53.2880, -1.8666) opp gated path to quarry pools.
5 mins, 53.2895, -1.8685 🏊📸❓

DELIGHTFUL DOVE

5 PIKE POOL

One of the most famous locations in the canonical 'Compleat Angler', with a dramatic shaft of limestone overlooking a deep, luxurious swim. Nearby is the curiously named Frank i' th' Rocks cave (see entry).

→ Head S out of Hulme End, take first L after campsite, signed Beresford Dale. Park carefully on R at end, beyond SK17 0HQ. Walk on to river, turn L before ford and follow footpath to pool before wooden bridge.
15 mins, 53.1271, -1.8096 🏊🚶🌲🛶🏕

6 STEPPING STONES, DOVEDALE

The perfect family day out: stunning scenery and refreshing paddles and dips in the River Dove. Walk on to Reynard's Arch and cave (see entry) or those wanting a challenge can climb Thorpe Cloud above the iconic stepping stones.

→ Signed off A515 just N of DE6 1NH, 2 miles N of Ashbourne. Follow road through Thorpe to car park signed R. Deeper pools beneath Dove Holes upstream (53.0795, -1.7883) nearer Milldale.
10 mins, 53.0597, -1.7760 🏊🌲🛶🚶👨‍👩‍👧📷

ANCIENT & SACRED

7 FIVE WELLS CHAMBERED TOMB

The highest barrow in the Peak District, where the remains of 17 burials have been found. Once extensive at 15m wide, the outer cairn is gone, and only one chamber stands.

→ From Buxton follow A6 E, and ½ mile beyond A5270 turning turn R at crossroads up no through road (opp road to SK17 9TQ) and park at end. Follow track and footpath L signed to top of hill.

10 mins, 53.2362, -1.8159 ✝🚴🚶🏕

8 PILSBURY CASTLE

Prominent earthworks of a once-substantial Norman motte and bailey, possibly built on an Iron Age fortification.

→ Take turn off A515 signed Pilsbury just S of Hurdlow (SK17 9QJ). Follow for 2 miles into Pilsbury (keep an eye out for limestone paving outcrop L at 53.1698, -1.8152), park at end of road and take track N to earthworks.

10 mins, 53.1716, -1.8299 🚴🏕📷

9 ARBOR LOW

Nationally significant Neolithic monument with a substantial henge surrounding a circle of 40 recumbent stones.

→ Signed from A515 2½ miles N of Newhaven, and then R dir DE45 1JS, follow signs into farm. £1 charge to access through private land.

6 mins, 53.1688, -1.7613 🚴🏕✝🏕

10 THROWLEY OLD HALL

This ruinous 16th-century manor stands regally surveying the rolling hillside of the Manifold Valley. One of the best-kept secrets of the area.

→ From Calton, follow signs for Throwley N for 1¾ miles dir DE6 2BB. As road passes through Throwley Hall Farm yard, turn R and park after 150m, beyond cattle grid. Manor to L on private land, be respectful.

3 mins, 53.0698, -1.8362 📷⛰

ROCKS & CAVES

11 SEVEN WAYS & THOR'S CAVES

Intriguing Neolithic cave with seven openings. It sits above the picturesque gaping mouth of Thor's Cave (pictured above), used by humans since the Palaeolithic.

→ From Wetton head W dir DE6 2AG, and after ¾ mile park in lay-by R where Manifold Way crosses road. Follow Manifold Way S

for ½ mile and take footpath and steps L signed Thor's Cave (53.0915, -1.8546). Follow footpath on around Thor's Cave up to the top, Seven Ways Cave is right on edge of cliff.
20 mins, 53.0916, -1.8543

12 ILAM ROCK, DOVEDALE

This incredible limestone shard, 25m tall, with fossils of sea creatures, has been a favourite of artists since JMW Turner immortalised the area.
→ Follow A515 for 5 miles N from Ashbourne, turn L signed Milldale. Follow ½ mile to Milldale car park, beyond DE6 2GB. Walk back to bend and follow footpath downriver to rock on R.
25 mins, 53.0753, -1.7900

13 WOLFSCOTE HILL

Rare, little outcrop of limestone pavement, away from the well-trodden paths. More can be seen near Pilsbury Castle (see entry).
→ In Hartington take Hall Lane S and turn R before SK17 0AT. Follow 1¾ mile (sharp R after ¾ mile) to pull off R by stone building before farm driveway. Walk on 400m to gate L and up to summit across open access land. GPS recommended.
15 mins, 53.1220, -1.7972

14 FRANK I' TH' ROCKS CAVE

A magical, ancient cave overlooking the River Dove as it gently babbles through Wolfscote Dale. Frank was said to live here in the 19th century.
→ Park as for Pike Pool swim (see entry) but walk across ford and over stile. Follow footpath across field and over stile. Cave up on L.
5 mins, 53.1226, -1.8051

15 REYNARD'S ARCH, DOVEDALE

A perfect arch and cave behind it, majestically overlooking the River Dove. Named after a local brigand who used it as his refuge.
→ Park and follow path as for Stepping Stones swim (see entry), cross at stepping stones and continue on path by river for ½ mile. Arch on R up steep incline.
30 mins, 53.0697, -1.7848

16 MAM TOR

Stunning views of the surrounding Peaks from 'Mother Hill', which was once topped by a huge and rare Bronze Age hillfort and still has two round barrows at the southern end. Can be extremely busy, but still worth it.

→ From A6187 W from Castleton, shortly after S33 8WP, take L fork signed Chapel-en-le-Frith. Follow 1¼ miles over summit of Winnats Pass (see entry) and turn R. Road bends L to Mam Tor/ Mam Nick car park (NT) R, and R turn beyond this leads to bottom of steps and very limited roadside parking: at peak times car park and roadsides fill up. Clear path to summit.

25 mins, 53.3504, -1.8084 🖼️🚶‍♂️🚴‍♂️⛺

17 PETER'S STONE

At 15m high, this limestone dome is said to resemble St Peter's in Rome. It was here in 1815 that Anthony Lingard was gibbeted, having murdered toll-keeper Hannah Oliver for her red boots. His bones allegedly remained for 11 years. Wonderful views.

→ Park at Three Stags' Head, Wardlow (SK17 8RW, see listing), take footpath across road and 100m W, after B6465. Follow ridge line for half a mile.

20 mins, 53.2740, -1.7407 🖼️🚶‍♂️

WOODS & WILDLIFE

18 HARTINGTON MEADOWS

A beautiful little limestone bowl in the hillside, in which nestles a meadow full of summer flowers, birdsong, and secluded spots for a romantic picnic.

→ Head E 2 miles on B5054 from Hartington (past SK17 0AZ) and take sharp R just before A515. Park in reserve gateway after ¼ mile on R.

2 mins, 53.1459, -1.7714 ♻️🚶‍♂️⛱️⛰️

19 GREAT SHACKLOW WOOD

Pretty woodland walk, with wild garlic in spring, old mill, and weir. Watch trout lazing in the river from the bridge.

→ From Ashford in-the-Water (DE45 1QP), follow A6 ½ mile W and park in lay-by R almost opp gateway and stile. Follow track beyond stile and footpath over river into woods.

5 mins, 53.2231, -1.7343 🅿️🌲🚶‍♂️

20 MILLER'S DALE QUARRY

Pretty walk up from the old railway route alongside the River Wye, lined with wild flowers and strawberries.

→ From B6049 in Miller's Dale take turn by bridge for Wormhill (dir SK17 8SL) and park in station pay car park L after ¼ mile. Follow signs to Monsal Trail and turn L; reserve entrance immediately R up steps.

5 mins, 53.2551, -1.7908 🚶‍♂️🚩

21 PRIESTCLIFFE LEES RESERVE

Wild flowers cover this steep limestone hillside. Breathe in the scent of thyme, and marvel at the cowslips in spring or the yellow mountain pansies in summer.

→ Park and start as for Miller's Dale Quarry reserve (see entry) but walk for ¾ mile to signed entrance on R.

5 mins, 53.2534, -1.7766 ⚂🏞

INDUSTRIAL HERITAGE

22 ODIN CAVE, MINE & CRUSHING CIRCLE

The entire small ravine is an ancient lead mine, but the cave extends 10m underground from the round opening, and next to it is the later underground mine entrance. On open-access land, but all a protected archaeological site, and the underground mine is dangerous. Bring a good torch and take care.

→ From Castleton (S33 8WP) follow A6187 W 1 mile and park L opp bus stop (road beyond is abandoned due to landslips). Mine L, crushing circle below R.

1 min, 53.3482, -1.8016 🏞🚶

23 MONSAL TRAIL TUNNELS

Bring bicycles or hire them in order to get the most out of this disused railway line.

The track disappears in and out of tunnels and gorges that cut straight through the stunning scenery.

→ Wyedale car park signed off A6 E of Buxton, opp SK17 9TE; card payments only. Follow path to Blackwell Mill Cycle Hire (01298 70838) which is at the start of trail; 5 miles to Monsal Head.

10 mins, 53.2393, -1.7192 🚴🚶♿🏞⟲

24 TIDESLOW RAKE, TIDESWELL

This unusual landscape is a real hidden gem. Bumps and hollows from centuries of lead extraction scar the slope, scattered with remains of workings and buildings.

→ From A623 at Tideswell turn up lane in front of The Anchor Inn, (dir Little Hucklow, SK17 8RT). Follow N for 1 mile and pull onto gravel by stile R. Stiles lead into the rake.

1 min, 53.2980, -1.7644 🏞🚶

25 BATEMAN'S HOUSE, LATHKILL DALE

The enchanting, lush green gorge of the River Lathkill shelters many lead mining relics. Bateman's House is a ruined pumping station sited above a cold, 12m-deep mining shaft with newly installed ladder to allow exploration below. There is also a Cornish beam engine at Mandale Mine.

→ Park in Over Haddon (DE45 1JE), descend S past St Anne's church, and take Lathkill Dale path to the R (upstream). Follow for ½ mile to Mandale Mine on R (53.1923, -1.7075) then a further ¼ mile along riverpath, Bateman's House signposted L across river.
20 mins, 53.1893, -1.7103 🏊🚶🅿

26 MAGPIE MINE

One of the most famous lead mines in the Peaks, not least for the murder charges following a fire underground in 1833. Picnic, wild camp, explore the rakes and buildings. All the shafts are safely capped.

→ Heading N out of Monyash, past church and DE45 1JJ, turn R at junction signed Sheldon. After ⅓ mile, park on verge L by gate, follow path to mine.
5 mins, 53.2103, -1.7432 🏊🚶✶

DALES & DINGLES

27 WINNATS PASS

A deep limestone cleft, home to rare wild flowers like purple Jacob's ladder and bright yellow Derby hawkweed. Spectacular views from the top.

→ From A6187 W from Castleton, shortly after S33 8WP, take L fork signed Chapel-en-le-Frith. Follow ½ mile and park at Speedwell Cavern on R. Follow path by road or head up the steep slopes either side.
2 mins, 53.3409, -1.7998 🏊🚶✶🚌

28 ILAM PARK

Swathes of wild garlic adorn the paths around this peaceful parkland in spring. Circular walk takes in a rope bridge, grotto, a natural playroom for the kids, a paddle in the river near the weir and the elegant 18th-century St Bertram's Bridge.

→ In Ilam, many park on Ilam-Moor Lane outside estate gates, DE6 2AZ. Also NT car park in estate near Ilam Hall YHA (see listing).
3 mins, 53.0522, -1.8032 🚶🚲🏕🌲🏊🛶🍴

29 SECRET VALLEY, CAVE DALE

A magical dale just off the tourist trail behind Peveril Castle. At the start the dry limestone walls are almost perpendicular and 50m high. Absolutely stunning; walking boots recommended.

→ Park in Castleton and follow Bargate to Cave Dale signed path, between Cavedale Cottage and Dale Cottage (near S33 8WQ).
5 mins, 53.3386, -1.7776 🚶🚌

SLOW FOOD

30 WETTON MILL CAFE & CAVE
Former watermill converted into cosy NT tearoom and picturesque picnic spot. Just above perches a cave with several mouths, well worth investigating (53.1025, -1.8591). Accommodation available.

➜ Wetton Mill Lane, Wetton, DE6 2AG, 01298 84838
53.1020, -1.8585 🍴🛏

31 HERBERT'S TEA ROOM, TISSINGTON
Converted barn with vintage crockery, freshly prepared lunches and delicious, home-made cakes.

➜ 1 The Green, Tissington, DE6 1RA, 01335 350501.
53.0672, -1.7391 🍴

32 THE OLD CHEESE SHOP, HARTINGTON
A quaint, little cheese shop selling a vast array of British and local cheeses including Peakland Blue and the salty, crumbly Peakland White, made at their own creamery.

➜ Market Place, Hartington, SK17 0AL, 01298 84935.
53.1411, -1.8107 🍴

33 THE GEORGE, ALSTONEFIELD
Family-run pub with large garden and fine dining, sourced from local suppliers.

➜ 1 Church Lane, Alstonefield, DE6 2FX, 01335 310205.
53.0972, -1.8053 🍴🛏

34 TINDALLS OF TIDESWELL
Award-winning, family-run bakery selling all manner of mouth-watering morsels.

➜ Commercial Road, Tideswell, SK17 8NU, 01298 871351.
53.2782, -1.7726 🍴

35 THE SAMUEL FOX COUNTRY INN
Delightfully refined, award-winning pub, which offers sublime food with first-class service. Excellent rooms available too.

➜ Stretfield Road, Bradwell, S33 9JT, 01433 621562.
53.3333, -1.7393 🍴🛏

36 OLD SMITHY TEAROOMS, MONYASH
Traditional stone-built café, bar and bistro, the ideal place to refresh after a long walk. Superb cakes and ice-creams.

➜ Church St, Monyash, DE45 1JH, 01629 810190.
53.1960, -1.7768 🍴

COSY PUBS

37 PACKHORSE INN, LITTLE LONGSTONE
Great place for a good, honest pint and delicious, locally sourced food. Three cosy rooms with flagstone floors and open fires, welcoming 'muddy boots, kids, and dogs'.
→ Main Street, Little Longstone, DE45 1NN, 01629 640471.
53.2422, -1.7162

38 THE QUIET WOMAN, EARL STERNDALE
Take a step back in time into this rare, unspoilt, no-frills village pub. Pop in for a pint and real conversation with landlord Ken. Named after the story that a landlord silenced his wife by chopping off her head!
→ Earl Sterndale, SK17 0BU, 01298 83211.
53.1999, -1.8666

39 CHURCH INN, CHELMORTON
Cosy, traditional 18th-century pub with rooms. Just down the road is a remaining pair of troughs fed by Illy Willy Water spring, the early water supply for the village.
→ Main Street, Chelmorton, SK17 9SL, 01298 85319. Troughs 150m down hill.
53.2771, -1.7301

40 THREE STAGS' HEADS, WARDLOW
Transport yourself back to the 1950s. A roaring fire and host of locals with their dogs add to the welcoming cosiness. Be prepared to share your settle, and don't order a lager!
→ Mires Lane, Wardlow, SK17 8RW, 01298 872268.
53.2771, -1.7301

41 COACH & HORSES, FENNY BENTLEY
Traditional 17th-century coaching inn. Good, home-cooked food and a range of ales.
→ Fenny Bentley, DE6 1LB, 01335 350246.
53.0473, -1.7394

42 SYCAMORE INN, PARWICH
Charming village inn and community focal point, serving hearty pub grub and doubling as the village store.
→ Parwich, DE6 1QL, 01335 390212.
53.0857, -1.7207

43 THE PACK HORSE INN, CROWDECOTE
You will be made to feel very welcome at this friendly and cosy 16th-century inn. Honest food and local real ales. A gem.
→ Crowdecote, SK17 0DB, 01298 83618.
53.1837, -1.8504

CAMP & SLEEP

44 CASTERNE HALL CAMPING
A lovely, country house B&B offering camping in the secret walled garden with superb views over the Manifold Valley.
→ Ashbourne, DE6 2BA, 01335 310489.
53.0686, -1.8174

45 DALE FARM CAMPSITE
Peaceful, rural idyll a short step away from the Monsal Trail and Bakewell. Hire bell tents and shop at the onsite farm store.
→ Moor Road, Great Longstone, DE45 1UA, 07734 190588.
53.2461, -1.7078

46 BELTONVILLE FARM SHOP & CAMPSITE

Fantastic farm shop selling raw milk and local produce. Enjoy fire pits in the farm's camping field or stay in the 14-person bunk barn with wood-burner.

→ Beltonville Farm, Millers Dale, SK17 8SS, 07813 325923.
53.2573, -1.7751 ▲ ▮

47 ILAM HALL YHA

17th-century Gothic manor converted into a well-thought-out and comfortable youth hostel in 84 acres of NT grounds. Manifold and Dovedale rivers on the doorstep.

→ Ilam, Ashbourne, DE6 2AZ, 0345 3719023.
53.0530, -1.8055 ▨ ▨

48 HADDON GROVE FARM CAMPING

A no-frills, family-friendly campsite with large, tree-lined grassy fields and plenty of space for children to run wild. Dogs allowed.

→ Haddon Grove, Over Haddon, DE45 1JF, 01629 812343.
53.1912, -1.7369 ▲

49 ALSTONEFIELD CAMPING BARN

Charming off-grid camping in a stone barn, set in a beautiful location with fantastic views and walks right from the door. Bring logs for the wood-burner. Room for up to 12.

→ Alstonefield, DE6 2FT, 01335 310349, pitchup.com.
53.1087, -1.8143 ▨ ▨ ▨

50 THE ROYAL OAK, HURDLOW

Camping and bunk house accommodation behind a friendly pub where a hearty breakfast is available.

→ Hurdlow, SK17 9QJ, 01298 83288.
53.1908, -1.8118 ▲ ▮ ▨

51 COLUMBINE CAMPING BARN

A stone barn conversion with two family bedrooms sleeping up to 8. Outside meadows burst with wild flowers and it's a short walk to the village.

→ Bradwell, S33 9HZ, campsites.co.uk.
53.3247, -1.7356 ▨

52 HULME END CAMPSITE

A large, spacious field behind the Manifold Inn with toilets and pot washing area. Arrive before 9pm, find a spot and pitch up.

→ Hulme End, SK17 0EX, 07800 659985.
53.1294, -1.8417 ▲

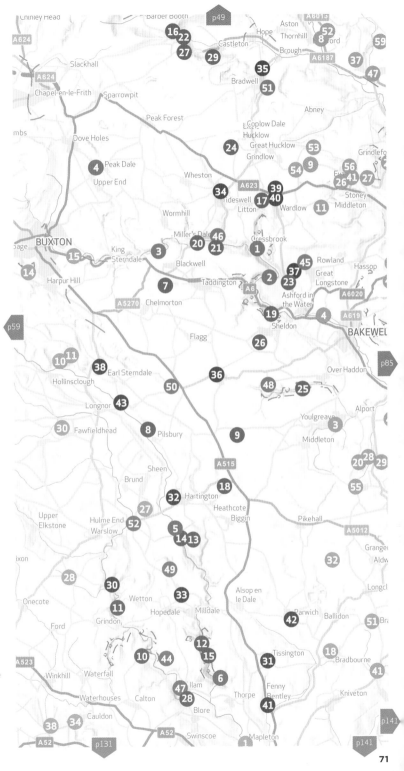

DARK PEAK

Our perfect weekend

→ **Treat** yourself to a picnic from Coleman's Deli to eat in a secluded glade at the delightful Wyming Brook Nature Reserve.

→ **Seek** out the graceful statue of Fair Flora before walking up through Padley Gorge and plunging into a refreshing pool near its top.

→ **Stand** in awe at the beautiful Cucklett Delf before marvelling at the murmurations of starlings over Middleton Moor.

→ **Swim** downstream from Calver Bridge in the gentle Derwent River or paddle in the rapids at the regal Chatsworth House.

→ **Scramble** around the fascinating shapes carved into the Rowtor Rocks, then treat yourself to an old-fashioned pint at The Flying Childers.

→ **Explore** the cascading water and mining remnants of Lumsdale Falls or walk along the dizzy heights of Giddy Edge high above Matlock Bath.

→ **Wonder** at the Neolithic chambered tomb of Minning Low then join in the frivolity of hen racing at the lively Barley Mow in Bonsall.

→ **Dip** into the refreshing bathing pool on the River Bradford after seeking out the fascinating hermit's cave at Cratcliffe.

→ **Join** in the dancing circle of Nine Ladies before singing songs around the campfire at The Campsite.

Glorious vistas over hundreds of miles on a clear day, walks that blow away the cobwebs, beautiful plateaus scattered with the remains of ancient settlements; the Dark Peak is the perfect antidote to our busy world. Here nothing interrupts the acres of purple heather, rocky outcrops, and beautifully wind-carved rock formations.

Called the Dark Peak due to the layer of rugged millstone grit and shale which sits over its limestone bed, the area reveals a dark history to match. Civil war ravaged the Peaks during the mid-1640s, when it was often a site of skirmishes. Not long after, in 1665, the Plague wreaked havoc on the ancient village of Eyam. Quarantining itself for 14 months, it prevented the spread elsewhere, but the toll on its villagers was devastating. The Riley Graves just outside the village are a haunting reminder of its impact on families: Elizabeth Hancock buried her husband and six children in the space of just eight days. The nearby Cucklett Delf, a natural, secluded craglet overhung with green vines, was a place of worship during the Plague, as open-air services were thought to prevent the spread of infection.

Lead mining was productive in the Peaks for over three millennia. The Romans settled here because of it and, in the 17th and 18th centuries, this was the most important lead mining area in the world. The Good Luck Mine and Sheep Pasture Incline offer both energetic uphill walks and a fascinating insight into the lucrative coal and lead industries. Lumsdale Falls, with rambling mill ruins cascading down a series of waterfalls in a wooded gorge, are great for a day's exploring with the kids.

The gentle River Derwent runs southwards from Bleaklow and powered the first-ever cotton mill at Cromford. When it reaches Calver Bridge and the Chatsworth Estate it is wide and luxurious, perfect for a lazy day messing about on the river. Wyming Brook Nature Reserve is enchanting: a pine tree-lined gorge with waterfalls, plunge pools and secluded glades. Padley Gorge, a wooded ravine with ancient oak trees, has larger pools and deep sections of the Burbage Brook to swim in as it tumbles down the hillside. The walk to the top rewards visitors with views across the purple heathland to Carl Wark and Higger Tor, standing proudly against the skyline.

Community spirit is at its best here, and visitors are welcomed like friends in many establishments. For an old-fashioned pint and a packet of crisps head to The Flying Childers, high up in the village of Stanton in Peak. A warm welcome awaits you at the lively Barley Mow in Bonsall, a truly locally spirited establishment that serves the most delicious Sunday roast as well as being home to the World Hen Racing Championship.

7

1 WYMING BROOK NATURE RESERVE

A simply stunning gorge lined by majestic pine trees, mossy crags and endless waterfalls. Perfect for a river walk or a paddle in the pool at the bottom.

→ From Redmires follow Redmires Rd 1¼ miles W from edge of village, past S10 4LJ. Entrance with car park on R. Follow footpath R dir Rivelin Dams.

15 mins, 53.3693, -1.5963

2 PADLEY GORGE

Mossy, twisted oaks and the bubbling Burbage Brook make this beautiful woodland gorge a popular spot for local photographers. There are some bracing plunge pools for the brave.

→ In Upper Padley (S32 2JA) park by Grindleford Station Cafe, cross railway and follow Padley Gorge Trail footpath on R. Waterfalls near wooden bridge after ⅓ mile, pool a further ⅓ mile.

20 mins, 53.3122, -1.6181

3 YOULGREAVE, RIVER BRADFORD

Short but perfectly formed river known for the clarity of its water. Stroll along and take a dip in the shallow 'swimming pool' above the little weir.

→ Follow Bradford Rd S from Youlgreave Church (DE45 1WL), keeping L at fork, park near footbridge and walk 200m upstream. For a longer walk, take Alport Lane from church dir Alport (DE45 1LG) ½ mile, park in lay-by L, walk over river and take footpath R.

10 mins, 53.1732, -1.6854

4 ASHFORD-IN-THE-WATER, RIVER WYE

Delightful riverside pools above a weir, with deep, clear sections and some shaded areas.

→ Heading E on A6, 230m after A6020 signed Ashton-in-the-Water, take L down short dead end over old bridge (opp turn to DE45 1PY) and park. Follow footpath downstream ½ mile.

15 mins, 53.2223, -1.6939

5 LOWER LINACRE RESERVOIR

Crystal-clear but cold waters are surrounded by attractive woodland trails. There are bluebells in spring and a good spot for a picnic.

→ From Overgreen, head E on B6050 (dir S42 7AX), reservoirs signed R after ½ mile. Car park after ¼ mile and path to water.

10 mins, 53.2480, -1.4976

6 CALVER BRIDGE, RIVER DERWENT

Probably the best place in the Peaks for a long, secluded river swim. Beautifully bracing water and jumps from bridge. Simply delightful.

→ From Froggatt take A625 dir Calver (S32 3WY) and park in lay-by L just before bridge. Follow footpath downriver or walk ½ mile up to Froggatt Bridge for a leisurely swim back.

2 mins, 53.2748, -1.6342

7 CHATSWORTH, RIVER DERWENT

Perfect place for a day out with family in a stunning parkland. Calm, deep river pool above downstream weir, shallows to paddle in below. Use discretion.

→ Park at Calton Lees pay car park off B6102 N of Beeley (DE4 2NX). Follow paths down to river in park and walk upstream for weir. There is also a long stretch of sheltered, secluded river upstream of house and bridge.

10 mins, 53.2199, -1.6125

8 BAMFORD MILL

Pretty bridge and stepping stones across the Derwent lead to a secluded and peaceful swim with rope swing.

→ Park in Bamford; some space to pull off along The Hollow (S33 0DU). Follow The Hollow down to mill, then footpath to river and across stones, turn R to rope swing.
10 mins, 53.3466, -1.6939 🏊🍴🌲🚶🏕️

WATERFALLS

9 WATERFALL SWALLET

Hidden inside an unassuming copse is a limestone cleft with this enchanting cascade of water, which is almost immediately swallowed by the ground. On private land, but access appears to be allowed.
→ From Foolow (S32 5QR) head E dir Eyam. After ½ mile there is a field track L opp Waterfall Farm. Track may be passable to gravel area around bend; otherwise pull off by road. Path L down to swallet off track.
10 mins, 53.2901, -1.7029 🏞️🍴⛰️❓

10 LUMSDALE FALLS

A beautiful, wooded gorge hiding historical mill ruins, where small waterfalls cascade into a series of ponds beside a warren of buildings and tunnels. A glimpse into a bygone era.
→ Head E from Matlock on A615. Turn L onto Lumsdale Rd and follow through Lower

Lumsdale to park in lay-by R opposite derelict buildings. Follow path up through gorge to falls.
10 mins, 53.1422, -1.5327 🏞️🚶🌲🍴

WOODLANDS & WILDLIFE

11 MIDDLETON MOOR MURMURATIONS

The reed beds here are one of the best places in the country to witness the stunning flocking of starlings as they settle in to roost. Called murmurations, the sight of hundreds of birds swirling in the sky is a real spectacle. Visit at dusk from October to March.
→ On A623 W of Eyam, 230m W of turning to S32 5QB, turn S (unsigned). After ⅛ mile take L signed Cavendish Mill only, and park at mining site after ½ mile. Follow footpath markers to hide; stay on track, the area is prone to quicksand!
10 mins, 53.2707, -1.6951 🐦

12 BUBNELL CLIFF FARM POPPY FIELD

Around June this field plays host to a vivid red sea of poppies. Access kindly permitted.
→ Walk W from Baslow (DE45 1RB) on Wheatlands Lane for ½ mile. Field on R at bend, just after farm entrance opp.
2 mins, 53.2454, -1.6400 🚶

16

13 FROGGATT WOOD
Charming woodland walks with babbling stream and old industrial remnants. Lead smelt mill and wood-drying kiln near brook.

→ Park on B6521 near Grindleford church and community shop (see listing, S32 2JG). Walk S on road to signed footpath L through gate by traffic light, follow diagonally across field to woodland entrance.

15 mins, 53.2927, -1.6318 🚶🏕🚗

14 ROSE END MEADOWS
Orchids, buttercups and bluebells abound in this mosaic of 16 small fields left free from fertiliser and herbicides.

→ In Cromford on B5036/Cromford Hill turn N onto Hawthorn Dr then L onto St Marks Close, dir DE4 3QD, follow L fork to park at end. Follow footpath through trees to reserve.

5 mins, 53.1057, -1.5653 🌸🚶🚶

15 SHINING CLIFF WOODS
Ancient, once-royal forest, home to an abandoned 19th-century manor and the shattered trunk of a veteran yew, fancifully claimed to be where Betty Kenny rocked her babies to sleep 'in the treetop' and gave rise to the rhyme.

→ Follow Higg Lane S from All Saints Church, Alderwasley (DE56 2SR), for ½ mile. Park at bend of road without blocking gate, follow footpath into woods and uphill to L. Manor is by old wireworks at 53.0659, -1.4934, yew is around 53.0774, -1.5028.

15 mins, 53.0683, -1.5206 🚵🍽📷

ROCKS & CAVES

16 BAMFORD EDGE
A dramatic limestone ridge with vast views over Ladybower Reservoir and the surrounding area. A climber's playground.

→ From Bamford (S33 0DY) take Ashopton Rd/A6103 N 1 mile. Turn R onto New Rd, after 1 mile, park in long lay-by L. Follow path uphill.

30 mins, 53.3608, -1.6898 🚶🏕🏔

17 CARL WARK & HIGGER TOR
Two impressive high points overlooking Burbage Brook, immediately recognisable as a setting in *The Princess Bride*. Great views all around with a surprisingly gentle climb. Toad's Mouth Rock is just up the road (see entry).

→ Follow A6187 from Hathersage for Sheffield 2½ miles (dir S11 7TZ), past Surprise View car park (magnificent views over two valleys to Mam Tor); 100m after

14

17

sharp R over bridge turn into car park L. Follow footpath uphill.

25 mins, 53.3292, -1.6106

18 TOAD'S MOUTH ROCK

Quirky rock formation in the shape of a toad. The eye may have been added as far back as the Mesolithic era.

→ Park as for Carl Wark rocks (see entry) and walk back to sharp bend. Toad Rock looks out over road.

5 mins, 53.3225, -1.6098

19 EAGLE STONE, BASLOW EDGE

Young Baslow men used to show their fitness for marriage by climbing the overhangs of this rock to the top, and you may still find some there keeping up the tradition in good humour.

→ From crossroads in Curbar head E, dir S32 3YR, ¾ mile to Curbar Gap pay car park L. Follow path across the road S for ¾ mile across plateau.

15 mins, 53.2607, -1.6079

20 ROBIN HOOD'S STRIDE

Legend has it that Robin Hood leapt the 5m gap between the tallest pinnacles. Fabulous entry-level climbing with the kids, though the pinnacles are trickier. In the woods nearby is Cratcliffe Hermitage (see entry).

→ Take B5056 NW of Winster, dir DE4 2LZ, for 1¼ miles and park in lay-by R (53.1538, -1.6592) just after lane L on bend. Cross into lane, turn R through gate, follow path up and over brow of hill to rocks on L.

15 mins, 53.1570, -1.6658

21 CORK STONE, STANTON MOOR

This striking, wind-eroded sandstone rock is shaped like a champagne cork and has grips added for an easy ascent. Stanton Moor is rich in other rocks and remains, such as Nine Ladies circle (see entry).

→ Take Main Street E out of Birchover, follow L for Stanton in Peak, dir DE4 2LR. Pull off R after ½ mile by signed entrance to Stanton Moor. Follow footpath to stone.

5 mins, 53.1616, -1.6374

22 BIRCHEN EDGE

Magnificent rocks providing wondrous views of Baslow and Chatsworth Estate. Popular with climbers and walkers. Visit the Nelson Monument by the inscribed 'Three Ships' rocks.

→ Take A619 E from Baslow and 1 mile after roundabout turn L dir Cutthorpe on B6050 to

car park L (DE45 1PU). Walk on past house L and take footpath next to driveway along and R up to edge.

25 mins, 53.2524, -1.5831

23 HIGH TOR & GIDDY EDGE

Claimed to be Britain's scariest footpath, with one stretch having a 90m drop awaiting a wrongly placed foot! There are handrails, but this is not one for children.

→ In Matlock some parking on Church St near DE4 3BZ, next to Pic Tor Lane. Follow lane to join footpath at end and head L. Linear walk continues past station along river, but becomes more urban.

20 mins, 53.1251, -1.5569

FOLLIES & RUINS

24 FAIR FLORA

Legends tell that this statue, originally from Chatsworth House, was either erected in memory of a girl who drowned in the Derwent River while eloping, or died at the hands of her lover, or was banished into the woods after bringing ill fortune in the house.

→ Head S on B6521 from Grindleford, take first R on New Rd (S32 2HW) and park

carefully on L where road is straight. Walk back to bend looking for path into wood opp, by Goatscliff Farm Lane. Follow path to statue.

5 mins, 53.2907, -1.6421

25 WINGFIELD MANOR

The still-majestic ruins of a 15th-century manor where Mary, Queen of Scots was imprisoned by the Earl of Shrewsbury.

→ Park in South Wingfield (near DE55 7NH). Walk S downhill, turn L onto bridleway where wall curves in. Follow 37m round bends, and after trees take footpath R towards manor; working farm beyond, respect paths. Pre-book tours with English Heritage.

15 mins, 53.0890, -1.4425

ANCIENT & SACRED

26 CUCKLETT DELF, EYAM

During the Plague quarantine, this natural amphitheatre was an outdoor church (still commemorated with a service every August) and the place where two lovers from different villages would call across the rocks to each other.

→ Follow footpath sign from bend on Dunlow Lane in Eyam (S32 5RD). After 150m Delf on L.

7 mins, 53.2826, -1.6781

27 RILEY GRAVES, EYAM

A poignant reminder, amidst stunning views, of the devastating effects of the Plague on the families of Eyam: six gravestones and a tomb of the Hancock family.

→ 10 miles SE of Chapel-en-le-Frith off A623 Baslow Road. Graves on Riley Road, ½ mile E of Eyam (past S32 5QY). Narrow lane, best park in Eyam and walk.

10 mins, 53.2838, -1.6586 ✝

28 CRATCLIFFE HERMITAGE

Fascinating 14th-century hermit's cave with carved crucifix on wall, positioned to be seen from the sleeping ledge. Fenced to deter climbers from using it as a shelter.

→ Park and walk up track as for Robin Hood's Stride rocks (see entry) then take path R to woodland and uphill to R to cave.

15 mins, 53.1577, -1.6612 ✝ ⚙

29 ROWTOR ROCKS

Carved by a local man in the late-18th century to resemble a Druidic ritual site. Fascinating rock formation with caves, altars, thrones, and symbols carved into the sandstone.

→ Park at the W end of Birchover (DE4 2BG) and follow the footpath from the car park of

Druid Inn up towards outcrop.

5 mins, 53.1560, -1.6497 ✝ ⚑

30 NINE LADIES, STANTON MOOR

The usual sanction for ladies dancing on a Sunday was to be turned to stone. This photogenic Bronze Age circle is the most complete and important of a number of monuments on the moor.

→ Park as for the Cork Stone climbing rock (see entry). Follow footpath on to crossroads and turn L up to summit for circle.

10 mins, 53.1679, -1.62896 ✦ ⚙ ✝ ✕ ✦

31 TRINITY CHAPEL, BRACKENFIELD

Hidden away in the woods above Ogston Reservoir are the romantic ruins of this little chapel, the roots of which date back to 1086.

→ From Brackenfield head W on School Lane past DE55 6DF and pull to side carefully 200m past Coldharbour Lane fork L. Enter field L by footpath sign and follow fence line into wood.

5 mins, 53.1299, -1.4654 ⚙ ✝

32 MINNING LOW

Impressive Neolithic chambered tomb hiding in a circle of trees and crowned with a copse, with two bowl barrows nearby.

→ Head E on A5012 from Pikehall (DE4 2PH), take first R signed Parwich Lane and follow just under 1 mile to car park entrance after bend. Follow High Peak Trail E for 15 mins then follow wooden sign to tree-lined mound. Concessionary footpath granted by landowner.
20 mins, 53.1124, -1.6887

33 CROMFORD BRIDGE CHAPEL
Tiny 15th-century travellers' chapel tucked away below the road and now ruined. The bridge also has a curious inscription about a horse and rider who missed the bridge yet survived the leap into the river.

→ Take Mill Road out of Cromford, past Mills and DE4 3RQ. Limited street parking L just after Mills (or park in Mills and get a coffee), pay car park R by bridge. Chapel on R below bridge before you cross river.
1 min, 53.1108, -1.5529

INDUSTRIAL HERITAGE

34 MILL CLOSE MINE, CLOUGH WOOD
Once said to be the largest lead mine in the world, all that remains after it was closed by a flood in 1939 is this two-storey engine house.

→ From Darley Bridge (DE4 2JY) follow Oldfield Lane W, take fork L after ¼ and park R of triangle ½ mile further. Follow footpath from S point of triangle R into woods 100m.
5 mins, 53.1530, -1.6160

35 GOODLUCK MINE
Perched high in the hills along the famous Via Gellia Road, this remnant of 19th-century lead mining offers an insight into bygone days and a beautiful view across the valley. Run by volunteers, mine tunnels open one day a month or by appointment, check website.

→ Take the A5102 NW out of Cromford 2 miles and park in lay-by on L by wooden bridge (1 mile after passing old mills at DE4 2AJ). Follow footpath up to spoil heap. Alternatively follow footpath up from Cromford along bubbling stream with wild garlic.
15 mins, 53.1052, -1.5985

36 SHEEP PASTURE INCLINE
It's hard to imagine trains being winched up this 1-in-9 gradient, and the catch pit at the bottom is a testament to runaways that didn't make it! Now a beautiful woodland walk, with remnants of the industrial era an integral part of the flora and fauna.

39

42

43

44

➜ Take Mill Rd out of Cromford, past station, dir Holloway. Follow 1½ miles to High Peak Junction car park L just before Holloway (DE4 5AA).
5 mins, 53.1003, -1.5360 🚶🚲

SLOW FOOD

37 HOPE VALLEY ICE CREAM

With over 300 years of dairy farming experience, the Marsden family offer daily tours and an onsite café.
➜ Thorpe Farm, Hathersage, S32 1BQ, 01433 650659.
53.3369, -1.6669 🍴

38 THE DEVONSHIRE ARMS, BASLOW

A cosy, relaxed pub serving delicious food. Loved by locals and visitors. Rooms available.
➜ Baslow, DE45 1SR, 01246 582551.
53.2459, -1.6133 🍴

39 GRINDLEFORD COMMUNITY SHOP

A community shop in the village church oozes warmth and serves light refreshments.
➜ St Helen's Church, Main Road, Grindleford, S32 2JG, 01433 631611.
53.2974, -1.6323 🍴

40 THE DEVONSHIRE ARMS AT PILSLEY

Sample towering Chatsworth burgers, chickpea curries and local ales within easy walking distance of the Chatsworth Estate.
➜ High St, Pilsley, DE45 1UL, 01246 565405.
53.2359, -1.6408 🍴🛏

41 VILLAGE GREEN, EYAM

A lovely little café with home-made food, organic, Fairtrade coffee and friendly staff. Part of the #MyPeakCup initiative to reduce waste cups.
➜ The Square, Eyam, S32 5RB, 01433 631293.
53.2842, -1.6710 🍴

42 CHATSWORTH ESTATE FARM SHOP

Thriving farm shop and café with mouth-watering home-grown and reared produce, alongside the best local and national goods.
➜ Pilsley, DE45 1UF, 01246 565411.
53.2340, -1.6381 🍴

43 CAUDWELLS CRAFTS & CAFE

Take a trip down memory lane to see lost crafts and relax in the old corn mill café with seating sourced from the local church.
➜ Caudwell's Mill, Rowsley, DE4 2EB, 01629 733185.
53.1886, -1.6189 🍴

44 SCARTHIN BOOKS

Sit alongside the old stove to sample the delicious, home-made vegetarian food, discover captivating editions old and new, or while away an hour reading in the armchairs of the old drawing room in this beloved bookshop.
➜ The Promenade, Cromford, DE4 3QF, 01629 823272.
53.1091, -1.5615 🍴

45 HIGHFIELD HOUSE FARM SHOP

Farm shop and tearoom with a real focus on celebrating local fare, Highfield is a favourite amongst locals.

→ Darley Rd, Ashover, S45 0LW, 01246 590817. 53.1982, -1.5040 🍴

46 TICKLED TROUT, BARLOW

High-quality food from local artisan ingredients in comfortable surroundings.

→ 33 Valley Road, Barlow, S18 7SL, 0114 2891111. 53.2745, -1.4959 🍴

47 COLEMAN'S DELI, HATHERSAGE

Fabulous old-school deli specialising in hearty local produce, ideal for a sumptuous picnic.

→ 5 Main Road, Hathersage, Hope Valley, S32 1BB, 01433 650505. 53.3307, -1.6537 🍴

COSY PUBS

48 THE FLYING CHILDERS INN

The embodiment of a Peak District traditional pub: real ales and real people, a snug and a garden. Richard and Sophie welcome all.

→ Main Road, Stanton in Peak, DE4 2LW, 01629 636333. 53.1753, -1.6417 🛏

49 THE THORN TREE INN

Dating from the 1800s, this real ale gem is small, friendly and traditional. The south-

facing terrace has great views over the Derwent Valley.

→ 48 Jackson Road, Matlock, DE4 3JQ, 01629 580295. 53.1442, -1.5532 🛏

50 BARLEY MOW, BONSALL

Home to the world Hen Racing Championship, this warm, eccentric pub is a national treasure. Regular live music, accommodation, locally sourced, organic food and a proud welcome from the locals. Maybe it is, as proclaimed, the best pub in the world.

→ The Dale, Bonsall, DE4 2AY, 01629 825685. 53.1189, -1.5896 🍴🛏

51 THE OLDE GATE INNE, BRASSINGTON

Step back in time at this pub with cosy rooms and antique furnishings, real ales and good food.

→ Well Street, Brassington, DE4 4HJ, 01629 540448. 53.0846, -1.6582 🍴🛏

52 THE ANGLER'S REST, BAMFORD

A community-owned pub, cafe and post office. Breakfasts, lunches, cakes and dinners all served by friendly staff. Choose to sit in the pub with its settles and wood-burner or in the café. Secure bike parking.

→ Taggs Knoll, Bamford, S33 0DY, 01433 659317. 53.3496, -1.6889 🍴🛏

53 THE BARREL INN, BRETTON

The highest pub in Derbyshire, with magnificent views, great food and real ale. This pub has everything you'd expect from the phrase 'old-world charm'.

→ Bretton, S32 5QD, 01433 630856. 53.2978, -1.7003

54 THE BULLS HEAD, FOOLOW

Relaxed, traditional inn with flagstone floors and open fires to welcome the weary walker.

→ Eyam, S32 5QR, 01433 630873. 53.2878, -1.7143

55 DUKE OF YORK INN, ELTON

Historic, unchanging pub, and a favourite with locals. Honest, no-frills charm.

→ Main Street, Elton, DE4 2BW, 01629 650367. 53.1452, -1.6699

CAMP, SLEEP & STAY

56 YHA EYAM

In the Hope Valley, surrounded by woodland Eyam's castellated Victorian youth hostel is popular and well run. Loved by groups and individuals, it's a great base from which to explore the area. Family rooms available.

→ Eyam, S32 5QP, 0345 371 9738, yha.org.uk. 53.2891, -1.6726

57 SHERIFF LODGE B&B

You won't find a friendlier, more comfortable stay, with a hearty breakfast cooked to your exact wishes! Lots of little extras like 7-foot beds to make your stay truly memorable.

→ 51 Dimple Road, Matlock, DE4 3JX, 01629 760760. 53.1422, -1.5609

58 TANNENBAUM CAMPSITE

Back-to-basics campsite or glamping options, with big skies, fire pits and stunning panoramic views.

→ Belper Road, Alderwasley, DE56 2RD, 07929 345622. 53.0631, -1.5214

59 NORTH LEES CAMPSITE

Idyllic, peaceful and basic National Park site, with four small fields, drystone walls and a babbling brook. Home to pied flycatchers, bats and water voles. Pods available.

→ Birley Lane, Hathersage, S32 1DY, 01433 650838. 53.3451, -1.6477

60 THE OLD LOCKUP, WIRKSWORTH

Once a magistrate's house, then a police station, now an intriguing B&B.

→ 46 North End, Wirksworth, DE4 4FG, 01629 826272. 53.0848, -1.5716

61 THE CAMPSITE

Gorgeous, private eco-campsite available to hire exclusively for a group. Wood-fired pizza oven and 18 acres to explore. Summer only.

→ Flash Lane, Darley Moor, DE4 5LJ, 07980 852831. 53.1899, -1.5618

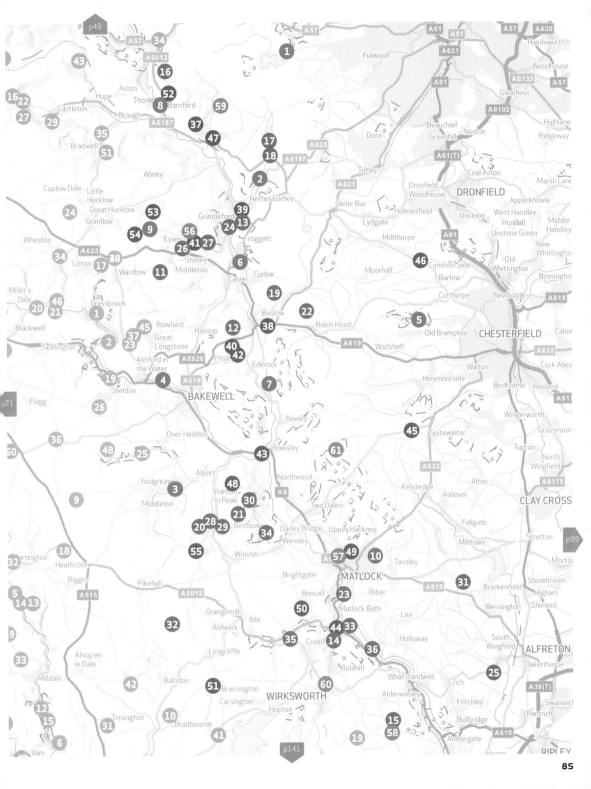

NOTTINGHAM-SHIRE

Our perfect weekend

→ **Paddle** the Soar from Normanton then explore the intriguing Hermit's Cave at Dale Abbey.

→ **Sample** award-winning pork pies at Nice Pie and experience Stilton heaven in the Vale of Belvoir.

→ **Dine** at The Cow Shed in front of the fire before relaxing in your own hot tub at the Tin and Wood shepherds' huts.

→ **Wander** the scenic countryside soaking up the fascinating stories of All Saints Old Church and Houghton Chapel.

→ **Explore** Robin Hood's county for St Edwin's Chapel Cross before relaxing in your own tree house hideaway in Sherwood Forest.

→ **Cycle** the endless woodland trails around the lake of Clumber Park, followed by a stay in the luxurious Brown's of Holbeck.

→ **Treat** yourself to some delicious local goodies from Maxeys Farm Shop then find the Ossington Sundial for a romantic picnic for two.

→ **Chat** with the locals and enjoy a pint in traditional surroundings at The Final Whistle in Southwell or The Bee Hive at Mapleback.

→ **Soak** up the sunset by swimming beneath the George Bentinck monument, staying to gaze at the stars as they light up in the night sky.

The beautiful county of Nottinghamshire, once part of the Kingdom of Mercia, lies across the Roman Fosse Way, providing visitors with a wealth of history and culture, tranquil spaces, undulating hills, and ancient forests full of folklore: an unexpected trove of history and archaeology. The legend of Robin Hood is synonymous with the county and is woven into the landscape and its narrative, while later literary and religious roots can be traced with Lord Byron, D.H. Lawrence and the Pilgrim Fathers all hailing from the area.

The vibrant city of Nottingham sits atop a subterranean network of over 800 sandstone caves, but travel further afield to discover more remote wonders such as the Hermit's Cave at Dale Abbey, carved out of the same ridge of rock in the 12th-century. Wander down to St Mary's Church in Colston Bassett which looks surprisingly intact until you inspect it further, its outer shell now being all that remains of this 12th century structure.

Creswell Crags has the most northerly cave art in Europe, dating from the ice age; most recently, the largest collection of 'witch marks' in Britain was found here. The homes of religious orders, like Mattersey and Newstead Abbey, offer hints of what life was like before ducal estates like Welbeck and Clumber built their dynasties. Clumber Park is now a stunning expanse of 3,800 acres perfect for families, with woodland trails, wild flowers, cycle routes, lakeside walks and secluded picnic spots to explore.

The popular and thriving River Soar offers multiple opportunities to explore the area by water. Drop a canoe into the river at Zouch or Normanton for a longer kayak. Further north, the River Trent meanders slowly through the countryside offering perfect spots like Littleborough or Burton Joyce for a leisurely swim or kayak.

Food is an integral part of the culture here, with an emphasis on local, high-quality, home-made goods straight from the producer. Head to the villages of Long Clawson, Cropwell Bishop and Colston Bassett in the Vale of Belvoir, for world-renowned, mouth-watering Stilton, or to Nice Pie in Old Dalby for award-winning pork pies. The Cow Shed at Dickies Butchery and Farm Dining is an experience not to be missed, and possibly the best steak you will ever eat. For a more refined meal, The Martin's Arms or The Crown Inn at Old Dalby offer high-quality, locally sourced food in charming surroundings.

LAKES & POOLS

1 NEWSTEAD ABBEY, RAVENSHEAD
Just beyond the quirky cannon fort is a great spot for a discreet swim, with the abbey ruins and Byron's home across the water. Walking in the park is free – or rent the gardener's cottage (see listing).

→ In Newstead follow Tilford Rd over railway (past NG15 0BT), turn R down Station Ave and follow to end. Park at barrier, continue walk and turn L at lake. Swim spot just past fort. To visit the ruins, house and gardens, too (£), use main gate on A60 in Ravenshead.

10 mins, 53.0792, -1.1992

2 CARBURTON FORGE DAM, RIVER POULTER
Wait until the sun starts to set to capture the true majesty of your surroundings from this dam; a memorial to the 19th-century politician George Bentinck can be seen just up the hill (53.2420, -1.1272). An enticing-looking dip from the grassy banks of the lake but private and popular for fishing.

→ Take Limetree Ave E out of Norton, dir S80 3BP. After 1½ miles turn L into car park for reservoir. Various entry points away from road. Monument is ⅓ mile back uphill on R.

4 mins, 53.2438, -1.1148

3 TREETON DYKE
There are a number of good access points at this delightful lake frequented by anglers, swans and mallards. Also used by powered vehicles, and has 'no swimming' signs, so exercise judgement.

→ From Sheffield Rd/B6200 turn into Falconer Lane (S13 9ZL) and find parking (limited). Follow path through gate at end of lane to lake

15 mins, 53.3767, -1.3477

4 HOVERINGHAM LAKES
A pretty riverside walk to these tranquil, old gravel pits. Great picnic spot. There is supervised swimming (fee) and activities in the summer. Other swims along the river.

→ Take Main St E out of Bleasby, over crossroads onto Boat Lane past NG14 7FT, and park at end. Follow footpath R for ¼ mile. See nowca.org for their activities. River swim at 53.0300, -0.9220.

15 mins, 53.0232, -0.9300

5 ST CHAD'S WATER
A hidden gem in the middle of the Derbyshire countryside, this nature reserve in a former gravel pit offers a peaceful picnic spot by a medieval church with a Saxon carved font.

→ In Draycott take Market Street and follow just over 1 mile to nature reserve car park, after DE72 3QH, opposite St Chad's Church.

1 min, 52.8823, -1.3359

6 NETHERFIELD LAGOONS
Secluded local nature reserve that was once a dump for coal slurry. Now a haven for wildfowl, rare birds such as the marsh warbler, wild orchids and dragonflies. A circular walk takes you around the various lagoons to the gravel pits and the river.

→ In Victoria Business Park in Carlton, take Teal Close L off the second roundabout and park near NG4 2PE, before the yellow lines. Walk on to bend, take path R over Ouse Dyke and ¼ mile along bank to footbridge into reserve. Follow the circular track.

20 mins, 52.9536, -1.0503

RIVER SWIMS

7 SEGELOCUM, RIVER TRENT
A serene section of the River Trent, just walk upstream and then swim with the flow. The tiny Norman church of St Nicholas (see listing) is worth a visit.

→ Park at St Nicholas Church in Littleborough (DN22 0HD, E of Sturton le Steeple) and walk

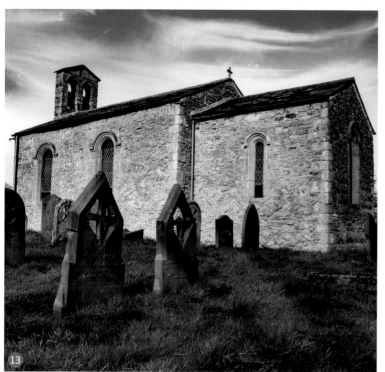

down to river. Footpath to L offers grassy bank for easy access. Walk ½ mile, keeping an eye out for the Chateau (rentable, see listing) between the trees on opposite bank.

5 mins, 53.3399, -0.7573

8 EATON BRIDGE, RIVER IDLE

A great spot for cooling off in the river on a hot summer's day.

→ On A638 just S of Retford, turn off to Eaton (DN22 0PR). Park just after bridge by footpath sign on R. Walk back over bridge and enter river by bench on R. Further entry points along bank for 100m where bank shelves to beach.

4 mins, 53.2943, -0.9371

9 NORMANTON ON SOAR

The perfect launch or landing point for a kayak adventure. Easy swims up- and downstream, or take advantage of the old chain ferry for access to walks along the riverbank.

→ Park on the main street in village (LE12 5HB). Slipway is down Soar Lane, beside pub. For chain ferry (operates May to September) head S, signed through gate R 130m beyond the church.

1 min, 52.8019, -1.2339

10 BURTON JOYCE, RIVER TRENT

Wide ½-mile swim or kayak with the flow along the River Trent. Some fast currents so competent swimmers only, and be careful of rocks on exit.

→ Park near to The Nelson pub (NG14 5DN, see listing). Take path from car park over railway lines and grass to riverside path and turn R. Walk 1 mile to The Ferry Boat Inn (NG14 5HX, 0115 9871232) for easy access, and swim back to The Nelson.

25 mins 52.9854, -1.0338

11 DRAYCOTT BEACH, RIVER DERWENT

A tranquil meander on the River Derwent with a gently sloping beach. Lovely little picnic spot.

→ From A6005 in Draycott turn S on Market Street and follow 1½ miles, past St Chad's Church (DE72 3QH), to park in lay-by R where road comes alongside river. Head over bridge and downstream to beach.

4 mins, 52.8777, -1.3300

12 ZOUCH, RIVER SOAR

Kayak the gentle meanders that surround Zouch, a lovely stretch of the River Soar, ideal for beginners or just for a lazy day out on the river.

→ On A6006 heading E in Zouch, turn L and park just after LE12 5EU and bridge. Kayak to The Otter near Kegworth.
1 min, 52.8068, -1.2471 🏊🚣

SACRED & ANCIENT

13 ST NICHOLAS CHURCH, LITTLEBOROUGH

Built in the 11th century and incorporating Roman tiles and Saxon pillars from earlier settlements on the spot, St Nicholas is one of the smallest churches in England. Swim in the river nearby at Segelocum (see listing).
→ From Sturton le Steeple follow Littleborough Rd E to the end (DN22 0HD). Church is up lane L just before river.
3 mins, 53.3339, -0.7631 ✝

14 CRESWELL CRAGS

Picturesque gorge with fascinating evidence of what life was like during the last ice age, including caves containing Britain's only known ice age rock art.
→ Entrance to museum/cave tours signed off B6042 ½ mile E of Creswell (dir S80 3LQ). Or, park in Creswell (nr S80 4AF), walk along Crag's Rd to track along gorge (½ mile).
5 mins, 53.2626, -1.1981 ♿🧍🚲⛺♨

15 LADY WELL, HEADON

Hidden in an ancient roadside holloway, the arch over this medieval spring has a keystone from the 1700s. Used as a water source until the 1930s.
→ Park carefully at junction of Lady Well Lane and Greenspotts Lane in Nether Headon (DN22 0RQ). Head back up Lady Well Lane hill. 65m after Brickyard Farm cut through into ravine to R. Well is at the base of the bank.
5 mins, 53.2932, -0.8787 ✝📷🧍

16 ST MARY'S CHURCH, COLSTON BASSETT

Solitary outside the village, much of this ruined church still stands proudly on a low rise. Centuries of adaptation, abandonment and restoration can be read in its walls.
→ From the Market Cross pillar at School Lane junction (near NG12 3FD), follow road NW out of Colston Bassett ½ mile, turn R onto New Rd. Park carefully on L after ⅛ mile opposite church and enter via gate.
1 min, 52.8975, -0.9683 ✝📷

17 HERMIT'S CAVE, DALE ABBEY

Hidden in the woods is a 12th-century hermit's cave, hewn out of the rock by a local baker-turned-recluse. Complete with windows, peephole, engraved cross, niche for

20

a light, and a well. Nearby is a majestic arch framing the rural landscape at the edge of an unassuming village field, all that remains of the abbey (52.9442, -1.3501).

→ Park at The Carpenter's Arms (DE7 4PP) and take The Village road S to All Saints Church (attached to a house). Follow the footpath to the R that leads behind the church up through the woods. Footpath over stile L at last bend leads up along field edge to abbey arch.

10 mins, 52.9420, -1.3484 🖼️✝️🚲⛳🏃🚶⛰️🏞️🐾

18

18 CODNOR CASTLE

Abandoned in 1692 and its stones promptly robbed for other structures, this atmospheric, and some say haunted, late-12th-century ruin overlooks the Erewash Valley. Usually quiet, check codnorcastle.co.uk for open days, events and longer walk-in routes.

→ From A610 take turn into N side of Aldercar, past NG16 4HA, then L onto Aldercar Lane. Follow 1½ miles (very rough road) to farm and castle on R. Parking in yard allowed.

2 mins, 53.0449, -1.3547 🐾🌳🏕️🖼️⛳

19

19 OLDOX CAMP

Experience stunning views of traditional patchwork countryside from the twin peaks of this hilltop overlooking this double-

banked enclosure. Just off the Robin Hood Way footpath, and perfect for picnics.

→ Head towards NG25 0RE N of Oxton, take R onto Greaves Lane, park carefully after ½ mile at 53.0800, -1.0577. Take path uphill to woods, turn R and follow woods to hilltop. Or park in Oxton behind The Old Green Dragon (NG25 0SS, see listing) and follow Windmill Lane and footpath 1 mile straight to hills.

20 mins, 53.0721, -1.0547 🐾🏃🏕️🖼️🐕✿

20 MATTERSEY PRIORY

By a remote farm lie the ruinous remains of a 13th-century priory, home to the uniquely English Gilbertine Order of nuns.

→ Take Abbey Rd E of Mattersey (DN10 5DX), park at the Private Rd sign and continue on foot for 1 mile. EH, free.

20 mins, 53.3981, -0.9439 ✝️🏃🖼️⛰️🏞️

21 OSSINGTON SUNDIAL

In the dappled shade of the extensive woodland beyond the church stands a sundial dating from the early 17th century. Snowdrops carpet the ground in spring – a delightful venue for a secluded, romantic picnic.

→ In Ossington follow Ossington Rd E, dir Carlton. Take L (dir NG23 6LH) and follow signs

through gates for Holy Rood Church. Park at church, sundial to rear.
3 mins, 53.1782, -0.8650 🖼️✝️

22 ALL SAINTS OLD CHURCH, ANNESLEY
Substantial ruins of a 14th-century church which still stand proudly on a mound. The building remains are Grade I listed and perfect for exploring and a picnic.
→ Just off M1 at J27; follow A608 signed Hucknall/Mansfield and Annesley, straight over roundabout, signed R after ½ mile (NG15 0AS).
2 mins, 53.0660, -1.2502 🅿️✝️

23 HAUGHTON CHAPEL
These secluded ruins in a clump of trees by the River Maun are all that remains of the village of Haughton, destroyed by enclosure in 1509.
→ Park in car park at bend on B6387 by DN22 8DY. Follow path along river E ½ mile to ruins.
8 mins, 53.2494, -0.9657 🖼️⛰️ℹ️🧍🖼️✝️

SHERWOOD FOREST

24 CLUMBER PARK, WORKSOP
The perfect family day: walks in the woods, cycle trails, lakeside walks, a Gothic church, and a café in the woods. NT but worth the entry price (cash only)!
→ Entry points all around park: from Limetree Ave NE of S80 3AE (at 53.2828, -1.0571) follow road straight to Hardwick Village and park at the Broomwagon Velo Cafe (S80 3PB).
5 mins, 53.2710, -1.04537 🚲🚶🧍🍴🖼️🐾🖼️

25 ST EDWIN'S CHAPEL CROSS
A metal cross on an ancient holy site dedicated to the beatified King Edwin of Northumbria, who died in battle against an Anglo-Welsh pagan alliance in AD 632.
→ Take A6075 from Mansfield E dir NG21 9HG, and ⅓ mile after Market Warsop double roundabout park in rough lay-by on L. Follow path along tree line, take first path on R after 400m, along tree line 200m.
4 mins, 53.1932, -1.1129 ✝️🖼️

26 RUFFORD ABBEY
Set in the grounds of the country park are these stunning remains of both a 12th-century Cistercian abbey and the later mansion they were incorporated into. Great walks around the grounds. EH, free but pay parking.
→ Signed off A614, 2 miles S of Ollerton (NG22 9DF).
5 mins, 53.1759, -1.0356 🖼️✝️🧍🅿️🐾🍴

27 SHERWOOD PINES

Set in the heart of Robin Hood's forest, miles of tracks through the pine trees are laid out for walking, cycling and adventures. Forest Holidays cabins and a campsite. Well-loved particularly by families who make the most of the kids' trails, activities and bike hire.

→ Signed off the B6030 east of Kings Clipstone (NG21 9JL)

1 min, 53.1557, -1.08598 🚶🚴🏊🐟🏕🅿🍴🏖⛺

WOODS & WILDLIFE

28 ATTENBOROUGH NATURE RESERVE

This back door entrance avoids the busy visitor centre and takes you straight to peaceful trails and the tranquil waters of the reserve. Renowned for its amazing winter wildfowl. Paths link up to the River Trent.

→ In Attenborough village, park on The Strand (NG9 6AU) and head into reserve at gate to R of cricket ground.

10 mins, 52.9027, -1.2273 🏊🏕🚴🚶🏖🔭🍴

29 TRESWELL WOOD

A lovely ash, oak and maple wood, this nature reserve is a haven for wildlife. Primroses and bluebells cover the ground in spring, and if you are very quiet you might catch sight of its elusive inhabitants such as roe deer, stoats, hares or woodpeckers.

→ Travel W from Treswell 1⅓ miles onto Wood Lane, parking at entrance to reserve on L after houses (DN22 0ED).

4 mins, 53.3106, -0.8588 🚶🏕🐕🚗🔭

30 BESTWOOD COUNTRY PARK

Once a bustling coal mine (some buildings have been restored), Bestwood is now an oasis of calm with many meandering paths through the woods to explore. Look out for deer, or migrating birds at the Mill Lakes.

→ From the B683 through Bestwood, N Nottingham, take Park Rd ⅓ mile, past NG6 8TQ, to park entrance R.

2 mins, 53.0229, -1.1688 🚶🚴🏕🚗🐕🐟

31 WILWELL FARM CUTTING

This nature reserve tucked in at the edge of the city is one of the best sites in the county for wild flowers and the vast array of butterflies that visit them.

→ Head ¾ mile N from Ruddington on B680 and take track forking L after NG11 6NA, just before bridge. Limited parking within, keep road gate clear.

5 mins, 52.9097, -1.1581 🔀🚶🏕

32 SHIPLEY COUNTRY PARK

With over 18 miles of walks, this 600-acre park provides a perfect chance to lose yourself amongst its varied meadows, woods and lakes. Enjoy a picnic and watch the sunset from its many vantage points.

→ Travelling into Heanor on A608, take Thorpes Rd just after New Inn/opp Jolly Colliers (DE75 7QL) continue to Slack Lane and pay parking.
5 mins, 53.0005, -1.3520 🐶🚶🚲♨️🚻🌳♿🅿️

33 DUKE'S WOOD

A lovely woodland nature reserve with a hidden industrial past: it was the country's first onshore oilfield, and some restored pumps stand along the trail. Spring and summer flowers and butterflies abound.

→ Park at entrance gate halfway along the Eakring to Kirklington Rd, just S of NG22 8PA.
6 mins, 53.1351, -0.9917 🏛️♿🅿️

REGAL RUINS

34 SUTTON SCARSDALE HALL

A splendid shell of a grand Georgian mansion built in 1724. It was sold and stripped of roof and interiors in 1919; conservation work recently started on what is left. You can't enter inside but you can enjoy its exterior stonework

and there are glorious views over the countryside and plenty of space to run wild.
→ At the end of Hall Drive, Sutton Scarsdale, beyond S44 5UR. English Heritage, free.
2 mins, 53.2153, -1.3398 🏛️🖼️

35 KING JOHN'S PALACE

A few ruinous walls are all that remains of a substantial 12th-century royal residence, visited by the infamous king no more than nine times. It sits on private land, be respectful; usually open for the village beer and cider festival each summer.

→ Take B6030 S out of Kings Clipstone. Just after bend to R at brow of hill, park on grass verge near NG21 9BN; or there is a lay-by further on. Walk back down to gate on R, into field.
6 mins, 53.1765, -1.0988 🖼️♿

SLOW FOOD

36 WELBECK FARM SHOP & CAFE

One of the county's best farm shops: onsite brewery, local produce, often from the estate, and its own award-winning, unpasteurised Stichelton blue cheese.
→ Worksop, S80 3LW, 01909 478725.
53.2617, -1.1796 🍴♿

37 GONALSTON FARM SHOP

A food lover's paradise! Fish counter, butchery, fresh bread, award-winning deli, local produce and friendly staff.

→ Southwell Road, Lowdham, NG14 7DR, 0115 9665666.
53.0147, -0.9918 🍴

38 THROUGH THE GATE (BOUVERIE LODGE)

Quirky smallholding specialising in bison and venison. Great on-site café open until 2pm, serving a range of food including meat from the farm. Ruth and her team are warm and friendly and encourage all visitors to wander freely around the farm.

→ Nottingham Road, Nether Broughton, LE14 3ES, 07976 409923.
52.8210, -0.9601 🍴

39 VALE OF BELVOIR, STILTON

Only six places are licensed to produce the blue veined Stilton cheese, and three villages here are recognised as the finest. Start at Cropwell Bishop and work your way south to Long Clawson (52.8360, -0.9344) and Colston Bassett (52.8916, -0.9567). A must for cheese lovers.

→ Cropwell Bishop Creamery, Nottingham Road, Cropwell Bishop, NG12 3BQ, 0115 9891788; Long Clawson Dairy, Long Clawson, LE14 4PJ, 01664 822332; Colston Bassett Dairy, Harby Lane, Colston Bassett, NG12 3FN, 01949 81322.
52.9126, -0.9872 🍴

40 NICE PIE

Step inside the wooden barn and you will enter a cosy café/shop adorned with vintage furniture, armchairs and a wood-burner, outside picnic benches look over the fields. Enjoy their much-acclaimed handmade pies, hearty breakfasts or traditional English tea, served with a wide range of sandwiches and tempting cakes.

→ Six Hills Lane, Old Dalby, Melton Mowbray, LE14 3NB, 07531 641893.
52.7979, -0.9804 🍴

41 MAXEYS FARM SHOP

A great farm shop full of high-quality products including meat from the farm, freshly made cobs from the deli, and coffee to take away.

→ Brickfield Farm, Hockerton Road, Kirklington, NG22 8PB.
53.1075, -0.9637 🍴

42 THE MARTIN'S ARMS, COLSTON BASSETT

A gorgeous Elizabethan farmhouse which is now a charming eatery. Its elegant rooms ooze country house charm with soft furnishings, old settles, and log fires. Delicious, home-made food served with a wide range of real ales.

→ School Lane, Colston Bassett, NG12 3FD, 01949 81361.
52.8914, -0.9637 🍺🍴

43 THE CROWN INN, OLD DALBY

Beautifully renovated village pub serving a simple menu executed to a high standard. Outstanding friendly and attentive service.

→ Debdale Hill, Old Dalby, LE14 3LF, 01664 820320.
52.8081, -1.0051 🍺🍴

44 DICKIES BUTCHERY & THE COW SHED

Unique, authentic and rustic, this tin-and-timber building contains a seasonally focused restaurant with a butchery behind. At one end of the restaurant lies a huge fire and at the other an open kitchen.

→ 45 Barkestone Lane, Plungar, NG13 0JA, 01949 869733.
52.9006, -0.8540 🍴🍴

45 MANOR FARM TEA SHOPPE, BLEASBY

Serving sublime cooked breakfasts and a tasty, varied lunch menu, this is the perfect place to meet friends. You can even book into the onsite shepherds' hut for the night.

→ Manor Farm House, Station Road, Bleasby, NG14 7FX, 01636 831316.
53.0425, -0.9461 🍴🛏

46 GATEHOUSE TEAROOMS

Originally the main entry to the priory built for Carthusian monks in 1343, the thriving tearoom serves delicious cakes and light lunches. Take a stroll around the priory ruins, open for the same hours (10am–4pm, Wed–Sun).

→ Beauvale Abbey Farm, New Road, Moorgreen, NG16 2AA, 01773 710682.
53.0360, -1.2668 🍴🚶🚲✝

47 CHEQUERS INN, WOOLSTHORPE

Award-winning inn with open fires in the cosy, traditional bar area, a spacious modern restaurant, and a garden out back for eating al fresco in summer.

→ Main Street, Woolsthorpe by Belvoir, NG32 1LU, 01476 870701.
52.8981, -0.7556 🍺🍴🛏

COSY PUBS

48 THE BEES' KNEES PUB
A great little pub with the Springhead Brewery next door. Food served each evening.
→ Main St, Laneham, DN22 0NA, 01777 228090.
53.2770, -0.7934 🏠

49 BEEHIVE, MAPLEBECK
This unpretentious, welcoming pub was once the smallest pub in England. The heartbeat of the village.
→ The Hollows, Maplebeck, NG22 0BS.
53.1389, -0.9397 🏠

50 THE FINAL WHISTLE, SOUTHWELL
Fabulous real ale and cider pub with a great outdoor seating area and many features from the redundant railway station.
→ Station Road, Southwell, NG25 0ET, 01636 814953.
53.0818, -0.9471 🍴

51 OLD GREEN DRAGON, OXTON
Award-winning, welcoming hostelry specialising in local real ales and ciders. Good-quality pub food.
→ Blind Ln, Oxton, NG25 0SS, 0115 9652243.
53.0587, -1.0616 🏠🍴

52 DIXIES ARMS, LOWER BAGTHORPE
Honest, unspoilt local with tiled floors and wooden beams. A focus on real ale and genuine hospitality makes this cosy pub a favourite in the area.
→ Lower Bagthorpe, Bagthorpe, NG16 5HF, 01773 810505.
53.0595, -1.2961 🏠🍴

CAMP & SLEEP

53 THE CHATEAU, GATE BURTON
Romantic miniature chateau by the River Trent; sleeps two in Georgian elegance, with a balcony and log fires.
→ landmarktrust.org.uk, 01628 825925
53.3412, -0.7549 🏠

54 GARDENER'S COTTAGE
Delightful, recently restored cottage in the grounds of Newstead Abbey (see entry).
→ Ravenshead, NG15 8NA, 01623 455900.
53.0782, -1.1929 🏠

55 BROWNS OF HOLBECK
Award-winning, boutique B&B in a beautiful countryside location. Sorry, no children.

→ The Old Orchard Cottage, Holbeck, S80 3NF, 01909 720659.
53.2539, -1.1864 🏠

56 LITTLE OAK CAMPING
Secluded and peaceful camping and glamping surrounded by open countryside. Fruit and vegetable garden.
→ Grove Coach Road, Retford, DN22 0PW, 07538 581476.
53.3094, -0.9215 ⛺🏠🚿

57 LANGAR NEAR THE HALL
A fusion of mod cons and tasteful vintage make this bright little cottage a favourite with both couples and families.
→ Langar, NG13 9HD, 07771 883273.
52.9024, -0.9256 🏠

58 ELTON BARN CAMPING & FISHERY
Enjoy your own cosy indoor BBQ in wooden lodges, sleep in shepherds' huts overlooking the fishing lake, or camp in the quiet field (no electrical hook-ups).
→ Elton Barn, Grantham Road, NG13 9EW, 01949 851720.
52.9398, -0.8831 🏠⛺

RUSTIC HAVENS

59 ODDHOUSE FARM GLAMPING
Luxury bell tents and gypsy caravan in a pretty meadow. Hampers of local food available and spa treatments onsite.
→ Owthorpe, NG12 3SF, 07951 985688.
52.8896, -0.9893 🏠🍴🚿

60 TIN AND WOOD SHEPHERDS' HUTS
Beautifully crafted shepherds' huts overlooking the Grantham Canal in a peaceful rural setting.
→ 17 Granby Lane, Plungar, NG13 0JJ, 07974 979506, canopyandstars.co.uk.
52.9013, -0.8605 🏠🚗♿

61 ARCHWAY HOUSE
This Victorian Gothic hunting lodge and folly offers accommodation for up to 8 people in the heart of a secluded patch of Sherwood Forest just a few minutes' walk from the River Maun. Niches contain statues of forest folklore such as Robin Hood, Maid Marion and Friar Tuck.
→ Archway Road, Kings Clipstone, NG21 9HF, 01623 824016.
53.1864, -1.0929 🏠

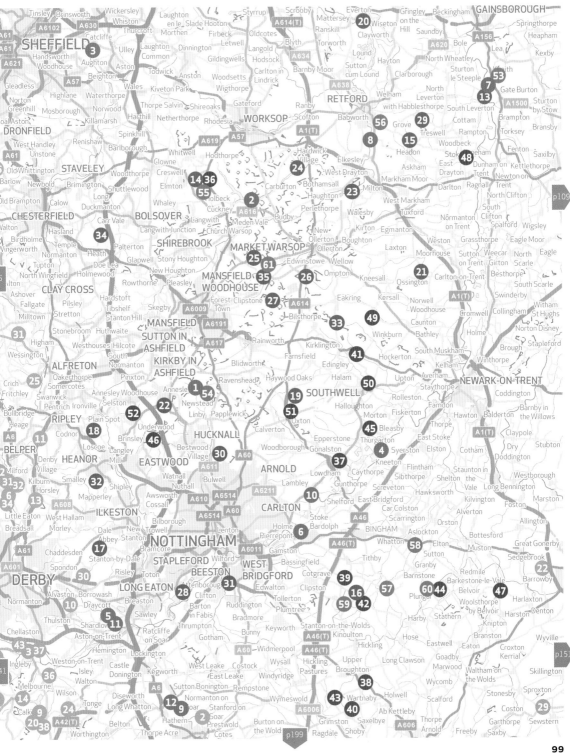

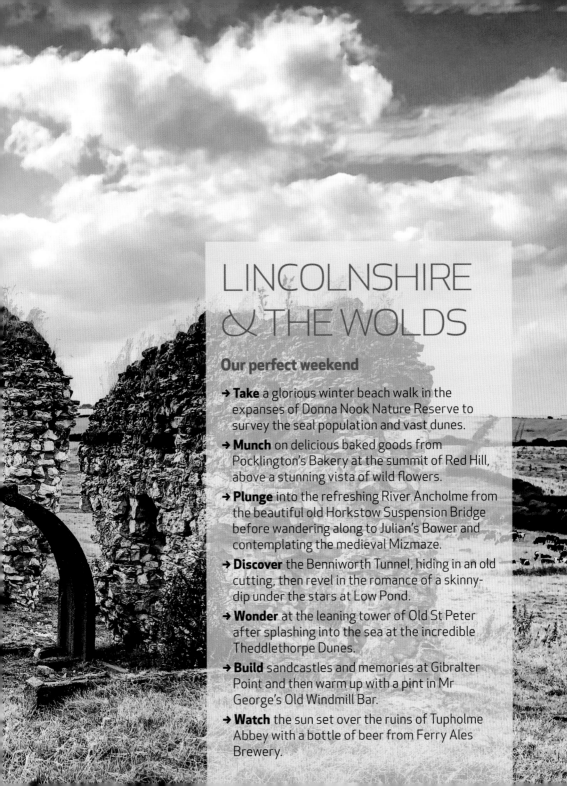

LINCOLNSHIRE & THE WOLDS

Our perfect weekend

→ **Take** a glorious winter beach walk in the expanses of Donna Nook Nature Reserve to survey the seal population and vast dunes.

→ **Munch** on delicious baked goods from Pocklington's Bakery at the summit of Red Hill, above a stunning vista of wild flowers.

→ **Plunge** into the refreshing River Ancholme from the beautiful old Horkstow Suspension Bridge before wandering along to Julian's Bower and contemplating the medieval Mizmaze.

→ **Discover** the Benniworth Tunnel, hiding in an old cutting, then revel in the romance of a skinny-dip under the stars at Low Pond.

→ **Wonder** at the leaning tower of Old St Peter after splashing into the sea at the incredible Theddlethorpe Dunes.

→ **Build** sandcastles and memories at Gibralter Point and then warm up with a pint in Mr George's Old Windmill Bar.

→ **Watch** the sun set over the ruins of Tupholme Abbey with a bottle of beer from Ferry Ales Brewery.

With its flat fenlands, vast expanses of unspoilt coastline and rolling wolds, Lincolnshire is a land of intrigues. Its marshy wetlands created the fertile plains of the Fens in the south, but when the Romans settled in the Wolds they developed an infrastructure of forts, three great roads, dykes, inland ports and straightened rivers.

These waterways, thriving and busy when they connected the bustling trades of the area with Europe, now offer plenty of serene opportunities for those wishing to swim, kayak or simply splash about. Brandy Wharf and the Louth Navigation Canal are great for a swim or kayak, or you can join the locals who jump off the listed suspension bridge at Horkstow. The Branston Island Loop is a great place for a longer swim, or Low Pond lake offers seclusion amongst nature. Be more cautious of the coastal areas, as many places are not recommended for swimming due to dangerous tides and currents. Access to the sea is safer at Moggs Eye, with long, unspoilt stretches of sand.

A Danish invasion in AD 865 paved the way for the settlement of Scandinavians and their Danelaw, ruling over 15 English counties at its height. Walkers can now hike along the Viking Way from the shores of the Humber across the Wolds right down to Rutland Water. The path passes the ruins of Norman abbeys at Barlings, Tupholme and Bardney in the Witham Valley, home to the highest concentration of abbeys in England. Few castles were built here, but some good examples still exist, such as Bolingbroke. More poignant are the deserted villages, such as Calceby, abandoned as livestock farming took over from crops and reduced the demand for agricultural labour.

More recently, there were over 46 RAF bases in Lincolnshire, critical for defending the eastern approaches during the Second World War. Many have now closed, but memories of that time still echo through the county. Wander through the nature reserve at Tattershall Carrs to discover old aircraft hangars and bomb shelters slowly rewilding. The Blue Bell Inn, a thatched 13th-century pub, was the favourite haunt of the Dambusters, who were based close by. The pennies of airmen are still lodged in the ceiling for their next pint, a haunting reminder of the number who never made it home.

Still a very rural area, dotted with market towns and villages, Lincolnshire has garnered a reputation for high-quality food production. Local specialities such as stuffed chine and plum bread are almost unknown outside the county, but other gastronomic delights like the sage-seasoned Lincolnshire sausage and golden Lincolnshire Poacher cheese are staples of British cuisine: find them all at sellers like the Cheese Shop and Pocklington's Bakery in Louth, or RJ Hirst butcher's in Woodhall Spa.

RIVER SWIMMING

1 BRANDY WHARF, RIVER ANCHOLME

An interesting swim or kayak in the narrow, diverted section of an old river that is now as straight as a Roman Road!

➔ Take Waddingham Rd/B1205 from South Kelsey 2 miles to Brandy Wharf. At second bend after bridge, turn L down track to river. Swim or kayak down to bridge.

2 mins, 53.4556, -0.4717 🏊🚣🏕

2 BRANSTON ISLAND LOOP

Swim the loop past Mrs Wright's former lock house at Bardney, around the lush, green fields of Branston Island, where the River Witham and Old River Witham join. There may be fishing: use discretion.

➔ Park in Bardney by Heritage Centre LN3 5UF. Cross road and follow Water Rail Way up to Bardney Lock. Use metal steps down into water on RH side to swim anticlockwise. Be aware that you need to exit on L side after the fishing site to navigate the weir before re-entering the water to finish the swim.

20 mins, 53.2157, -0.3477 🏊🚣🏃🚶🧍🏕

3 HORKSTOW BRIDGE

The beautiful Grade II listed suspension bridge is a fantastic place to leap into the Ancholme. Popular with locals on a hot day.

➔ From South Ferriby take High St/B1204 S 1 mile, turn R onto Bridge Lane by DN18 6BE, drive to limited parking at end. Follow footpath down to river near bridge.

2 mins, 53.6583, -0.5282 🏊🚣🍴

4 LOUTH NAVIGATION CANAL

Despite its less than appealing name, this river is no longer used for navigation and is ideal for a long swim down through leafy green pastures.

➔ From A1031 in Tetney, take Tetney Lock Rd E 2 miles and over bridge to park near DN36 5UW. Walk back over bridge to take path L. Enter river after 100m on bend. Exit at sluice 400m down, or continue on for a longer swim.

5 mins, 53.4976, 0.0196 🏊🚣

LAKES & SPRINGS

5 SWANHOLME LAKES

Wild spaces such as this offer a handy escape from urban life and many opportunities for fun. Beautifully clear lakes (SSSI, No Swimming) with tantalising islands and paths winding through the woods dappled in sunlight.

➔ In Lincoln take Doddington Rd/B1190 opp Methodist church (LN6 8RZ), after 1⅓ miles turn R into Birchwood Av and park. Walk back to footpath sign at bus stop on main road. Follow R fork in path around fences to lake.

5 mins, 53.2051, -0.5940 🚶❓🏕

6 TETNEY BLOW WELLS

Artesian springs once used for a watercress farm and to provide the locals with water. Crystal-clear waters, but be wary of very cold temperatures and signs saying no swimming. Pipistrelle bats haunt the trees at dusk.

➔ Park in Tetney close to footpath from Church Lane, opposite Primrose Lane (DN36 5PJ). Follow path through field to first blow well in front of you to L of field.

15 mins, 53.4872, -0.01035 🏊ℹ️❓🚗

7 LOW POND, DONINGTON ON BAIN

A secluded lake, dappled by shade, offering the perfect spot for skinny-dipping on a hot summer's evening.

➔ Follow B1225 south of Ludford 4½ miles, past LN8 6JT, turn L signed Donington on Bain. Follow ½ mile and park on verge R as road bends L. Follow footpath over stile and R at field end, past first lake.

20 mins, 53.3247, -0.1557 🏃🚶🏕🏕🔢

BRILLIANT BEACHES

8 MOGGS EYE

A long, sandy, often deserted and unspoilt beach. Perfect for a run, dip, kite-flying, or picnic.

➜ Heading N on Roman Bank coastal road, take first proper road R (not gravel) after Anderby Creek and PE24 5XJ, signed Moggs Eye. Car park at end. Be aware of tide times.
2 mins, 53.2725, 0.3188 🏖🚶👨‍👩‍👧⛱

9 GIBRALTAR POINT

A beautiful, unspoilt expanse of coastline incorporating sand dunes, salt marshes and freshwater lakes in the nature reserve. Access to the beach but be aware of tide times and the tidal creek.

➜ Take Gibraltar Rd S out of Skegness. Park in Beach car park (PE24 4ST) and follow path down to beach. Other trails on map in car park.
15 mins, 53.0968, 0.3354 🏖🌊🚶👪👨‍👩‍👧⛱

10 THEDDLETHORPE DUNES RESERVE

Walk through the dunes to a quiet, sandy beach with extensive walks either way: look for orchids and listen for noisy natterjack toads. A couple of miles N is a Second World War tank.

➜ Heading N from Mablethorpe turn R off A1031 at Theddlethorpe St Helens. Both roads here lead to dunes (past LN12 1NW or LN12 1NR), and are crossed by foot- and cycle paths, and have car parks at end. Tank at 53.3959, 0.2206.
5 mins, 53.3803, 0.2316 🏖🚶⛱🚴

ANCIENT & SACRED

11 BARLINGS ABBEY

Along the Viking Way, the single remaining wall section of a once-majestic 12th-century abbey is still a commanding presence on the hillside.

➜ In Langworth on A158, take Barlings Lane S signed Barlings at LN3 5DA. Follow 1½ miles, take L signed Low Barling, follow 1 mile to Viking Way footpath and park (53.2480, -0.3718). Follow footpath E past farm.
3 mins, 53.2479, -0.3689 🔆🏛✝⛱

12 TUPHOLME ABBEY

Interesting remains of monastic building, framing a perfect picnic spot just off the Viking Way. With a map, can make circular walk to Bardney Abbey (see entry).

➜ Take Horncastle Rd/B1190 from Bardney (LN3 5TY) dir Bucknall, after 1¾ miles park in lay-by R on bend and walk up track.
5 mins, 53.1983, -0.2885 🔆✝⛱

13 BARDNEY ABBEY

Read the outline of this monastery, founded in AD 697 by King Æthelred of Mercia, in the knee-high lumps and bumps in the grass. With a map, can make circular walk to Tupholme Abbey (see entry).

→ In Bardney take Abbey Road past LN3 5XA to end, through farmyard, to small parking area by the wooden monk.

3 mins, 53.2203, -0.3335 👟✝⛺

14 THORNTON ABBEY & GATEHOUSE

Remarkably majestic gatehouse at entrance to ruins of abbey. The spiral staircases and maze of corridors are truly wonderful. English Heritage, but well worth the fee.

→ From B1206 at Barrow upon Humber take College Rd signed East Halton. Abbey signed R after 3 miles (DN39 6TU). Short walk from Thornton Abbey station.

3 mins, 53.6553, -0.3138 ✝🖼️🚂🎫

15 OLD ST PETER, SALTFLEETBY

Nestled in a small, atmospheric graveyard, this 15th-century church tower tilts in a very peculiar way. The rest of the church was relocated in 1877.

→ Heading E on B1200 through Saltfleetby

St Peter, turn L at crossroads onto North End Lane then unsigned R after 300m onto Charles Gate, at LN11 7SP. Tower is R at bend after 700m, with limited parking space.

2 mins, 53.3867, 0.15723 ✝👟

16 KIRKSTEAD ABBEY & CHAPEL

Only a shard of the south transept of the church remains standing, but surrounding earthworks reveal the extent of the Cistercian monastery. It was founded in 1139 by monks from Fountains Abbey in Yorkshire; its beautiful chapel in the trees was spared in the dissolution and is still in monthly use.

→ Take Tattershall Rd/B1192 S from Woodhall Spa (LN10 6TL) about ¼ mile, turn R at Abbey Lodge Inn. Park at gate to abbey L after ¼ mile at bend in road. Woodhall Spa Churches group hold keys to St Leonard's chapel, visible further along track.

5 mins, 53.1386, -0.2236 🚶⛺👟➕✝

17 JULIAN'S BOWER, ALKBOROUGH

Situated high over the Alkborough Flats, the rare, medieval turf Mizmaze offers an excellent viewpoint over the estuary and Alkborough Flats. Lots of paths along estuary for a walk with views and birdspotting.

→ Parking easiest on Front St, Alkborough (DN15 9JW). Follow brown signs down Back Street and then footpath to maze.
2 mins, 53.6848, -0.6687 ⚑♿♿

REMNANTS & RUINS

18 BOLINGBROKE CASTLE
Substantial remains of a hexagonal castle built in the 13th century, badly damaged by Cromwell's forces in 1643 and 'slighted' after the Civil War.
→ Park on Moat Lane in Old Bolingbroke, near Black Horse Inn (PE23 4HH, 01790 763388). Walk S along lane to gate.
2 mins, 53.1651, 0.0175 ♿▦⛩

19 CALCEBY DESERTED VILLAGE
All that remains, except for lumps and bumps in the field, is the isolated ruins of St Andrew's Church. They stand on the top of the hill as a reminder of the village doomed by changes in farming 400 years ago.
→ Signed from A16 3 miles S of Burwell at staggered crossroads, dir LN13 0AX, opp South Thoresby turning. Lay-by R after ⅓ mile and field gate to remains just before the T-junction.
2 mins, 53.2601, 0.0820 ▦♿⛩

20 THE WHITE LADY OF NORTH ORMSBY
Believed to be Roman in origin, this life-size statue was erected in 1850 as a monument to an unfortunate lady who lost her life in a riding accident. Traces of a lost village can be seen in the ridges of the landscape.
→ Head SW through North Ormsby (LN11 0TJ). Park by white house on L after ½ mile. On private land, but knock on door for friendly access.
5 mins, 53.4179, -0.0752 ♿?

WOODLANDS & WILDLIFE

21 CHAMBERS FARM WOOD
A charming medieval woodland with many paths wandering through it, noted for butterflies.
→ Signposted off B1202, N of Bardney. Car park at end, after farm (LN8 5JR).
15 mins, 53.2530, -0.2658 ⛐♿♿⛩

22 LINWOOD WARREN
This area of northern Lincolnshire's wind-deposited 'coversands' is a rare, heather-rich scrubland fringed with trees, alive with butterflies, moths and birds. Take a hammock and settle down to watch the wildlife.

→ Take Legsby Rd out of Market Rasen dir LN8 3QT. After 1½ miles, park in lay-by R, after golf course entrance L, just before Wild Pines L.
5 mins, 53.3722, -0.2977 🅿🚶🔀⛩

23 DONNA NOOK NATURE RESERVE
One of the best places in the country to spot seals, especially early winter when they come ashore to pup. Huge expanse of dunes and coastline for walks; keep out of MOD areas when red flags are flying.
→ During pupping season, follow the signed one-way system, restrictions and overflow pay car parks that are in place to cope with large numbers. Otherwise, take Marsh Lane N out of N Somercotes past LN11 7NT. Follow straight to end and car park.
4 mins, 53.4765, 0.1407 🚗🚶🐕

24 CORONATION MEADOW, RED HILL
Once a barley field, this chalkland meadow transforms in spring and summer to a colourful, tapestry of wild flowers. Across the road the overgrown quarry of Red Hill is rich in fossils.
→ Take A153 for 5 miles NE of Hornchurch, turn L for Asterby. After ⅓ mile turn R again, then follow 1 mile to turn R at Manor Farm (LN11 9UD). Parking L after ⅓ mile, just after LH bend, meadow lies to L of farm track opp.
1 min, 53.3080, -0.1021 🚗⛩

25 TATTERSHALL CARRS
Two Woodland Trust alder woods famed for bluebells, often used by the famous RAF Dambusters. Remnants of the bomb shelters and aircraft hangars are now home to bats. Paths can be muddy all year.
→ On B1192 in Tattershall Thorpe head N past The Blue Bell Inn (LN4 4PE, see listing). Park on verge to L alongside end of woodland, just before Thorpe Camp Visitor Centre. Woodland through wooden gate. For other wood take footpath at S of pub over first field, turn L along hedge into wood.
2 mins, 53.1196, -0.1828 🏛🅿🔀🚶⛩

26 RIGSBY WOOD, ALFORD
A little path winds among the trees of this ancient woodland, with sunshine dappling through the branches. Butterflies abound. Beautiful in all seasons, especially in spring when carpets of bluebells unfurl.
→ Take the Rigsby turning (dir LN13 0AN) off the A1104 SW of Alford, and after just over 1 mile park on corner where road bends L. Track here leads to woodland.
5 mins, 53.2639, 0.1296 🅿🚗🔀🚶⛩

27 BENNIWORTH TUNNEL
Hidden in an old hillside cutting is this elegant brick railway tunnel from 1875. You can still walk through the 500m from one end to the other.
→ B1225 south of Donnington Rd. After ½ mile park at track entrance of R, just after Belmont House Farm. Follow track on R to cutting.
10 mins, 53.3301, -0.1835 🏞🚶⛩🛈

28 RIVER WITHAM WATER RAIL WAY
This 33-mile, road-free cycle route is part of National Cycle Route number 1. Along the way are sculptures inspired by local themes and the poems of Tennyson, and numerous swim spots. Start in Lincoln city centre or in Bardney, with cycle hire at both.
→ By the bridge at Waterside South, LN5 7FB has some public parking, see hirebikelincoln. co.uk for information on the city bike scheme. Bardney Heritage Centre is at LN3 5UF, see Branston Island swim entry.
1 min, 53.2269, -0.5250 🚲🔀

29 HOPE & ANCHOR, SOUTH FERRIBY

Award-winning, 19th-century gastropub in a tucked-away location overlooking the Humber. Don't be put off by its rather uncharming exterior, it's welcoming inside and there's a garden with views of the water.
→ Sluice Road, South Ferriby, Barton-upon-Humber, DN18 6JQ, 01652 635334. 53.6774, -0.5242 🍴🍷⛵

30 TEA HOUSE & KINEMA IN THE WOODS

A lovely, traditional tea house, first opened in 1903, serving an extensive range of delicious meals and a great Sunday lunch. Next door in a converted pavilion is the only full-time cinema in the country to use back-projection, open since 1922. A must-see!
→ Spa Grounds, Coronation Road, Woodhall Spa, LN10 6QD, 01526 354455. 53.1548, -0.2128 🍴

31 RJ HIRST BUTCHERS

When in Lincolnshire.... visit a great family butcher's selling a range of local delicacies, from the famous sausage to the lesser-known Lincolnshire stuffed chine.
→ Station Road, Woodhall Spa, LN10 6QL, 01526 352321. 53.1519, -0.2160 🍴

32 MYERS BAKERY, ALFORD

Traditional family baker, café and deli selling their famous Lincolnshire plum loaf, local cheeses, and other delights.
→ 20 Bull Ring, Alford, LN9 5HU, 01507 525871. 53.2084, -0.1148 🍴

33 THE CHEESE SHOP, LOUTH

The most amazing savoury pies in Lincolnshire, freshly prepared with local ingredients. Outstanding selection of cheese.
→ 110 Eastgate, Louth LN11 9AA, 01507 600407. 53.3673, -0.0020 🍴

34 STEAMING KETTLE BUFFET

Converted train carriage café at the station of a heritage steam train route. Delightful! Volunteer-run and open on running days and special events: call or see railway website.
→ Lincolnshire Wolds Railway, Ludborough Station, DN36 5SQ, 01507 363881. 53.4448, -0.0309 🚂🍴

35 POCKLINGTON'S BAKERY, LOUTH

Traditional family bakers, selling speciality plum loaf, bread and savouries, made using local ingredients as much as possible.
→ 2 Market Place, Louth, LN11 9AA, 01507 600180. 53.3666, -0.0045 🍴

36 FERRY ALES BREWERY

Award-winning micro-brewery selling their beers from the 'shed-shop' out front.
→ Ferry Road, Stainfield, LN3 4HU, 0800 9993226 . Ring ahead to check opening times. 53.2321, -0.3746 🍷

37 MR GEORGE'S WINDMILL BAR

Charming Batemans Brewery bar housed in a former bakery windmill, used by the brewery since the start of the century to bottle their wares. Shop, food, brewery tours and campsite all available. A rare real ale pub.
→ Wainfleet, PE24 4JE. 01754 880317. 53.1040, 0.2322 🍴🍷⛺

38 THE INN ON THE GREEN, INGHAM

Tucked away at the corner of the village green, this Grade II listed limestone pub offers a fantastic Sunday roast.
→ 34 The Green, Ingham, LN1 2XT, 01522 730354. 53.3403, -0.5794 🍷🍴

39 THE KINGS HEAD, TEALBY

The oldest pub in Lincolnshire with a thatched roof. Real ales and lovely summer beer garden.
→ 11 Kingsway, Tealby, LN8 3YA, 01673 838347. 53.3987, -0.2626 🍷

40 THE BLUE BELL INN

Built in 1257, this pub has seen its fair share of iconic historical figures, from royal fugitives to the Dambusters. A favourite haunt of the RAF, with many names scrawled on the ceiling and pennies left in the beams for their next pint.
→ Thorpe Road, Tattershall Thorpe, LN4 4PE, 01526 342206. 53.1183, -0.1797 🍷

41 THE SHIP INN, BARNOLDBY LE BECK

Traditional pub with good food and an interesting collection of Edwardian curiosities.
→ Main Road, Barnoldby le Beck, DN37 0BG, 01472 822308. 53.5112, -0.1372 🍷

CAMP & SLEEP

42 BAINLAND COUNTRY PARK

Safari tents and other glamping options, some with hot tubs, suitable for families or groups.

→ Horncastle Road, Woodhall Spa, LN10 6UX, 01526 352903.
53.1597, -0.1852 🛶

43 THREE HORSESHOES, GOULCEBY

Glorious views over the countryside from this well-kept camping field, with glamping options and a warm welcome in the pub (though weekends only in winter).

→ Shoe Lane, Goulceby, LN11 9WA
53.2935, -0.1211 ⛺🍴🛶🍴

44 DEAN HOUSE CAMPSITE

Sit around an open fire and enjoy some stargazing at this back-to-basics, adults-only camping field.

→ Gautby, Horncastle LN9 5RW,
07944 247811, pitchup.com
53.2389, -0.2278 ⛺🍴

45 WAINFLEET CONTROL TOWER

The ultimate in quirky accommodation: the former RAF Wainfleet observation tower complete with Westland Lynx helicopter in the grounds, containing a double bed!

→ Sea Lane, Friskney. hostunusual.com
53.0615, 0.2362 🛶

45

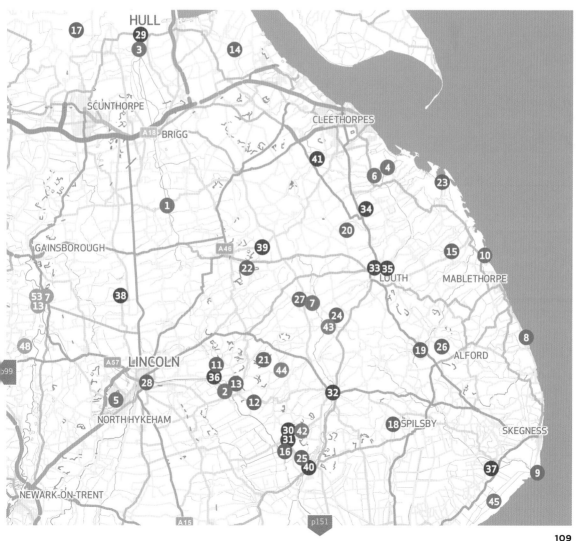

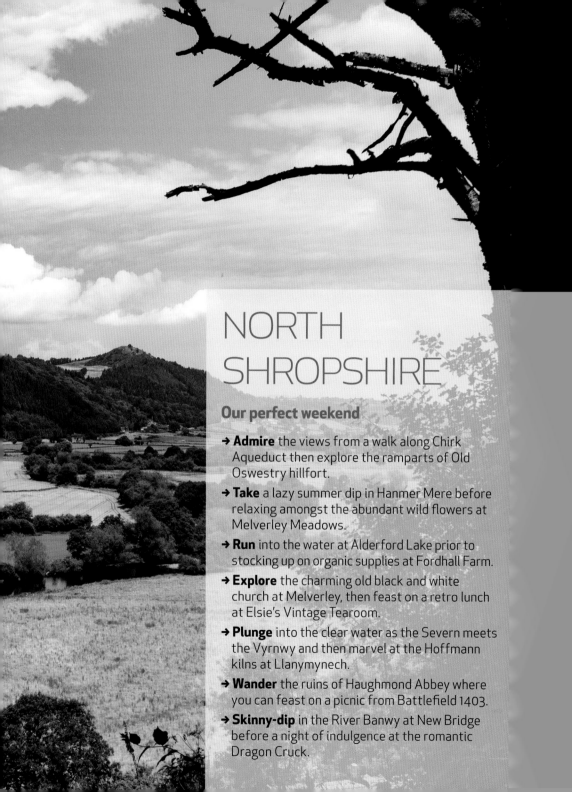

NORTH SHROPSHIRE

Our perfect weekend

→ **Admire** the views from a walk along Chirk Aqueduct then explore the ramparts of Old Oswestry hillfort.

→ **Take** a lazy summer dip in Hanmer Mere before relaxing amongst the abundant wild flowers at Melverley Meadows.

→ **Run** into the water at Alderford Lake prior to stocking up on organic supplies at Fordhall Farm.

→ **Explore** the charming old black and white church at Melverley, then feast on a retro lunch at Elsie's Vintage Tearoom.

→ **Plunge** into the clear water as the Severn meets the Vyrnwy and then marvel at the Hoffmann kilns at Llanymynech.

→ **Wander** the ruins of Haughmond Abbey where you can feast on a picnic from Battlefield 1403.

→ **Skinny-dip** in the River Banwy at New Bridge before a night of indulgence at the romantic Dragon Cruck.

The undulating plains of North Shropshire are an old, mystical and largely rural landscape. The glaciers of the last ice age left meres and mossy wetlands to the north, and a more rugged western edge along the border with Wales. One of the quietest areas of Shropshire, this offers its visitors breathtaking views over the plains and a warmth of welcome found only in remote, sparsely populated communities.

A land of myth, settlements here can be dated back to the Bronze Age. The magnificent Iron Age hillfort at Old Oswestry is one of the best-preserved examples in Britain, and celebrated in legend as the birthplace of King Arthur's Guinevere. Whittington Castle, not far away, is a strikingly beautiful, community-owned castle in the home town of the legendary Dick Whittington, and a Roman onyx cup kept in its chapel was believed to be the Holy Grail. Further to the south, along the Roman Watling Street, is the curiously hand-carved Kynaston's cave where Shropshire's Robin Hood, Wild Humphrey Kynaston, retreated when he was outlawed for murder.

This was predominantly a densely wooded land through the Roman occupation and the Saxon period, until religious orders cleared areas for grazing pasture and arable farming. Their monastery ruins, such as the well-preserved and extensive Haughmond Abbey, are atmospheric places to visit. Many woodlands have survived almost untouched through the ages despite being used to pave Watling Street and as royal, medieval hunting grounds. Nature reserves, such as the fascinating Brown Moss, have become incredibly important in preserving the fragile landscapes of heath and woodland with their many varieties of wildlife, both flora and fauna.

The rivers Banwy and Vyrnwy meander through the north and west offering secluded beaches for paddling and deep, clear pools for swimming. Head to Melverley for a delightful swim beneath the old 12th-century black and white church. The young River Severn cuts through the lower half of the county, offering a gloriously placid swim where it meets the Vyrnwy at Crewgreen. Alternatively, kayak down from Royal Hill to Shrawardine, a firm family favourite. The meres at Colemere Country Park and Hanmer are warm, shallow and crystal-clear, the perfect spots for a picnic and a dip.

Eating fresh, local produce is easy, with a range of farm shops and pubs serving high-quality, home-produced fayre. Battlefield 1403 farm shop showcases the best local meats in its butchery, whilst Elsie's Vintage Tearoom serves up the most delicious local pies in the area. For a stylish meal, head to The Haughmond Inn, with a tasty menu and picturesque garden, or the lovingly restored White Lion Inn at Ash Magna.

RIVER SWIMMING

1 NEW BRIDGE, RIVER BANWY
A beautiful location for a family day splashing in the shallows. Deeper pools for swims or drift down to where the Vyrnwy merges.

→ Head W out of Meifod on A495. Turn L after traffic lights, park on L in lay-by. Scramble down to river on R just before bridge.

3 mins, 52.6928, -3.2692

2 MEIFOD, RIVER VYRNWY
A delightfully deep section of the Vyrnwy with a pebble beach. Perfect for a longer, secluded swim.

→ Follow sign for Rugby Club in Meifod (SY22 6DA). Park just over bridge.

3 mins, 52.7073, -3.2499

3 ROYAL HILL, RIVER SEVERN
A family favourite thanks to shingle beaches, grassy banks and easy access to a swim or longer, secluded kayak to Shrawardine (see entry). Pub and camping opposite.

→ From Pentre, follow lanes to SW (National Cycle Route 81) 1 mile and park opposite the pub, SY10 8ES.

2 mins, 52.7498, -2.9627

4 SHRAWARDINE, RIVER SEVERN
A lovely, grassy-banked section of the young River Severn with an easy entry point next to the ruined railway bridge. A good take-out point if kayaking from Royal Hill (see listing).

→ In Shrawardine take lane NW dir SY4 1AJ (National Cycle Route 81). Park by last houses, follow footpath sign to L to river.

15 mins, 52.7330, -2.8996

5 SEVERN/VYRNWY CONFLUENCE, CREWGREEN
A glorious stretch of deep, tranquil water where the Severn and Vyrnwy meet. Perfect for jumps, dives and swimming.

→ At E end of Crewgreen (SY5 9AT) take lane N signed Melverley (National Cycle Route 81) for ⅓ mile. Park R just before bridge and follow footpath R down, then L under bridge.

5 mins, 52.7359, -2.9966

LANGUID LAKES

6 COLEMERE COUNTRY PARK
A beautiful, warm glacial mere. No Swimming signs due to its rare lilies and SSSI status, but people sometimes swim from the gently sloping beach by the boardwalk. Blue-green algae blooms in summer.

→ Signed from A528, 2 miles S of Ellesmere, down lanes past SY12 0QL then L at T-junction to car park. Follow boardwalk to beach.

8 mins, 52.8910, -2.8402

7 HANMER MERE
Wander through the woods past carpets of bluebells until you reach an open meadow and small, secluded, sandy beach, perfect for a swim.

→ Hanmer is signed 6 miles W of Whitchurch on A539. Park at Glendower Place (SY13 3DF) and follow footpath through gate on corner 500m L through woods, keeping the mere on your R.

10 mins, 52.9469, -2.8147

8 ALDERFORD LAKE
This pretty lake, with good water quality, is a spot popular with wild swimmers and triathletes. It is also a peaceful place for a walk (50p donation) or bring your own kayak or paddleboard. Swimmers are asked to sign in and pay. Café onsite.

→ From roundabout on A41 just south of Whitchurch (SY13 3JQ) take B5476 signed Wem. Entrance L after ⅓ mile.

4 mins, 52.9522, -2.6742

ANCIENT & SACRED

9 ST PETER'S CHURCH, MELVERLEY

A beautiful 12th-century black and white church built of timber, wattle and daub and featuring exquisite Jacobean carving. Open daily. The River Vyrnwy passes behind and in summer is slow and chest-high.

→ In Melverley turn down dead end by pub just S of SY10 8PJ and park by church.
5 mins, 52.7425, -2.9903

10 CHIRK AQUEDUCT

It feels as if you are walking in the air as you stroll across Telford's elegant, imposing yellow sandstone aqueduct, 21m above the River Ceiriog.

→ Heading into Chirk from S on B5070, turn hairpin to Chirk Bank L just before bridge, signed Weston Rhyn, and park in car park R by bridge, opp Canal View (LL14 5BY). Follow path W for 500m along canal.
7 mins, 52.9281, -3.0621

11 THE CASTLE, RUYTON-XI-TOWNS

This castle, built in the 12th century, was the major manor of 11 local townships and gave the town its unusual name. It now lies in ruins in the churchyard.

→ Head into Ruyton on B4397. Ruins in John the Baptist churchyard, near SY4 1LG. Park on streets off main road.
3 mins, 52.7935, -2.8993

12 OLD OSWESTRY

One of the best-preserved Iron Age hillforts, in the country. Panoramic views across England and Wales.

→ Follow Llywyn Rd out of Oswestry, past SY11 1EW. Parking ½ mile on, opp gate and path up to fort.
10 mins, 52.8711, -3.0510

13 SYCHARTH CASTLE

Once the home of Owain Glyndŵr, the rebel leader and last native Prince of Wales, the castle was burned to the ground in 1403 during his uprising. The grassy mound is now a haven of tranquillity and makes a perfect playground and picnic spot.

→ Head S from Llansilin on B4580. After 2 miles turn L signed Llynclys at SY10 9JZ. Parking signed L from road after ¼ mile.
7 mins, 52.8245, -3.1808

14 QUINTA STONE CIRCLE

Enchanting and strangely familiar, this half-

size, near replica of Stonehenge was built around 1850.

→ From roundabout by church in Weston Rhyn, take High St N out of village past SY10 7RN. Park on lane, or space for 2 cars by gate just after start of national speed limit. Follow path beyond gate for 400m through woods, W then turning N.

6 mins, 52.9198, -3.0716 ⊹☕

15 WHITTINGTON CASTLE

One of the first community-owned castles in the UK. These pictureque, half-moated, ruins date back to the 11th century and are perfect for a picnic or combined with a visit to its cafe (open Sun–Wed 10am–4pm) and little second-hand bookshop. Legends about the castle range from the Holy Grail being kept in its chapel, to Dick Whittington living in a cottage nearby.

→ Castle St in Whittington, SY11 4DF.

2 mins, 52.8737, -3.0032 ☕🚶🎣

16 HAUGHMOND ABBEY

Impressive ruins of an abbey, perfect for a game of hide-and-seek. Enjoy a picnic within the sprawling ruins and finish with a walk through the woods up to Haughmond Hill.

→ From A49 roundabout at Shrewsbury take B5062 E. Car park L down bumpy track after approx ½ mile, shortly after SY4 4RW.

2 mins, 52.7318, -2.6804 ▦🚶🛶🎣🚴🐾

17 MORETON CORBET CASTLE

Striking and extensive ruins from two different eras, a medieval stronghold and an Elizabethan manor, badly damaged in the Civil War and disused since the 18th century. Look out for the carved mythical beasts.

→ Take B5063 N from Shawbury, signed R and visible after ½ mile, shortly past SY4 4RH.

1 min, 52.8041, -2.6536 ▦🖼

ROCKS & RAMBLES

18 CORBET WOOD & GRINSHILL CLIFF

A woodland and quarrying site rich in birds and butterflies, with maze of paths ideal for a family stroll. Superb views across the Welsh Borders from the sandstone ridge of Grinshill.

→ Follow High St E out of Clive signed Preston. Wood signed R after ¾ mile, dir SY4 3BU. Car park at end of lane.

3 mins, 52.8093, -2.7060 🐾🚶📷🔩

19 KYNASTON'S CAVE, NESSCLIFFE HILL

Marvel at the extensive carved staircase leading up to the hideout of the notorious highwayman Wild Humphrey Kynaston, Shropshire's very own, very real Robin Hood figure. Hillfort remains in woods above.

→ Park at The Old Three Pigeons pub in Nesscliffe (SY4 1DB, 01743 741279) where Kynaston was reputedly a regular. Signed entrance to parkland across road and fork signed Hopton. Follow path up and L to cave.

10 mins, 52.7734, -2.9118 🚶🅿️♿🎒

20 ADMIRAL RODNEY'S PILLAR

Imposing pillar within a hillfort on Breidden Hill, thought to be the last stand of Caractacus against the Romans. Energetic walk.

→ Signed from B4393 just W of Crewgreen. Follow 1½ miles to Breidden car park L. Trails shown on board.

90 mins, 52.7227, -3.0450 🚶🅿️📷🚌

WILDLIFE MEADOWS

21 IFTON MEADOWS, ST MARTIN'S

A diverse area of wilderness in a former colliery with bluebells and wild garlic, skylarks, and sweeping views over the Welsh countryside.

→ Signed from B5069 in St Martin's, along Colliery Rd, L on Glyn Morian Lane past industrial estate (SY11 3DA), and R signed Pentre to signed parking L.

4 mins, 52.9301, -3.0130 🚻🅿️♿

22 MELVERLEY MEADOWS & BROWN MOSS

Stunning wild flower hay meadow farmed in the traditional way since 16th century. Visit in summer for best flowers. Nearby is Brown Moss SSSI Local Nature Reserve, a rich, diverse landscape of woodland, heathland, marshes and pools.

→ From Ash Magna follow Church Lane (one way at start) past SY13 4EA, park R next to gateway just beyond the first small lane on R. Or park at Brown Moss (52.9503, -2.6501) and follow footpaths and lanes between reserves.

2 mins, 52.9596, -2.6262 🚶🅿️♿

23 LLYNCLYS COMMON NATURE RESERVE

A pretty patchwork of woodland and meadows across the hillside, offering orchids and wild garlic in spring.

→ Park in the lay-by at houses ⅓ mile W of Llynclys crossroads on A495 (SY10 8LN). Walk up Turner's Lane opp to paths into reserve.

10 mins, 52.8054, -3.0806 🚶🅿️♿🎒📷♿

INDUSTRIAL HERITAGE

24 LLANYMYNECH KILN

Fascinating Hoffmann kiln that burned continuously in a sequence of chambers; the only one in the country with its chimney intact. Pretty walks up the incline plane to the magnificent quarry rock face, with industrial relics dotted along the way.

→ Nature reserve car park signed off A483 just N of canal and Llanymynech (SY22 6EZ) but easily missed. Path from parking to kilns.
8 mins, 52.7838, -3.0861

SLOW FOOD

25 FORDHALL FARM, MARKET DRAYTON

Inspiring, community-owned organic farm, farm shop and organic café. Home-reared, grass-fed meats, local produce, farm trails and glamping amongst the buttercups in Shropshire-made Mongolian-style Yurts.

→ Tern Hill Road, Market Drayton, TF9 3PS, 01630 317531.
52.8927, -2.5250

26 LLYNCLYS HALL FARM SHOP

A rustic farm shop selling local meat, bread, honey and fresh produce grown on the farm.

Gluten-free cooking ingredients and an extensive pumpkin field in the summer and autumn. Open daily.

→ Llynclys, SY10 8AD, 01691 652434.
52.8152, -3.0605

27 BATTLEFIELD 1403

Destination farm shop with café, falconry and nature trail to local medieval church. Focus on locally sourced Shropshire fare.

→ Upper Battlefield, Shrewsbury, SY4 3DB, 01939 210905.
52.7534, -2.7203

28 ELSIE'S VINTAGE TEA ROOM

A superb little tearoom and pie parlour offering top-quality food and home-made pies all served on vintage china with a warm, friendly smile.

→ Tan Y Bryn Barn Business Park, Coedway, SY5 9AR. 07864 810704. Wed–Sun.
52.7292, -2.9833

29 DERWEN FARM SHOP

A great farm shop run by someone with a passion for good quality, local produce. Meat, bread, cheese, fruit and vegetables and an interesting deli counter.

→ B4392, Guilsfield, SY21 9PH.
01938 551586.
52.6887, -3.1553

30 THE LAZY COW CAFE

A small, friendly café on a working farm,
serving all-day breakfasts, light lunches,
home-made cakes, tea and coffee. Small,
enclosed playground and outdoor seating
overlooking the fields and animals.

→ Lyneal, Ellesmere, SY12 0LG,
07572 131475. Follow the signs!
52.8882, -2.8244

31 CHURNCOTE FARMSHOP & COTE KITCHEN

Great selection of home-reared beef, pork
and lamb all in a traditional 18-tie cowshed.
Onsite café.

→ Bicton Heath, SY3 5EB, 01743 851081.
52.7164, -2.8236

32 THE HAUGHMOND, UPTON MAGNA

Coaching inn with stylish, modern decor,
well-maintained garden and great views over
the local countryside. Superb tasting menu.
Featured in Michelin Guide in 2019.

→ Pelham Road, Shrewsbury SY4 4TZ,
01743 709918.
52.7076, -2.6581

COSY PUBS

33 NAVIGATION INN, MAESBURY MARSH

A quirky, cosy, laid-back pub sitting
alongside the canal. Real ale, cider, locally
sourced pies. Dogs, muddy boots and
children welcome.

→ Maesbury Marsh, Oswestry, SY10 8JB,
01691 672958.
52.8183, -3.0198

34 THE WHITE LION COMMUNITY INN

Community-owned pub in lovingly restored
17th-century school building, with features
in keeping. Serves home-made pies and
hearty meals.

→ The Old School, Ash Magna, Whitchurch,
SY13 4DR, 01948 663153.
52.9528, -2.6380

35 CROSS KEYS INN, SELATTYN

Wonderfully cosy little local serving craft
ales from local breweries and locally sourced
homemade food.

→ Glyn Road, Selattyn SY10 7DH,
01691 653347.
52.8984, -3.0913

RUSTIC HAVENS

36 DRAGON CRUCK

An enchanting, hand-crafted cabin with
its own outdoor kitchen nestled into the
hillside above the Vyrnwy Valley. A romantic
getaway or perfect honeymoon location.

→ Sunny Lea, Meifod, SY22 6YA.
canopyandstars.co.uk
52.7069, -3.2406

37 NINK'S WAGON

A stunningly beautiful 1920s showman's
wagon once owned by the ringmaster
himself. Complete with a mirrored living
area with a wood-burner, a little kitchen and
one cosy bedroom. The perfect escape from
modern life.

→ Frankton Grange, English Frankton,
SY12 0JZ, quirkyaccom.com
52.8706, -2.8215

38 CAMPIO-GLAMP

Quirky but cosy converted single-decker bus
set in private, secluded field. Sleeps four and
great for kids

→ Hindford, SY11 4NR. 07564127555.
52.8890, -2.9929

CAMP & SLEEP

39 ST WINIFRED'S WELL

A beautiful, tiny, black and white chapel built
over the spring, which still feeds the three
pools today, so you can dip in the reputedly
healing waters. There is also a modern,
separate bathhouse.

→ Woolston, Oswestry, SY10 8HY,
landmarktrust.org.uk
52.8132, -3.0071

40 THE BOAT HOUSE CAMPING

An immaculately kept and friendly little
campsite on the banks of the River Severn.
Kayak hire onsite.

→ The Boat House, Llandrinio, SY22 6SG,
07814 598591.
52.7462, -3.0411

41 CANAL CENTRAL

A great place to relax next to the canal.
Pitches for tents, vans and caravans, a jolly
little café (open Wed–Sun), canoe hire and
self-catering accommodation above the café.

→ Coed-y-Rae Lane, Maesbury Marsh, SY10
8JG, 01691 652168.
52.8174, -3.0258

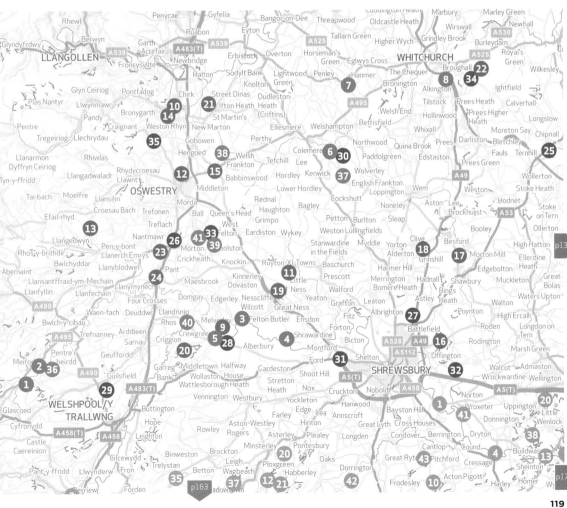

CENTRAL STAFFORDSHIRE

Our perfect weekend

- → **Book** a stately stay at the Tixall Gatehouse to check out Shugborough's Triumphal Arch and cool off in the Trent by Essex Bridge.

- → **Cycle** the infamous 'Follow the Dog' at Cannock Chase and then float around enjoying the dramatic cliffs of Brocton Pools.

- → **Seek** out the sacred Gawton's Well before clambering up to the views from the folly castle at Mow Cop.

- → **Seek** out Calwich Abbey fishing temple, then take a dip in the River Dove at the beautiful, white-painted Toad Holes Bridge.

- → **Step** back in time and marvel at the music machines at the Yew Tree Inn over lunch, followed by a wander around the humps and hollows of Thornwood.

- → **Swim** in the deep pools at Ellastone then spend the night in the eco-friendly Farm On The Hill campsite.

- → **Explore** the woodland and search for a sea of snowdrops at Loynton's Moss before being amazed at the evening murmurations at Aqualate Mere.

- → **Discover** the curious Devil's Ring and Finger and then dine at the fabulous Fitzherbert Arms.

Tucked under the wing of the Peaks, Central Staffordshire shifts from wild, hilly moorland in the north to rolling agricultural fields and woods intersected by a network of canals as you travel south.

On the edge of the Peak District is the typically rugged landscape of Thorswood Nature Reserve, with its lead mines, ancient burial mounds, and glorious wild flower meadows, giving stunning views across the Dove Valley. The beautiful forest and heathland of Cannock Chase here is an Area of Outstanding Natural Beauty, a wildlife haven where you may see foxes, deer, badgers and green woodpeckers. There are miles of cycle trails for all abilities and ages, woodland walks, picnic and BBQ areas, secluded pools and even a campsite for those wishing to extend their visit. A project to restore the red squirrel in the area is currently underway, and conservation is always a top priority here.

Further west, where the plains of Staffordshire meet the rural beauty of North Shropshire, it feels like time stands still. Here you can find the Neolithic stones of the Devil's Ring and Finger, the lonely, misplaced relics of a long-vanished Neolithic monument. Even more ancient, Loynton Moss is a rustic wetland landscape scooped out by retreating ice sheets, adorned with snowdrops in spring and alive with birds.

The source of the River Trent is on the moorland near Biddulph in the east of the county, from where the young waterway winds its way south. A popular place to swim and paddle is the elegant Essex Bridge, a medieval packhorse crossing on the edge of the Shugborough Estate. Near here is the Tixall Wide, an unusual swim in the canal which was made to look like a lake to suit a Capability Brown parkland. Also in the east is a meander of the tranquil River Dove, where the swim above the weir at Ellastone is secluded and deep.

This is the home of the Staffordshire oatcake, Marmite and a brewery industry dating back to the Middle Ages, so there are many well-established eateries offering high-quality fare. The Duncombe Arms at Ellastone and The Holly Bush Inn at Salt come highly recommended for locally sourced, well-cooked food. Denstone Hall Farm Shop is a thriving business selling produce from the farm and local area, and its café serves delicious oatcakes. For a more traditional – but highly individual – approach, The Yew Tree Inn is a fascinating inn crammed full of antiques and memorabilia, or try the Black Lion Inn at Consall Forge, a thriving old alehouse at the end of a dusty track.

6

LANGUID LAKES

1 KNYPERSLEY SERPENTINE POOL

Country Park with 114 acres of old estate woodland, waterfalls, grottoes, follies and lakes. The lower reservoir is used by anglers, but shoreside paths leads on up to the more secluded upper lake and pool.

→ Greenway Bank Country Park signed from A527 S of Biddulph, 1¼ miles to entrance with car park L, before ST8 7QX.

15 mins, 53.0966, -2.1662 ▣☒⛵👟🎋🏊❓

2 THE BROAD WATER, TIXALL

When asked if the canal could cross his land, Lord Clifford agreed only if it could be made to look like a lake in front of his house, to match his Capability Brown grounds. The result, also known as Tixall Wide, makes an unusual swim.

→ Head E out of Tixall dir ST18 0XN, park in lay-by L by railings and trees after ½ mile. Cross road and walk on to take bridleway R by octagonal house down to canal, cross and turn R onto towpath. Variable water quality.

15 mins, 52.8019, -2.0250 ⚓⛴👟⛵

3 STONYBROOK POOL, CANNOCK CHASE

Sandy lakes in open heath and woodland of Cannock Chase. Upper (Fairbook) pools very popular with anglers, but lower Stonybrook pool much more secluded.

→ Take Penkridge Bank Rd W out of Rugeley 1⅓ miles, forest is signed L on Birches Valley (dir WS15 2UQ), car park 130m on L. Walk or cycle on new path behind car park up valley to find two lakes, followed by two more ½ mile further up.

15 mins, 52.7446, -1.9759 ⚓❓🎋

4 BROCTON QUARRY, CANNOCK

Wild, serene and secluded lake in a former gravel pit, with trees sweeping down to the water and an island. There is a bird hide at the north-west corner.

→ Head N from Cannock on A34, turn R before Brocton, signed Pye Green. After ½ mile (past ST17 0SS), just after Cannock Chase markers, park in lay-by L and take footpath back through woods, descending on far side.

10 mins, 52.7654, -2.0473 ⚓❓👟⛵🎋🏊🔱

5 BLITHFIELD RESERVOIR PENINSULA

A quiet, secluded beach can be found on the tip of the peninsula, a pleasant place to relax and watch the varied birdlife, including goosander and widgeon. Check for blue-green algae blooms if you paddle.

→ On B5013 N out of Abbots Bromley, take L at fork just after WS15 3EJ, on Newton Hurst Lane. Blithfield Walks signed L after 1 mile. Take signed footpath from car park through woods or walk on road to end of peninsula.

25 mins, 52.8195, -1.9175 🎋⛵

RIVER SWIMMING

6 ESSEX BRIDGE, RIVER TRENT

A beautiful location below a substantial 16th-century packhorse bridge on the edge of Shugborough Estate.

→ Park in Great Haywood and walk down Trent Lane (ST18 0ST) 150m, under railway and over first bridge.

3 mins, 52.8007, -2.0085 ⚓🍴⛵🏕️

7 ELLASTONE, RIVER DOVE

The idyllic, meandering River Dove pools near the bridge, offering the perfect spot for a refreshing dip. Head upstream near weir and downstream of bridge for other swim options.

→ Head SE of Ellastone on B5033 past DE6 2GY, park in lay-by R just before bridge and follow path R from kissing gate to river. Cross bridge to explore upstream footpath on L.

5 mins, 52.9787, -1.8231 👟🎋

8 **TOAD HOLE FOOTBRIDGE, SNELSTON**

Simple, white-painted bridge over the River Dove. Swim, picnic, relax.

→ On B5033 S out of Ellastone, take L onto Sides Lane signed Snelston at Norbury (DE6 2EQ). After 1½ miles, pull off L at footpath opp turning R. Follow footpath to river.
3 mins, 52.9905, -1.7877 🏊🏕

9 **CONSALL FORGE, RIVER CHURNET**

Once home to a thriving lime furnace, the area now offers a peaceful and tranquil swim in the river – with the sighting of a steam train on some days!

→ From Consall (ST9 0AE) follow signs for Consall Forge no through road 1¾ miles then L at fork for Black Lion pub (see listing) and park in car park at end. Follow river on for 200m.
5 mins, 53.0416, -2.0028 🏊🚶🏕🍴

ANCIENT & SACRED

10 **ST. CATHERINE'S WELL, SUGNALL**

Small 18th-century well head with pyramidal roof, probably built to capture the bubbling spring water when a temple was constructed here. Situated on a beautiful circular walk on a permissive path.

→ Entering Sugnall (ST21 6NF) from S on B5026 from Eccleshall, turn L at crossroads and park in business centre R. Walk on along lane past Walled Garden (lovely café, see listing) 350m to small ornate gate L into wood. Follow to well on L.
20 mins, 52.8724, -2.3056 🏞🕂🏃

11 **DEVIL'S RING AND FINGER**

Exceptional stones, one ridged, one holed (big enough to slither through), assumed to have been moved here centuries ago from a lost Neolithic tomb.

→ Approach bridleway from either end. In Norton Hales (TF9 4AT) take Forge Lane no through road S and park as close as possible to farm at end. Bridleway runs through yard and field R ahead to copse, stones are on far edge. From Napley (TF9 4DS) follow B5415 SW, take next R for Oakley Hall and park R 20m in. Walk up lane to bend L and cottages, bridleway stile is R just beyond these. Follow along field edge to copse, then R side of copse.
20 mins, 52.9366, -2.4369 🏞🕂🏞

12 **GAWTON'S WELL AND STONE**

Hidden in woodland adjoining Knypersley Reservoir seek out the beautiful well pool set in a yew grove and the vast stone on supports,

both of which are claimed to have healing powers.

→ Greenway Bank Country Park signed from A527 S of Biddulph, 1¼ miles to car park L opp ST8 7QY. Follow paths either way around reservoir to Wardens Tower on far shore, take footpath to R and follow signs to well or waterfall walk. Stone at 53.0957, -2.1537.
20mins, 53.0970, -2.1536 🚶🌲🥾👕✝️🛶🍽️🚗↩️

13 CALWICH ABBEY TEMPLE
A Jacobean-style fishing temple perched on the bank of the River Dove. Enjoy views across the valley and surrounding countryside.

→ On B5023 S from Ellastone, turn L onto B5033. After ¼ mile, shortly past DE6 2GY, park L and follow footpath through the old Calwich Estate and past Orchard Cottage, take path R through field down to river and temple.
25 mins, 52.9857, -1.8052 📷🚶

14 DOVERIDGE YEW TREE
This grand, old yew tree has presided over the village for an estimated 1,400 years and is claimed to have been where Robin Hood and Maid Marian married. Visitors to the church enter under a tunnel of mighty boughs that continue to flourish with a little love and support from the local community.

→ Doveridge is off the A50 1½ miles E of Uttoxeter, and St Cuthbert's Church stands where Hall Dr meets Church Lane in the SW of the village, near DE6 5NN.
1 min, 52.9042, -1.8317 ✝️

15 CROXDEN ABBEY
Magnificent remains of the 12th-century abbey tower over visitors, casting wonderful evening shadows from soaring window arches.

→ Signed from the Roman road E of Hollington, turn dir ST14 5JF, follow ¾ mile and pull off by gate. EH, free entry.
1 min, 52.9546, -1.9042 📷❓✝️🛝

HILLTOP FOLLIES

16 TRIUMPHAL ARCH, SHUGBOROUGH
One of many follies and features on the NT estate, this magnificent copy of Hadrian's Arch in Athens was built in 1765 to salute local Baron, George Anson, First Lord of the Admiralty during the Seven Years' War.

→ Estate entrance is signed 6 miles E of Stafford (near ST17 0UR) on A513, immediately off main road.
10 mins, 52.7918, -2.0211 👕🚶🌲🐾📷🚗

17 MOW COP CASTLE

Sitting atop Mow Cop Hill is a majestic folly castle, which can be seen for miles around. No access inside, but panoramic views.

→ In Mow Cop, on lanes W of Biddulph, NT car park is on High St, ST7 3PA.

7 mins, 53.1126, -2.2147 🚻🏕️💬📧

WOODLANDS & WILDLIFE

18 LOYNTON MOSS

A juxtaposition of changing landscapes: in late winter drifts of snowdrops adorn the banks of a wetland, surrounded by moss and lichen-rich trees, but in the summer the reserve transforms into an abundant, flower-rich meadow.

→ Follow A519 1 mile SW from Woodseaves, past ST20 0NX. Park in lay-by on L just after bridge or car park R 250m further, both with paths into woods and NE to wetland and snowdrops near canal footbridge.

15 mins, 52.8175, -2.3149 🚻💬🚗

19 PARROT'S DRUMBLE, TALKE

A hidden oasis of ancient woodland with a copper-coloured stream running through its middle. Come in April and May and revel in the incredible display of native bluebells.

→ Gravel parking at bend next to National Veterinary Services on Pit Lane in business estate (near ST7 1XW), with sign and path into reserve.

10 mins, 53.0692, -2.2727 🚻💬🚗

20 HAWKSMOOR NATURE RESERVE

The beauty of this reserve has inspired artists for centuries. The result of a complex geology rich in everything from fossils to iron and copper, this is a great place to walk and collect your thoughts.

→ From Cheadle, follow Queen St/B5417 E for 2 miles from mini-roundabout in centre to car park signed L through stone gateway, just before R turn to ST10 3AP. Paths signed from car park.

2 mins, 52.9952, -1.9496 🚻🏕️🐾💬🚗

21 THORSWOOD NATURE RESERVE

A captivating, higgledy-piggledy landscape of ancient bowl barrows, lead mines hiding among the trees, and beautiful wild flower meadows. Breathtaking views across the stunning Dove Valley. Walk quietly and you may see hares.

→ Take A52 NW out of Ashbourne. After 4 miles turn L to stay on A52. After ¾ mile turn L onto Dale Lane, signed Stanton, dir DE6 2BY.

Small car park ½ mile on R, with info board.
10 mins, 53.0206, -1.8344 [icons]

22 DOWNS BANKS

A valley with wonderful walks in the
woodland by the brook (look out for
kingfishers), rising to open heath with
panoramic views.

→ From NE end of Stone or from A34 junction
(near ST15 8UX) follow Washdale Lane ¾
mile NE to lay-bys either side at ford, or 200m
further to main car park L.
6 mins, 52.9312, -2.1507 [icons]

23 AQUALATE MERE

Large, natural lake and wetland and good
place to view the swirling black murmurations
of up to 250,000 starlings as they settle
down to roost at dusk (best Nov–Feb). Visit
the bird hide, see the 300-year-old heronry
and look out for osprey, otters, barn owls
and the hundreds of wildfowl and birds that
overwinter or breed in this special National
Nature Reserve. Bluebells in spring.

→ From Mere Park roundabout, Newport
take A518 E (past TF10 9BY) 2½ miles, turn
L signed Stafford. Car park L after ½ mile,
footpath to mere and bird hide.
10 mins, 52.7781, -2.3380 [icons]

24 CANNOCK CHASE FOREST

This former royal forest is now a designated
AONB and a joyful recreational area,
with really wild areas and myriad trails
for walkers, horses and cyclists. Try the
infamous 'Follow the Dog' or 'Monkey' cycling
trails if you are brave enough.

→ Take Penkridge Bank Rd W out of Rugeley
1¼ miles, forest is signed L on Birches Valley
(dir WS15 2UQ), car park 130m on L.
2 mins, 52.7510, -1.9725 [icons]

SLOW FOOD

25 SUGNALL WALLED GARDEN

Picturesque café serving a brunch-style
menu, with weekly specials reflecting their
seasonal garden produce. Country house
accommodation available.

→ Sugnall, Eccleshall, ST21 6NF, 01785 851556.
52.8749, -2.3022 [icon]

26 DENSTONE HALL FARM SHOP & CAFÉ

Award-winning farm shop and café, using
their own and local produce.

→ Denstone, nr Uttoxeter, ST14 5HF,
01889 590050.
52.9652, -1.8504 [icons]

33

27

28

27 THE FITZHERBERT ARMS, SWYNNERTON
Everything about this glorious pub makes you smile: the food, the decor, the staff, the ambience, the views, the local ales. Well worth a visit.
→ Swynnerton, nr Stone, ST15 0RA, 01782 796782.
52.9174, -2.2220 🍴📷

28 HETTY'S TEA SHOP, FROGHALL
Delightful canalside tearoom serving scrumptious home-made delights and with rooms above. Stroll along the towpath to see the pretty Cherry Eye Bridge (53.0308, -1.9802). Open Tues–Sun.
→ Foxt Road, Froghall, ST10 2HJ, 01538 266288.
53.0264, -1.9615 🍴🚲

29 CANALSIDE FARM SHOP & CAFÉ
In a lovely location right next to the canal, offering home-cooked food, delicious local produce at farm shop, and PYO.

→ Mill Lane, Great Haywood, ST18 0RQ, 01889 881747.
52.8055, -2.0083 🍴📷

30 THE DUNCOMBE ARMS, ELLASTONE
Fantastic modern food with a rustic twist, served in a beautiful, recently revived country inn. Well-kept ales and friendly staff.
→ Ellastone, Ashbourne, DE6 2GZ, 01335 324275.
52.9861, -1.8264 📷🍴🚲

COSY PUBS

31 HOLLY BUSH INN, SALT
Beautiful thatched inn with church pew seating and staff that go the extra mile. Highest-quality, locally sourced food. Garden overflowing with flowers offering a brick pizza oven and plentiful seating.
→ Willowmore Banks, Salt, ST18 0BX, 01889 508234.
52.8474, -2.0633 📷🍴

34

32 THE HAND & TRUMPET, WRINEHILL

A beautiful vintage interior with open fires makes this an ideal cosy retreat to dine on a well-prepared menu.

→ Main Rd, Wrinehill, CW3 9BJ, 01270 820048. 53.0231, -2.3693

33 THE BLACK LION, CONSALL FORGE

A delightful real ale pub with original character and old-fashioned values and pub food, right by the canal and heritage railway.

→ Consall Forge, ST9 0AJ, 01782 550294. 53.0396, -2.0012

34 THE YEW TREE INN, CAULDON

Extraordinary, unique, traditional alehouse, chock full of fascinating antiques and curios, including pianos, symphoniums, and a penny farthing . Roaring fire, great landlord and pies.

→ 3 Church Lane, Cauldon, ST10 3EJ, 01538 309876. 53.0407, -1.8873

HISTORIC HIDEAWAYS

35 TIXALL GATEHOUSE

Stunning 16th-century gatehouse owned by Landmark Trust. The hall it served, where Mary, Queen of Scots was held for two weeks in 1586, is long gone.

→ Tixall, ST18 0XT, landmarktrust.org.uk. 52.8040, -2.0324

36 ALTON STATION

The old station, built in 1849, has been lovingly renovated as a holiday let for four. Walk the Churnet Way along the disused railway route right from your door.

→ Farley, ST10 4BY, landmarktrust.org.uk 52.9814, -1.8963

CAMP & SLEEP

37 CALWICH UNDER CANVAS

Proof that luxury and simplicity can go together: beautiful, sumptuous yurts

35

36

with state-of-the-art cooking and shower facilities. Log-burners give a cosy feel, and the wood-fired hot tub and sauna make a stay extra-special.

→ Foxgloves, Calwich Rise, Ellastone, DE6 2HE, 07376 744147.
52.9916, -1.8036 🏕️🛁

38 SECRET CLOUD HOUSE HOLIDAYS
The ultimate in opulent glamping. Yurts with private, wood-fired hot tubs, spotless luxury washrooms and even an onsite therapy room and sauna.

→ Limestone View Farm, Stoney Lane, Cauldon, ST10 3EP, 01298 687036.
53.0390, -1.9057 🏕️

39 THE PARLOUR AT GREENACRES BARN
Luxury shepherd's hut next to an orchard, surrounded by open countryside. Wood-burner, fire pit, beautiful views.

→ Alton Road, Denstone, ST14 5DH, 01889 590647.
52.9680, -1.8611 🏕️

40 FARM ON THE HILL CAMPING
A peaceful eco campsite set in 12 acres of orchards, wild flower meadows and new woodland. Smaller pitches offering seclusion and larger spaces for groups.

→ Manor House Farm, Prestwood, ST14 5DD, 07597 841939.
52.9803, -1.8431 ⛺

41 INGLENOOK BOATYARD, RUDYARD
A unique wooden boathouse hideaway for two, with stunning vistas over Rudyard Lake.

→ Rudyard, nr Leek, hostunusual.com
53.1301, -2.0809 🏕️🚣🏊🚶🚴

42 FORESTSIDE FARM CAMPING
A small campsite with views over the Weaver Hills and Dove Valley. Has camping pods.

→ Forestside Farm, Marchington Cliff, ST14 8NA, 01283 520353.
52.8600, -1.8116 ⛺🐾📶

43 CHASE CAMPING
Campsite with fire pits and optional bell tents set in 30 acres of AONB. Spacious, with never more than three caravans or camper vans onsite. Walks, cycle trails, wildlife just across the road.

→ Four Oaks Farm, Penkridge Bank Road, Rugeley, WS15 2NE, 01543 427977.
52.7539, -1.9708 ⛺🐾🚴🚶🏕️

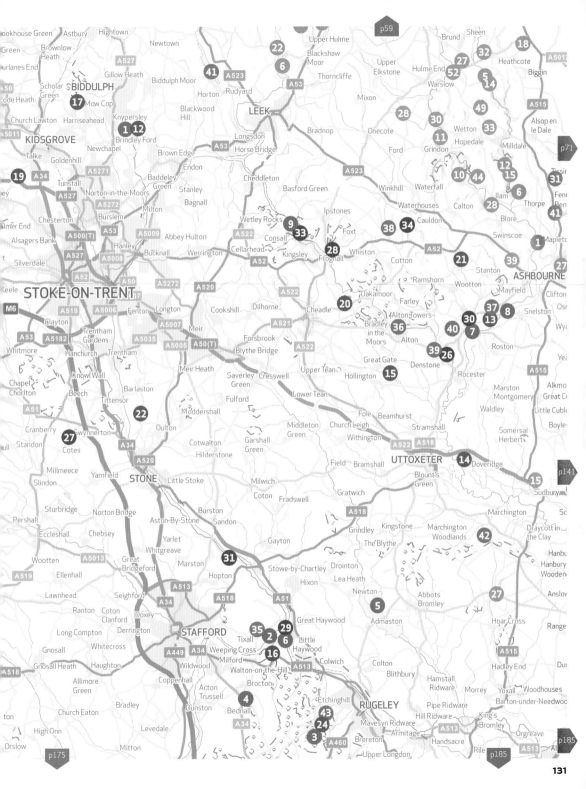

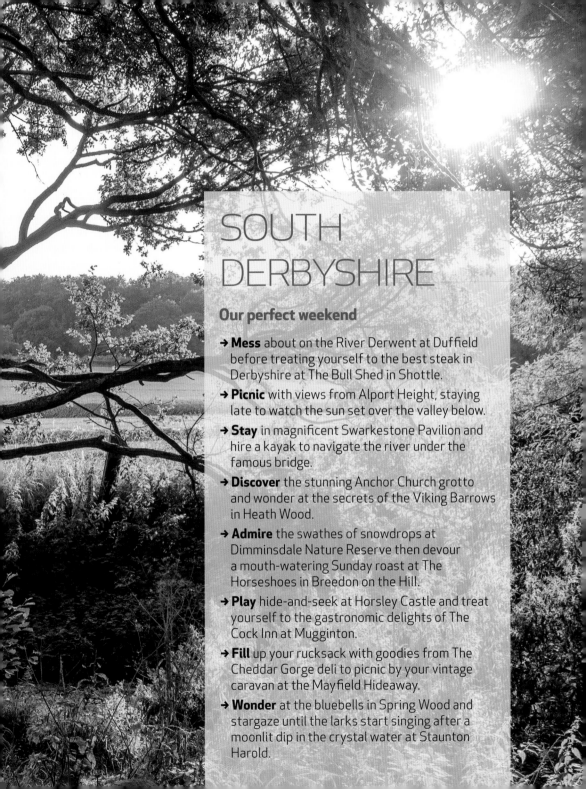

SOUTH DERBYSHIRE

Our perfect weekend

→ **Mess** about on the River Derwent at Duffield before treating yourself to the best steak in Derbyshire at The Bull Shed in Shottle.

→ **Picnic** with views from Alport Height, staying late to watch the sun set over the valley below.

→ **Stay** in magnificent Swarkestone Pavilion and hire a kayak to navigate the river under the famous bridge.

→ **Discover** the stunning Anchor Church grotto and wonder at the secrets of the Viking Barrows in Heath Wood.

→ **Admire** the swathes of snowdrops at Dimminsdale Nature Reserve then devour a mouth-watering Sunday roast at The Horseshoes in Breedon on the Hill.

→ **Play** hide-and-seek at Horsley Castle and treat yourself to the gastronomic delights of The Cock Inn at Mugginton.

→ **Fill** up your rucksack with goodies from The Cheddar Gorge deli to picnic by your vintage caravan at the Mayfield Hideaway.

→ **Wonder** at the bluebells in Spring Wood and stargaze until the larks start singing after a moonlit dip in the crystal water at Staunton Harold.

South Derbyshire, the foothills of the Peak District unites beautiful lowland valleys and rolling hills, rocky outcrops and picturesque villages. Many pass through without stopping, but this a county soaked in history rich in wildlife and offering endless adventure.

When the Anglo-Saxons and Vikings coexisted here, the land was covered entirely by forest. Take a journey back in time and seek out Heath Wood and its unique Viking cemetery, or visit the fascinating Saxon crypt beneath the church in the village of Repton. Today, the National Forest is a huge playground for everyone, with opportunities for walking, cycling, horse riding, kayaking and even llama-trekking. The Industrial Revolution brought phenomenal changes to the landscape, and slowly it is recovering, reclaimed by nature once more. Still there are captivating hints and traces of an ever-changing world to be seen, starting with the 12th-century Horsley Castle, which offers a great picnic spot and somewhere for the kids to lose themselves in the trees and the past. A walk through the countryside will bring you to Vernon's Folly, a splendid 18th-century red sandstone structure built purely for the lord's herd of deer! More down-to-earth are the 19th-century Morley Park Furnaces, slightly forgotten in a Derbyshire field.

Finding a place to swim in the area is relatively easy: there are a multitude of rivers, gravel pits and reservoirs, all with easy access. For a great river swim, head to the mile-long, medieval Swarkestone Bridge which was the turning point for Bonnie Prince Charlie. The River Derwent at Duffield offers the quintessentially English backdrop of a cricket match to a picnic and plunge, while the River Dove, which has shaped much of this area with its gentle, winding meanders, offers a serene dip at the old Okeover Bridge, also the location of a New Year's Day jump. The crowning glory of this area is an invigorating, safe swim on an offshoot of the Trent under the stunning Anchor Church, a grotto cave from the 6th century, hand-carved by the hermits who inhabited it over the centuries.

The county is also home to grand estates such as those at Calke, Elvaston Castle and Calton Hall. These have given the area the classic sweeping parkland landscape. Elvaston Castle is a fantastic destination for families to get out and about in the fresh air, with riverside walks, ancient woodland, hide-and-seek opportunities among the curious follies and a welcoming tea room. Pubs and farm shops such as the Barley Mow at Kirk Ireton, the Holly Bush Inn at Makeney and Croots Farm Shop thrive here, in the close-knit villages that continue the traditions, fêtes and festivals that bind communities together and were once so commonplace in Britain.

DELIGHTFUL DOVE

1 OKEOVER BRIDGE, RIVER DOVE

The small but beautifully formed River Dove winds its way through this lowland area. Here, a stony beach leads to a deep section for swimming by the bridge, where there is a traditional New Year's Day jump.

→ Follow Mapleton Rd from Ashbourne to park at Okeover Arms, Mapleton (DE6 2AB, 01335 350305). Walk on to next L to bridge.

2 mins, 53.0302, -1.7570 🏊🎋🍴

2 TUTBURY CASTLE, RIVER DOVE

A deep, rural stretch of the Dove above a weir, with a view back to Tutbury Castle ruins on the bluff.

→ Tutbury Mill picnic area is signed on A511 roundabout at N of Tutbury (N of DE13 9LZ). Park and follow path over meadows, along millstream to weir, ¾ mile.

15 mins, 52.8613, -1.6986 🏊🍴🎋

RIVER TRENT

3 SWARKESTONE BRIDGE, DERBY

Britain's longest stone bridge, at nearly a mile including the causeway section, is where Bonnie Prince Charlie turned back his Jacobite rebels and ended his advance on London. Some fancy they can still hear approaching hoofbeats on quiet nights.

→ On A514 heading N through Swarkestone, car park of Crewe & Harpur pub is on L (DE73 7JA, 01332 700641). Walk down to bridge. Path L down to entry point, or cross bridge, turn R signed Ingleby and find path down to river R after 50m.

1 min, 52.8529, -1.4534 🏊🚣🛶

4 NEWTON SOLNEY, RIVER TRENT

Several easy entry points from grassy banks along the river for a day adventuring, exploring and kayaking. Kayak down past Anchor Church to Swarkestone Bridge swim spots (see listings).

→ In Newton Solney Trent Lane becomes a path to river near DE15 0SE. Hire kayaks from Trent Adventure, Twyford DE73 7HJ, 07876 751599.

3 mins, 52.8308, -1.5851 🚣🛶

5 ANCHOR CHURCH, RIVER TRENT

Exceptional grotto cave thought to have been the home of St Hardulph, a 6th-century anchorite. Safe swimming in this gentle offshoot of the Trent.

→ Head N from Ticknall on Ingleby Lane for 2 miles dir DE73 7HW. Park on R in lay-by just before bend. Follow footpath through gate opp 1 mile down to and along river to crag. In high water you may need to follow path above crag and drop down.

25 mins, 52.8415, -1.4975 🏊🚶🛶🎋🚴♿

RIVER DERWENT

6 DUFFIELD, RIVER DERWENT

Immerse yourself in the cooling waters of the River Derwent and idle in the gentle current under the dappled shade against the quintessentially English backdrop of the village cricket team playing nearby.

→ In Duffield follow Makeney Rd (DE56 4BD) E over bridge and turn R on Church Dr. Follow ½ mile beside railway to car park L by cricket club and cross cricket pitch to bend in river to NW. Various jetties and gaps in vegetation. If busy, park in Duffield and follow path past medical centre (DE56 4GG) under bridge to cricket pitch.

5 mins, 52.9893, -1.4832 🏊🛶🚶🎋🚂

POOLS & RESERVOIRS

7 CUTLER'S BROOK

A secluded pool below a weir, dappled in sunlight, at the edge of the Kedleston

Estate. Plunge, paddle and picnic.

→ Park near Kedleston Country Hotel (DE22 5JD, some pulling off R shortly up Inn Lane). Head back down road to footpath sign R (52.9595, -1.5139). Follow path to and over brook, follow brook to R to pool.

25 mins, 52.9568, -1.5212 🏊🚶🅿️

8 FOREMARK RESERVOIR

Ideal location for a splash with the kids: clear-water coves and sandy beaches surrounded by woodland with a multitude of paths to wander under the leafy canopy.

→ Take Repton Rd signed Milton from A514 W of Ticknall, dir DE65 6EG. Reservoir and car parks signed L after 1 mile. Walk past café and crowds to sandy coves.

5 mins, 52.8111, -1.5042 🏊❓🐚🚶🅿️👪

9 STAUNTON HAROLD & SPRING WOOD

Staunton Harold Reservoir near NT Calke Abbey is a popular place for a lakeside walk or cycle with wild flower meadows, bird hides and a children's playground. But head to aptly named Spring Wood Nature Reserve and you will be rewarded with quiet woodland that is carpeted with bluebells in late spring. To access the reserve you will need to call Derbyshire Wildlife Trust 01773 881188 to obtain the code for the reserve entrance gate and bird hides.

→ Take B587 S of Melbourne past DE73 8BJ, turn R signed Calke after 2 miles. Park at Calke Car Park overflow L after ½ mile. Gate into wood opp and 20m to R of car park entrance. Follow path through reserve over wooden walkway and 200m after end of walkway take L spur to the bird hide.

10 mins, 52.7995, -1.4409 🚲🚶⛰️🅿️

RUINS & FOLLIES

10 ELVASTON CASTLE

The grounds of this Gothic Revival 'castle' are crammed with a jumble of secret nooks and crannies, ornamental arches, a Moorish temple, giant trees to climb, and secluded, romantic corners. Good café in courtyard.

→ From the A6 SE of Derby, take the B5010 through Thulston and Elvaston dir DE72 3EN. Pay car park L about ½ mile after Elvaston.

5 mins, 52.8931, -1.3929 🎨🚶🅿️🚲📷

11 MORLEY PARK FURNACES

A rare remnant of the Industrial Revolution, this pair of unique iron smelting blast furnaces now nestle, forgotten, in the corner of a field.

15

→ On B6374 W out of Ripley, turn L onto Street Lane. Just after DE5 8HT turn R onto Park Rd, park on L just under bridge. Follow track on past farmhouse and signed footpath L across field.
15 mins, 53.0386, -1.4347

12 FIRING WALL

An unexpected 5m high wall alongside a quiet countryside path, with firing platforms nearby, built in 1800 for the local militia to practise target shooting.

→ In Milford park on Sunny Hill no through road (DE56 0QR). Walk on up North Lane bridleway for ¾ mile.
20 mins, 53.0101, -1.4968

13 HORSLEY CASTLE, COXBENCH

The perfect 'hide-and-seek' location, with remains of a 12th-century Norman castle atop undulating earthworks. Wild daffodils and bluebells carpet the woods, birdsong floats in the air, and childhood memories are re-lived and made.

→ In Coxbench, turn R off main road onto lane opp Horsley Lane by A38 bridge (dir DE21 5BD) and park. Walk on past driveway L and follow paths into woods.
10 mins, 52.9849, -1.4427

14 CALKE LIME PITS

A collection of dips and hollows hint at the industrial past of these limekilns, tramway and caves, now hidden away in the dappled shade of the trees. Nearby is NT Calke Abbey and Staunton Harold Reservoir (see listing).

→ Park in Ticknall (DE73 7JZ) and at E end of Main Street and follow footpath sign R (52.8123, -1.4680) into woods. Or walk from NT Calke Abbey (20 mins)
2 mins, 52.8119, -1.4660

15 VERNON'S FOLLY

The whimsical nature of the landed gentry is captured in Lord Vernon's 18th-century red sandstone enclosure, which he built to contain his deer herd; how the other half lived! It now stands in a farmer's field opposite Sudbury Hall. Narrow lanes, best visited with a bike or a long walk.

→ At A40 roundabout at E of Sudbury, take Aston Lane N ¾ mile, past DE6 5HG. Take even smaller lane L on bend. After ⅓ mile take signed footpath L across field and along hedgerow. Folly on R. Alternatively, signed car park and footpath in Sudbury, near DE6 5HS. Follow path under A50 along field edge. Folly to L at far end of field.
30 mins, 52.8919, -1.7600

13

14

19

17

18

→ Parking at entrance to All Saints Church, Bradbourne, DE6 1PA. Cross in churchyard.
1 min, 53.0714, -1.6909 ⚡ ✝

ANCIENT & SACRED

16 VIKING BARROWS, HEATH WOOD

An extraordinary collection of 59 Viking barrows from the late-9th and early 10th centuries. The earliest and best examples of Viking graves in Britain and the only cemetery.

→ Take Ingleby Lane N from Ticknall (past DE73 7JX), park on L after 1¼ miles and follow footpath L into woods.
10 mins, 52.8300, -1.4936 ⚡ ✝ 🚶 🐕 ☂ 🚗

17 ST WYSTAN'S CHURCH, SAXON CRYPT

The original Anglo-Saxon crypt, built in the 8th century and the mausoleum of King Æthelbald, was lost for centuries until rediscovered in 1779. A stunning place, and one of the oldest surviving examples of Anglo-Saxon architecture.

→ Parking outside church on Willington Rd, Repton, DE65 6FH.
1 min, 52.8411, -1.5516 ⚡ ✝ 🍴

18 BRADBOURNE SAXON CROSS

The shaft of a 9th-century Saxon cross, one of the oldest Christian artefacts in the area. It was rescued and reassembled in the 1880s, having been used as the posts of a stile.

NATURAL WONDERS

19 ALPORT HEIGHT

Offering panoramas over the rural Derbyshire countryside, Alport Height is the first 300m+ hill you will encounter before the Peaks. Just keep your back to the radio masts! Couple with the Ecclesbourne Way Walk along the river: see signs for info.

→ NT car park on hill, entrance with sign off Alport Lane between Shottle and Belper, just N of DE56 2DQ.
2 mins, 53.0604, -1.5481 📷 ✖ 🚶 🏕

20 DIMMINSDALE NATURE RESERVE

Blankets of snowdrops signal the start of spring in this limestone quarry, now gracefully reclaimed by nature. Wild garlic runs riot along bubbling stream banks and ancient quarry pits, perfect for dipping a toe on a hot summer's day.

→ Park as for Staunton Harold Reservoir (see entry). Walk on 30m to L. Snowdrops beyond quarry pits.
5 mins, 52.7908, -1.4467 🚶 🅿 📷

SLOW FOOD

21 THE HORSESHOES, LONG LANE

A modern twist on a traditional country inn. Enjoy a pint of Pedigree next to the cosy fire or treat yourself to an award-winning meal in the modern dining room overlooking the pretty garden.

→ Long Lane, Longlane, DE6 5BJ, 01332 824625. Electric car charging point.
52.9395, -1.6297 🚺🍴

22 THE COCK INN, MUGGINTON

Modern meets tradition in this stylish gastropub. Well-presented food, with vegan and gluten-free menus, in comfortable surroundings with attentive staff. Tuck into the Derbyshire lamb shank washed down by a pint of Landlord. Delightful!

→ Bullhurst Lane, Mugginton, DE6 4PJ, 01773 550703.
52.9923, -1.5737 🚺🍴

23 THE BULLS HEAD, REPTON

Extensive gastropub split into distinct areas, each with its own identity, stylishly decorated. Stocks over 100 beers and ciders to pair with their delicious wood-fired pizzas.

→ 84 High Street, Repton, DE65 6GF, 01283 704422.
52.8360, -1.5470 🚺🍴

24 THE THREE HORSESHOES

Mouth-watering Sunday roasts are served by friendly bar staff in this warm and welcoming 18th-century dining pub. Exposed beams and brickwork, open fires, flagstone floors and real ales. Don't miss the quirky, old village lock up across the road.

→ 44 Main St, Breedon on the Hill, DE73 8AN, 01332 695129.
52.8020, -1.3982 🚺🍴

25 THE BULL SHED & SHOTTLE FARM BREWERY

Down a bumpy farm track and behind the old bull shed door lie a roaring log fire, friendly staff and unpretentious steak and pizzas. The Grumpy Farmer's own goat's cheese and beer brewed onsite are the best around. A small venture on a working farm, open Fridays and Saturdays only, strictly by reservation and preorder (by text). Wear layers in winter!

→ Handley Farm, Wilderbrook Lane, Shottle, DE56 2DT, 07877 723075.
53.0417, -1.5199 🍴🚺

26 THE SARACEN'S HEAD, SHIRLEY

Derby Dales village pub renowned for its high-quality modern English food and award-winning head chef. Open fires, a beer garden and a deli in the back.

→ Church Lane, Shirley, DE6 3AS, 01335 360330.
52.9712, -1.6760 🚺🍴

27 THE CHEDDAR GORGE, ASHBOURNE

Super little café and deli specialising in cheese (typically 75 different kinds in stock), pies and cakes.

→ 9 Dig Street, Ashbourne DE6 1GF, 01335 344528.
53.0166, -1.7333 🍴

28 CROOTS FARM SHOP & CAFÉ

Friendly, family-run farm shop stocking a vast array of mouth-watering local produce, much of which is from the farm. Perfect picnic bites on the deli, or try the award-winning sausages from the butcher's counter, which are simply scrumptious.

→ Farnah House Farm, Wirksworth Road, Duffield, DE56 4AQ, 01332 843032.
52.9844, -1.5113 🍴

29 HACKWOOD FARM

A picturesque courtyard farm shop and café. The butcher's counter and deli are crammed full of delicious, home-made and local produce, whilst the café serves a great range of lunches and afternoon tea fit for a queen.

→ Radbourne Lane, Radbourne, DE6 4LZ, 01332 528300.
52.9211, -1.5498 🍴

30 THE APPLE TREE, OCKBROOK

Pretty little tearoom and gift shop serving good home-made food and irresistible cakes. Booking strongly advised for lunch.

→ 6 Flood Street, Ockbrook, DE72 3RF, 01332 987001.
52.9180, -1.3729 🍴

31 CHEVIN STUDIO CAFÉ

Delightful, tiny cafe in beautifully restored cowshed sitting alongside a curious sighting tower built by Stephenson to ensure the straight line of the Duffield to Milford Tunnel. There's a lovely walk along the ridge line to Farnah Green.

→ North Lane, Milford, DE56 0QS. Park on Sunny Hill and walk up.
53.0022, -1.4866 🍴

COSY PUBS

32 HOLLY BUSH, MAKENEY

Reputedly a regular haunt for Dick Turpin, this timeless 17th-century inn has retained all of its character and charm. Marston's Pedigree still served from a jug and a strong selection of local and national real ales make it popular with enthusiasts and walkers enjoying a pork pie and a pint.

→ Holly Bush Lane, Makeney, DE56 0RX, 01332 841729.
52.9982, -1.4771

33 THE BARLEY MOW INN, KIRK IRETON

A real, honest gem that time passed by, dripping with warmth and charm. At the turn of the century, patrons would order from the hatch and pay the landlady sitting by the fire.

→ Main St, Kirk Ireton, DE6 3JP, 01335 370306.
53.0477, -1.6041

34 THE TOWN STREET TAP, DUFFIELD

A Tollgate Brewery micropub serving a lot more than ale including Crafternoon Tea, ale served with cakes and sandwiches.

→ 17 Town Street, Duffield, DE56 4EH, 01283 229194
52.9867, -1.4877

35 THE COW, DALBURY LEES

Stripped-back, quintessentially English inn offering everything you could want from your friendly local. Great food, local ales and quirky features like milk urns for bar stools. Rooms and electric car charging available.

→ The Green, Dalbury Lees, DE6 5BE, 01332 824297.
52.9315, -1.6076

RUSTIC HAVENS

36 HARDINGE ARMS

Stylishly decorated, comfortable rooms in the converted old stables, some with original features such as beams and bare stone walls. Delicious breakfast!

→ Main Street, King's Newton, DE73 8BX, 01332 863808.
52.8317, -1.4260

37 SWARKESTONE PAVILION

Rolling Stones fans may recognise the majestic Tudor structure, iconic from the *Beggars' Banquet* album poster when it was a ruin. Built as a grandstand to overlook the enclosure, which might have hosted from bear-baiting, but more likely bowls!

→ Swarkestone, DE73 7JB, landmarktrust.org.uk
52.8539, -1.4451

38 DEERPARK LODGE, STAUNTON HAROLD

Situated in the private parkland of the impressive Staunton Hall Estate, this contemporary timber lodge offers luxurious accommodation with a wood-burning stove for the winter months.

→ Staunton Harold, LE65 1RT, 01332 864435.
52.7869, -1.4349

39 MAYFIELD HIDEAWAY

Secluded accommodation in a cosy barn conversion or an upcycled vintage caravan in the South Derbyshire countryside.

→ Upper Mayfield, near Ashbourne, 01335 418468.
53.0198, -1.7833

40 MARTIN GREEN, POPLARS FARM

A cosy, converted horse box for two, in a tranquil spot alongside the River Trent. Kingfishers, martins and otters all spotted regularly. Canoe hire run from the farm.

→ Poplars Farm, Twyford, DE73 7HJ, canopyandstars.co.uk
52.8483, -1.5053

CAMP & SLEEP

41 THE PUDDING ROOM

Camp on one of the 20 simple pitches at this award-winning bakery and you have a café and shop onsite selling indulgent food made with local ingredients.

→ Near Carsington Water, DE6 1NQ, 01629 540413.
53.0624, -1.6544

42 FOUR OAKS CAMPSITE

A lovely campsite with communal BBQ, pizza oven and incredibly welcoming owners.

→ Buckford Lane, Stenson, DE73 7GB, 07939 152101.
52.8649, -1.5200

43 HILL FARM CAMPING

A quiet, simple campsite next to the canal, with easy access to the River Trent. If the weather is not on your side there are wooden pods with heating to rent.

→ Moor Lane, Barrow-on-Trent, DE73 7HZ, 01332 705165.
52.8589, -1.4701

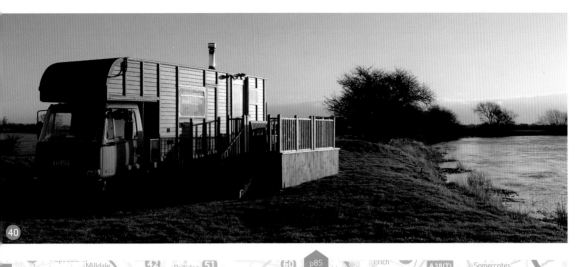

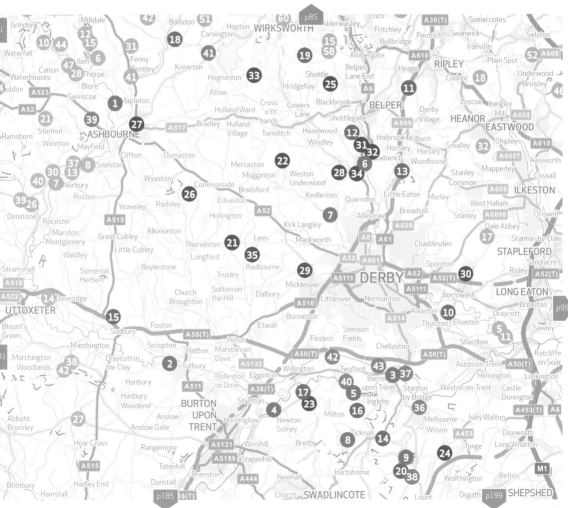

SOUTH LINCOLNSHIRE & RUTLAND

Our perfect weekend

→ **Admire** the rare pasque flowers at Ancaster Valley before indulging in a lavish evening meal at the Brownlow Arms.

→ **Explore** the wilderness of Launde Big Wood, taking a picnic with artisan bread from the Hambleton Bakery.

→ **Climb** up the hill to the Bellmount Tower to enjoy a sunset with panoramic views, then quench your thirst at The Green Man in Ropsley.

→ **Bathe** in the clear waters at Sykes Lane beach and marvel at Normanton Church before sampling the charcuterie at The King's Arms.

→ **Seek** out the Gothic folly at Fort Henry reflected in the lake, then be amazed at the layered chancel arch at St Peter's.

→ **Walk** beneath the awe-inspiring black brick arches of Harringworth Viaduct, and enjoy a private paddle in the Welland at Turtle Bridge afterwards.

→ **Discover** the ruins of Exton Park Old Hall or wonder at the curious shapes of the Yew Tree Avenue at Clipsham.

→ **While** away an afternoon amongst the rare orchids of Merry's Meadow before retreating to your own luxury geodome and hot tub at The Stix.

England's smallest county, Rutland, entices visitors with its country lanes that wind through a picture-postcard landscape bursting with ancient woodlands, pretty limestone cottages and friendly local pubs. Cross the border and the countryside flattens, the distance between villages increases, and the vast skies of Lincolnshire accompany you to its marshy coastline.

An ancient land with evidence of Neolithic, Bronze and Iron Age settlements, this area prospered during the Middle Ages with the rise in markets and trading routes. Hints of past greatness can be seen at the imposing 9th-century Crowland Abbey, which is still partly in use as the parish church, or the 12th-century St Peter's Church at Tickencote, famed for its magnificent Norman chancel arch. The 'sunken' Normanton Church, built in the 14th century, stands still proud, though partly buried overlooking Rutland Water. In the 19th century, Harringworth Viaduct was constructed, straddling the Welland Valley: its 82 arches still carry freight today. An impressive feat of engineering, maintenance workers say the imprints of children's hands and feet can be seen on the bricks from when they were made.

Rutland Water itself is the UK's largest man-made lake, and offers a superb family day out. There are sun-dappled cycle routes and walks around the perimeter, secluded picnic spots and a dedicated swimming area at Sykes Lane. It is also a great place for wildlife: many species of birds overwinter here and it is a breeding site for osprey. The gentle Welland is the principal river in the area, and meanders its way across the Rutland and Lincolnshire countryside to The Wash estuary. Head to the Windpump at Cottingham for pebbly beach shallows leading down to a deep, luxurious pool, or find the rope swing in a secluded stretch of river below the 14th-century Turtle Bridge.

Many patches of ancient woodland still survive from medieval times. Launde Big Wood is a wild, overgrown playground sitting atop a hill with glorious views across the surrounding countryside, while Bourne Wood is flora- and fauna- rich, with bluebells and primroses, kingfishers and herons. The perfect picnic spot can be found at Merry's Meadow, where wild flowers including the rare frog orchid grow in abundance.

Communities here have always been strong and self-sufficient, largely due to the sheer distance between them, and one result of this is the high-quality community shops and pubs to be found. The award-winning Hambleton Bakery is synonymous with quality, artisan bread, served in many local pubs and restaurants. The Olive Branch in Clipsham serves excellent food and The White Horse at Baston shines with its policy of sourcing locally.

RIVER SWIMMING

1 PINCHBECK SLIPE, RIVER GLEN

Arrow-straight, slow-moving aquamarine river in nature reserve of flood-meadows. Easy access to spot nesting birds and for a relaxing, secluded swim.

→ From West Pinchbeck (PE11 3NG) on the A151 take Slipe Drove turn just S of river, follow approx ½ mile and park L next to the lone small barn. Cross ditch opposite barn and small, wooden bridge across the marsh at telegraph pole. Crest the levee to reach the river.

2 mins, 52.7962, -0.2370 🏊🤿🐾

2 COTTINGHAM, RIVER WELLAND

Tranquil section of the Welland near old windpump. Pebble beach perfect for kids, leading into a gloriously deep pool near the bridge.

→ Take Ashby Road N from Middleton dir Ashley (past LE16 8YJ) 600m to bend L. Park carefully if barrier on track straight on is locked, and walk on along bumpy track to the bridge, 400m.

5 mins, 52.5103, -0.7678 🏊🌲🏞️🐾

3 STAMFORD, RIVER WELLAND

A lovely section of river with numerous beaches and deeper sections upstream. If you get a chance, grab a pint and pizza at the Tobie Norris after (see listing).

→ Park at the Cattlemarket car park in Stamford (PE9 2WB). Walk N over the footbridge and turn L onto Meadows footpath. Walk 500m along river to small beach on bend.

10 mins, 52.6461, -0.4843 🚶🧍🍴🏞️🏊

4 TURTLE BRIDGE, RIVER WELLAND

This quiet stretch of the Welland shelves gently down to deeper pools with a rope swing upstream. Perfect for a family picnic.

→ From A47 just S of Morcott, take B672 at LE15 9EB, signed Caldecott. Drive ¾ mile, to bend R, turn L and park immediately in end of bridleway. Walk ½ mile down bridleway to river.

10 mins, 52.5763, -0.6320 🏊🏞️🧍🏔️

LANGUID LAKES

5 SYKES LANE, RUTLAND WATER

Sykes Lane beach on the north shore is a recently designated official swimming site. With lifeguards on duty from July to September, this is the perfect spot for those new to wild swimming and those with young children. The beach can be crowded on peak days. Hambleton Peninsula is also lovely to explore, with views to Normanton church.

→ Sykes Lane Tourist Centre (LE15 8QL) is signed off A606 E of Oakham.

4 mins, 52.6625, -0.6174 🏊🐾🏘️🏞️🧍

6 NORMANTON CHURCH, RUTLAND WATER

The backdrop of Normanton church, half-buried to save it from erosion when the reservoir was filled, makes this a picturesque but popular location. This is not designated as a swimming site.

→ From the A606 ½ mile S of Empingham, take turn signed Normanton and car park at Rutland Water S (LE15 8HD, small charge).

4 mins, 52.6461, -0.6232 🏘️🏞️

7 FORT HENRY LAKE, EXTON PARK

Admire the magical waterside Gothic folly (now a wedding venue) reflected in clear waters edged with water lilies.

→ In Exton head S past LE15 8AW and turn L. Follow road 1½ miles and park at 52.6849, -0.5940 just before trout farm. Follow signed footpath 1 mile from field corner up to shores of lower lake, then to upper lake with folly.

25 mins, 52.6987, -0.5976 🏔️🖼️

145

ANCIENT & SACRED

8 ASHWELL WISHING WELL

This substantial holy well on the edge of Ashwell village was reputed to have healing properties. Come and make a wish.

→ In SW corner of Ashwell village (LE15 7LW), well is in trees just to W of junction of Oakham Rd and Langham Rd. Space for one car.

1 min, 52.7134 -0.7217 ✝🐾

9 ST PETER'S, TICKENCOTE

Absolutely stunning 12th-century vaulted chancel with a layered arch, each layer with its own design. The rest of the church was built up around it when restored in the 1700s, but it does nothing to detract from this masterpiece.

→ Take B1081 NE out of Stamford to Tickencote. Just before road joins A1, turn L then immediately L again onto Church Lane, signed Tickencote only (PE9 4AE). Church on bend after 200m.

2 mins, 52.6741, -0.5365 ✝🐾

10 CROWLAND ABBEY

The striking remnants of a Benedictine abbey, its north aisle still in use as the parish church. Croyland was an island in the fens when Guthlac the monk first came to live as a hermit here. See also the curious three-way bridge over nothing in the town!

→ In Crowland, N of Peterborough on A16, abbey remains at E end of East St (PE6 0EN), with car park. Trinity Bridge is at other end.

1 min, 52.6763, -0.1651 🐾✝

WOODLANDS & WILDLIFE

11 YEW TREE AVENUE, CLIPSHAM

Curious line of pepper pot yews, once the grand carriage drive to the stately home.

→ Take Castle Bytham Rd NE out of Clipsham (LE15 7SH) for 1 mile. FC car parking signed on L just after avenue itself.

2 mins, 52.7409, -0.5493 🚶🎋

12 MERRY'S MEADOW

A beautiful and diverse wild flower meadow in a ridge-and-furrow pattern, hidden among vast, modern fields. Rare frog orchid along with many others. Perfect picnic spot.

→ Take Great Lane out of Greetham (starts by LE15 7NL), park at end. Cross road, follow signed track for 400m to reserve entrance, crossing through hedge on R on the way.

15 mins, 52.7308, -0.6124 🌸🎋

13 LAUNDE BIG WOOD

Hidden ancient woodland adjacent to the old Launde Estate. Lose yourself in the impressive array of rich flora carpeting the floor.

→ From Loddington (LE7 9XE) take Main St NE dir Launde ¾ mile to staggered tracks into woods L and R. Park (52.6235, -0.8267 limited space) and walk 650m to end of track L and along field edge, enter woods at the SE edge.

8 mins, 52.6266, -0.8410 🚶🏕🐕🚗

14 FREISTON SHORE NATURE RESERVE

Remote RSPB site with wildlife in abundance on the saltwater lagoons. Second World War pillboxes hint at the area's place in history.

→ In Freiston turn at church signed Freiston Shore and follow Shore Rd 1¾ miles; reserve signed L (just past PE22 0NA). Follow path from car park.

10 mins, 52.9606, 0.0796 🏊🚶

15 ANCASTER VALLEY NATURE RESERVE

This steep-sided, narrow valley is one of the best places in the country to see limestone wild flowers such as pasque flowers and bee orchids, with a beech woodland to explore too. A wonderful place to escape modern life.

→ Park in Ancaster near St Martin's Church

(Ermine Street, NG32 3PW). Walk S and turn L dir Sleaford. Bridleway entrance to reserve on R after 50m.

7 mins, 52.9780, -0.5350 🚶🏕🐕🖼🌸

16 BOURNE WOOD

Peaceful, ancient woodland packed full of broadleaf trees, ferns, primroses and bluebells. Spot herons and kingfishers in and around the natural ponds and stop for a picnic in the many sun-dappled clearings.

→ Take West Rd/A151 out of Bourne W dir PE10 0LG; woods signed R ½ mile after roundabout, free FC car park.

4 mins, 52.7704, -0.4009 🚗🚶

RUINS & REMNANTS

17 EXTON PARK OLD HALL

Partially destroyed by fire, this 17th-century mansion now stands forlorn in the private estate of its replacement.

→ Take A606 E out of Oakham 3½ miles to Whitwell, turn L signed Exton. Church is signposted L as you enter Exton (opp LE15 8AX) just before Fox & Hounds (see listing). Ruins are visible over wall to rear of churchyard.

2 mins, 52.6909, -0.6380 ✝🏛🚴❓

18 BELLMOUNT TOWER

A proud folly built around 1750, primarily as a viewing tower. Although it cannot be entered, its hilltop location offers fine views over the National Trust parkland to the west. This is part of the Belton House Estate (house and garden are open for visits).

➜ Take Londonthorpe Lane out of NE Grantham past NG31 9SL. Take unsigned L after ½ mile and drive ¾ mile to parking R in view of tower on hill. Follow path uphill to folly.
15 mins, 52.9382, -0.5894 ⛔🏃🚼🐕📷🗑

19 HARRINGWORTH VIADUCT

The blackened brick arches of this imposing viaduct stretch for ¾ mile across the Welland River Valley. An impressive feat of engineering from 1878. Afterwards refuel on delicious coffee, cakes and lunches at Spokes pop-up café in Harringworth (Meadow Cottage, Wakerley Road, 01572 747974, closed in winter).

➜ Pull off by on B672 under viaduct N of Harringworth, ½ mile E of LE15 9HZ. Various paths through fields. Or at the S end, head W out of Harringworth past NN17 3AD, and walk W 70m to signed footpath.
15 mins, 52.5635, -0.6543 🐕👟📷

20 THE FOX & HOUNDS INN, EXTON

Overlooking the village green, this beautifully presented inn offers high-quality food and overnight stays in a luxurious, distinctive interior.

➜ 19 The Green, Exton, LE15 8AP, 01572 812403.
52.6902, -0.6336 🍴🍺🛏🚲

21 THE OLIVE BRANCH, CLIPSHAM

A 17th-century pub that has kept its old-world charm and grown a reputation for seriously great food from local produce.

➜ Main Street, Clipsham, LE15 7SH, 01780 410355.
52.7342, -0.5646 🍴🍺🛏

22 THE CAKEHOLE, BARROWBY

Deli and café, also called Dougie's, with set menu bistro nights in the dining room (book in advance). High-quality dishes served Wednesday–Saturday.

➜ 1 Main Street, Barrowby, NG32 1BZ, 01476 564250.
52.9171, -0.6920 🍴

23 BARROWDEN & WAKERLEY COMMUNITY SHOP

A thriving community shop and café serving light lunches, home-made cakes, Fairtrade coffee and local produce and crafts. Outside eating area for sunnier days.

→ 22 Wakerley Road, Barrowden, LE15 8EP, 01572 748748.

52.5912, -0.5992 🍴

24 HAMBLETON BAKERY, EXTON

Bread baked the traditional way, with slow-rise methods and no additives. The result is award-winning, mouth-wateringly tasty bread, cakes and savouries.

→ 2 Cottesmore Road, Exton, LE15 8AN, 01572 812995.

52.7028, -0.6491 🍴

25 WINDMILL TEAROOMS, WYMONDHAM

Vintage-styled tearoom among local boutique shops at a partly restored windmill, serving meals from local produce and huge slices of home-made cake.

→ Butt Lane, Wymondham, LE14 2BU, 01572 787304.

52.7642, -0.7406 🍴

26 THE WHITE HORSE, BASTON

Sympathetically renovated interior provides a relaxed atmosphere for drinkers and diners alike. A well-crafted menu features many local ingredients – including the exceptional Fen Apiaries honey, also sold from Grace's house a few doors down. A must-try

→ 4 Church Street, Baston, PE6 9PE, 01778 560923. Honey at 30 Church Street.

52.7115, -0.3538 🍴

27 THE WOODHOUSE ARMS, CORBY GLEN

Attractive inn with a central island bar, serving quality ales. Dine outside in the summer or settle by the fire in the colder months. Comfortable rooms and a well-prepared menu.

→ 2 Bourne Road, Corby Glen, NG33 4NS, 01476 552452.

52.8115, -0.5184 🍴

28 NORTHFIELD FARM SHOP

Award-winning farm shop specialising in rare and traditional British breeds on its butcher's counter. Lovely cottage available.

→ Whissendine Lane, Cold Overton, LE15 7QF (sat nav LE15 7JD), 01664 474271.

52.7014, -0.7990 🍴

29 TOLLEMACHE ARMS, BUCKMINSTER

Great food and ale served by friendly staff in this grand, stone-built inn from the 19th century.

→ 48 Main Street, Buckminster, NG33 5SA, 01476 860477.
52.7961, -0.6957

30 8 SAIL BREWERY, HECKINGTON

Friendly, small brewery shop and cosy bar serving their own draught ale, sited near the titular, working eight-sailed windmill. Open to 9.30pm Fri, 12.00–3.00pm weekends. Shop open to 4.00pm most days, closed Weds.

→ Hale Road, Heckington, NG34 9JW, 01529 469308.
52.9770, -0.2950

31 KING'S ARMS, WING

A top-quality country pub that produces its own charcuterie and baked goods and even has a smokehouse onsite. Award-winning food served by friendly staff with a well-kept bar. Accommodation available.

→ Top Street, Wing, Oakham, LE15 8SE, 01572 737634.
52.6169, -0.6838

32 THE BROWNLOW ARMS

Beautiful 17th-century inn. Friendly staff welcome you to relax in the deep armchairs by the fire or dine from the excellent menu. Thoroughly recommended. Closed Mondays.

→ Grantham Road, Hough-on-the-Hill, NG32 2AZ, 01400 250234.
53.0065, -0.6268

33 THE BUSTARD INN, SOUTH RAUCEBY

Lesley and Julian greet you warmly as you enter this tasteful pub built in 1860. Large flagstones add a sense of grandeur, backed up by fabulous food cooked using herbs from their own garden.

→ 44 Main Street, South Rauceby, NG34 8QG, 01529 488250.
52.9979, -0.4730

COSY PUBS

34 THE BLUE BALL, BRAUNSTON

Delightful, 17th-century thatched inn with roaring log fires, cosy seating and delicious food. Pop into the churchyard and see the enigmatic stone 'goddess' by the tower.

→ 6 Cedar Street, Braunston, LE15 8QS, 01572 722135.
52.6510, -0.7699

35 THE JACKSON STOPS INN, STRETTON

Great food served in a delightful, quintessentially English thatched building. It was once for sale so long that it was renamed for the estate agent's sign.

→ Rookery Lane, Stretton, LE15 7RA, 01780 410237.
52.7322, -0.5950

36 THE GREEN MAN, ROPSLEY

Charming, friendly local pub with exposed brick, wood-burner, quirky touches, plenty of character, and honest food.

→ 24 High Street, Ropsley, NG33 4BE, 01476 585897.
52.8958, -0.5239

37 THE BERKELEY ARMS, WYMONDHAM

Delightfully cosy, refurbished village pub, offering sumptuous Sunday roasts from local produce. Recent CAMRA Pub of the Year.

→ 59 Main Street, Wymondham, LE14 2AG, 01572 787587.
52.7603, -0.7399

38 THE WHEATSHEAF, GREETHAM

Well-made pub grub in this family-friendly, traditional inn. Freshly baked bread and ginger pudding are particularly recommended.

→ 1 Stretton Road, Greetham, LE15 7NP, 01572 812325.
52.7189, -0.6247

39 TOBIE NORRIS, STAMFORD

A 19th-century pub in a 13th-century building, serving great food from local produce. Lots of wonderful nooks and quirks in the historic interior (but for that reason no pushchairs allowed).

→ 12 St Paul's Street, Stamford, PE9 2BE, 01780 753800.
52.6542, -0.4735

CAMP & SLEEP

40 IN THE STIX, OAKHAM

Glamping as you've never seen it: luxury geodesic domes with leather Chesterfield sofas, double beds, mezzanine bedrooms, showers, wood-burners, and wood-fired hot tubs, all with outdoor cooking and campfires.

→ Brook Farm, Oakham, LE15 7SN, inthestix.co.uk.
52.7189, -0.6103

41 THE HOUSE OF CORRECTION

This grand entrance is all that survives of a prison intended to intimidate the idle and

sorderly. Once home to the turnkey, now
available as a unique place to stay.

▶ Folkingham, NG34 0SG, landmarktrust.co.uk
2.8879, -0.4043

2 LANTERN AND LARKS, EXTON PARK
All the fun of camping but in a luxury safari-
style tent, within the beautiful grounds of
Exton Park.

▶ Oakham, LE15 8AN, lanternandlarks.co.uk
2.6961, -0.6446

3 CUCKOO FARM CAMPSITE
Simple camping field on a working organic
farm. Buy the farm's own organic eggs,
chicken, lamb, venison, pork, sausages and
burgers. Wildlife can be spotted everywhere,
including the cuckoos in the title.

▶ Cuckoo Farm Lodge, Stamford, PE9 3UU (do
not use sat nav, see website), 07796 130923.
2.6147, -0.5726

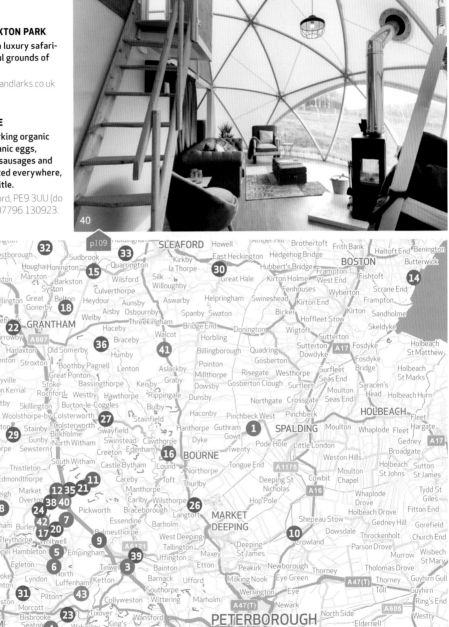

SHROPSHIRE HILLS

Our perfect weekend

→ **Bathe** in the river below the majestic Clun Castle, followed by a stroll up the ancient Green Lane Holloway.

→ **Dip** into the pools of the River Rhiw at Berriew and then sample the sublime cheese souffle at Checkers Pantry for lunch.

→ **Explore** the old mines at Snailbeach then watch the sunset from the Devil's Chair, high up on the Stiperstones.

→ **Scale** the vast earthworks of Bury Ditches and then down a well-earned pint at the jovial Bridges pub at Ratlinghope.

→ **Fuel** up on a Sunday roast at the charming Tally Ho Inn before walking up to Boyne Water for a secluded plunge.

→ **Soak** in the tranquil surroundings of the Carding Mill Valley and then feast on zero-food-miles game at Upper Shadymoor Farm.

→ **Wander** around the ruins at Lower Down Castle followed by a night in one of the wonderfully quirky cabins at Walcot Hall.

Diverse geology, stunning scenery and wide-open spaces beckon visitors to the Shropshire Hills. In this Area of Outstanding Natural Beauty you will find wild, craggy ridges leading to rugged heathland, rocky tors separated by deep valleys or 'batches', and ancient wooded hills sloping down to riverside meadows.

This is the perfect place for some off-the-beaten-track adventures, whether that be scaling the heights of the Stiperstones with their jagged outcrops of rock, or following the Portway medieval trade route along the plateau of the Long Mynd, so rich in archaeology, to search out hillforts and burial mounds. To the east of this, the area around Church Stretton was called Little Switzerland by the Victorians, due to its Alpine lookalike hills and valleys. Here, Carding Mill offers a delightful walk up to a beautiful waterfall or the tantalising treat of a dip in the reservoir.

To the west, along the Welsh borderlands, a double line of castles and fortifications hint at the turbulent past, chronicling invasions and rebellions. These picturesque remains offer a secluded swim below the ruins of Clun Castle, where the kids can splash around and swim in deep pools after a lazy riverbank picnic. Further west again, the Severn winds its way along the border. A strategically important ancient ford at Rhydwhyman promises a luxurious swim in the dappled shade of the trees, while the River Rhiw at Berriew tempts bathers with a series of cascading waterfalls and plunge pools, perfect for a cooling off on a hot summer's day.

Mining and farming have shaped much of the landscape in the area. Old quarrying communities have left their marks, which make fascinating sites for exploration. A rewarding hike to the top of Brown Clee Hill, the highest peak in Shropshire, offers an insight into the scale of excavations and leaves you in no doubt as to its prominence as an Iron Age hillfort. Snailbeach Mine, much less of a walk, is the most complete example of mining buildings in the country and intriguing to explore.

Shropshire wool also brought prosperity to the area, and public houses such as the iconic The Three Tuns inn, Bishop's Castle, The Stables Inn at Hopegate, and The Tally Ho Inn at Bouldon, sprang up as the backbone to rural communities. 'Hundred Houses', where chosen nobility met to discuss local issues and hold trials, have long since lost their power, but many still survive in the guise of pubs, like The Crown Country Inn at Munslow. The food festival in Ludlow, just to the south of this area, has had a halo effect over the years, ensuring fresh local produce is always sought for the top-quality food in many of these places.

RIVER SWIMMING

1 RIVER SEVERN, ATCHAM

Dip your toes at this calm, shallow bend in the River Severn or walk upstream and swim down through the languid, deeper waters.

→ Park at Atcham, 1½ miles from Shrewsbury ring road on B4380. Long lay-bys on road W of and opp Mytton and Mermaid Hotel (SY5 6QG, 01743 761220), or use hotel car park. Footpath at E end of old bridge down to a shallow sandy beach.

5 mins 52.6790, -2.6812 🏊🚶🏊🏕️

2 BERRIEW, RIVER RHIW

A series of secluded mini-waterfalls cascade along the edge of the village and offer a number of delightful swim spots.

→ Take road SW signed Bettws (National Cycle Route 81) out of Berriew over bridge, and park on lane immediately to R (SY21 8PJ). Railing ends 130m along lane.

4 mins, 52.5992, -3.2028 🏊🥾🏕️

3 RHYDWHYMAN, RIVER SEVERN

An ancient ford across the river, strategically important for centuries as the main route from mid-Wales into England, where Henry III relinquished his title of Prince of Wales to Llywelyn ap Gruffudd in 1267. Swim here, or upstream.

→ Follow B4385 NW from Montgomery and turn R after railway bridge, signed Caerhowel. Parking on L in wooded area after ¾ mile (opp turn to SY15 6HD). For upstream spot stay on B4385 for ½ mile after railway bridge, over river, and turn first R. Park at fork (limited space) and walk down R fork 500m and across grass to river beach.

1 min, 52.5775, -3.1700 🏊🏕️

4 RIVER SEVERN, CRESSAGE

Access points on both sides of the river, offering a great opportunity to wallow in the water under Cressage Bridge. Watch out for nettles!

→ From Cressage (SY5 6DE) take the B4380 N. After ⅓ mile, take footpath on L just before bridge and follow down to the riverside. Walk or cycle from village.

7 mins, 52.6378, -2.6010 🏊🏊

5 CLUN CASTLE

Swim at a bend of the River Clun below a wonderful ruined Norman castle sitting atop a natural elevation of rock. Lots to explore.

→ In Clun head W on High St/B4368 (SY7 8JB), and follow signs for castle L onto Bridge St, over river, then immediately R to car park on R. Follow signs from car park. Free entry to the castle.

5 mins, 52.4218, -3.0342 🏕️🏊🏕️🖼️

LAKES

6 BOYNE WATER, BURWARTON

Beautiful, peaty, warm water in a very secluded, tranquil location in the Clee Hills. Set in open-access land. Said to hold parts of aircraft that foundered on Brown Clee Hill (see entry).

→ Park in Burwarton and head out of village dir Cleedownton to pick up footpath to R after 5 mins (52.4593, -2.5660). Follow footpath across fields and around N side of woods, turning L to water. Can be muddy.

40 mins, 52.4587, -2.5904 🏊🥾🏕️

7 CARDING MILL RESERVOIR & WATERFALL

A beautiful walk up the path or scramble up the river to a waterfall and refreshing swim in the disused reservoir. Perfect day out and picnic spot, or a refreshing dip after a long walk on Long Mynd (see entry).

→ Signed Carding Mill Valley from B5477/High St in Church Stretton, Shropshire. Continue past SY6 6JG to furthest NT pay car park and

follow signs. Other paths lead up Long Mynd.
30 mins 52.5460, -2.8328 🖼🏞🏕🏖🌳🚶🏃🚻

8 LEA QUARRY, WENLOCK EDGE

Enjoy spectacular views from the Wenlock Edge ridge. Below are the dramatic turquoise waters of Lea quarry–the blue colour is from dissolved limestone. Sometimes the way down to the lake is open and people swim.

→ From Much Wenlock follow B4371 SW. Park at Wenlock Edge Car Park after 3 miles on R, before TF13 6DQ. Follow footpath up and NE to above quarry. Interesting kilns at 52.5751, -2.6126. Quarry is private, observe signs.
15 mins, 52.5770, -2.6109 🖼❓🚶🏞

RUINS & REMNANTS

9 LOWER DOWN CASTLE

A ruinous motte with a few fragments of the shell keep. Let yourself be transported back to when it was a local Norman stronghold and this quiet land was hard-fought.

→ Take B4385 S from Bishop's Castle 1½ miles and turn R signed Brockton (SY7 8BA). After 1½ miles, beyond village, park on R next to phone and postboxes (52.4557, -2.9765). Follow path through gate.
3 mins, 52.4553, -2.9780 🚲🏞♿

10 ACTON BURNELL CASTLE

This graceful red sandstone castle was started in 1284 by Bishop Burnell, a year after the first full English parliament met and passed laws in a barn here. Abandoned in the 15th century, it is managed by English Heritage (free entry). Spring flowers make this a picturesque spot for a quiet walk and a picnic.

→ From Shrewsbury follow lanes S to Pitchford and then Acton Burnell (SY5 7PA). Turn L at crossroads and then first R, park on lane near church. Castle behind church.
3 mins, 52.6128, -2.6898 🏰🐾🚲🖼

11 MONTGOMERY CASTLE

Impressive ruins of the Norman castle built by Henry III in 1223. Give the kids free rein to scramble, or bring a picnic and watch the sunset. Free entry. The Castle Kitchen in Broad St (SY15 6PH) offers great home-made cakes and refreshments.

→ Small car park next to castle at Kerry Road, SY15 6PD, or park lower in Montgomery and walk up hill.
5 mins, 52.5634, -3.1499 🐾🚲🏞

12 SNAILBEACH LEAD MINE

A fascinating insight into one of the biggest, richest, and now most complete

13

ollections of mine buildings in the country. nderground tours available, see Shropshire lines Trust website for details.

▶ Signed off A488 at Ploxgreen. Follow 1 ile and park next to village hall in Snailbeach efore SY5 0NX) and walk up hill to mine. mins, 52.6139, -2.9250 🐕🚶🏊🧍

SUNSET HILLTOPS

3 DEVIL'S CHAIR, STIPERSTONES

raggy, cobbled limestone path meanders nrough swathes of purple heather to the ors. Take a book, picnic on the rocks, and erch on the devil's chair on a misty day to inch with Lucifer himself.

▶ Head NW from The Bridges pub near atlinghope (SY5 0ST, see listing). Turn at T-junction then immediate R signed tiperstones. Follow 1¾ miles to car park. ollow path through first gate by information oard uphill.
0 mins, 52.5818, -2.9348 🧍🏕️🖼️🚶

4 BROWN CLEE HILL

n interesting assortment of ruins are cattered around the twin summit of hropshire's highest peak, from ancient illforts to mining buildings, aircraft control

towers, and aircraft remains; the hill is said to have suffered more wartime crashes than any other. Stunning views from the top.

▶ Head N and W from Cleobury North dir signed Ditton Priors (dir WV16 6TA). Follow to sharp R turn and park in second lay-by R after 400m, opp gate. Follow footpath uphill.
30 mins, 52.4750, -2.5994 🖼️🏕️🎋

15 BEECH TREE AVENUE, LINLEY HILL

A beautiful walk up this old drovers' road, now part of the Shropshire Way. Majestic trees, planted to commemorate the Napoleonic Wars, and magnificent views.

▶ A mile W of Norbury, turn R just before SY9 5HL, signed Cold Hill/The Bog. After ½ mile find small lay-by and Shropshire Way marker on R. Park here (room for one) and follow path NE.
5 mins, 52.5371, -2.9578 🧍🖼️🎋💧

16 GREEN LANE HOLLOWAY, CLUN

Charming and ancient sunken section of a path winding its way up towards Radnor Woods, which conceal an ancient hillfort.

▶ Head N on Guilden Down from YHA Clun Mill (SY7 8NY), park on R next to signed footpath and gate on bend after ¼ mile. Follow footpath turning L uphill and into sunken lane. Path continues to woods, hillfort is at

14

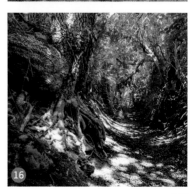

16

19

52.4295, -3.0014 along forestry tracks.
15 mins, 52.4279, -3.0185 🚶🚵

17 BURY DITCHES

Stunning views are awarded to those who ascend this formidable Iron Age hillfort. Well-preserved defensive earthworks.

→ Signposted on a lane that runs from the B4368 in Clunton (turn N past SY7 0HX) to the B4385 E of Lydbury North (turn S past SY7 8BA). Drive 1¾ miles from either end to FC car park at summit of road. Follow uphill R path.
20 mins, 52.4480, -2.9898 🐾🚶🎋🏞🚵

18 CAER CARADOC

Imposing Iron Age hillfort with stunning views to the Long Mynd (see entry). Man-made cave just below, where it is claimed Caratacus hid after his final stand against the Romans, and Comley Quarry, where Britain's first trilobites were found.

→ Leave the A49 N of Church Stretton, to and past SW6 7JN, to parking for 1 car at bend: 52.5636, -2.7619. Comley Quarry is through kissing gate then 100m across field 52.5639, -2.7627. Footpath up Caradoc is 200m along road, cave is on W flank.
45 mins, 52.5530, -2.7727 🚶🎋🏞🚵🚵

17

20

19 THE LONG MYND

A rich heathland plateau almost 7 miles long, topped with hillforts and Bronze Age barrows galore.

→ Start from NT car park at Carding Mill Reservoir (see entry). Follow signed path uphill then head west along the Shropshire Way to the summit of Pole Bank, the highest point on the Mynd. Walking boots and map advised.
2 hours, 52.5446, -2.8639 🚶🏞🚵🏔

WOODS & WILDLIFE

20 POLES COPPICE, PONTESBURY

Follow one of the paths through this ancient woodland with views over to the Iron Age forts at Callow Hill. Bluebells and orchids, dormice and bats in the old quarry buildings.

→ From Pontesbury follow Lower Rd through Pontesbury Hill, past SY5 0YL, to limited parking at the end of the road. Larger car park with slightly longer walk in 1 mile W from Habberley (SY5 0TP).
3 mins, 52.6365, -2.9018 🚶🏞🚗

21 THE HOLLIES & BROOK VESSONS

A spellbinding collection of wizened holly trees, some 400 years old. A mile along the ridge is Brook Vessons, with ancient, twisted

pple, birch and rowan trees, some of the rgest in the area. A place of peace and ontemplation.

▶ Park as for Snailbeach Lead Mine (see ntry). Walk up hill past mine. At top, take track to Lord's Hill chapel. Go through gate, take R ork in track. Hollies is on the L. Brook Vessons a mile along the ridge, 52.6023, -2.9131.
0 mins, 52.6105, -2.9121 🚶♿🚻

2 CLUNTON COPPICE

abulous all year round, a rich array of olours make this oak woodland stand out om many in the area. Great place to see e deer and, if you are lucky, the rare pine arten.

▶ On the B4368 travelling W in Clunton turn by Crown Inn (SY7 0HU, 01588 660265) ollow narrow lane over bridge and uphill to car ark ½ mile on the R.
mins, 52.4187, -2.9733 🐾🚶⛺♿♿

3 HARTON HOLLOW NATURE RESERVE

s you walk through the gnarled, mossy ees in the woods, you are treading on ncient coral reefs. Orchids, herb-paris and weet woodruff thrive atop this limestone, hich was cut from the abandoned quarries cattered in the wood.

▶ From Westhope (SY7 9JL), take lane N gned Ticklerton for 1 mile. Parking R at start f woods, with signed footpath.
mins, 52.4850, -2.7657 🚶♿♿

4 RECTORY WOOD, CHURCH STRETTON

ardens influenced by Capability Brown. ake a walk through the peaceful yew oodland to a pool with a ruined folly, ice ouse and summerhouse. There are also couple of ancient lime trees on the way. ollow the path further to Carding Mill eservoir (see entry).

▶ Limited parking on Church St by St aurence's church (SY6 6DQ). Gate in wall up to the gardens. Bear to the right of the hill or the pool.
0 mins, 52.5392, -2.8123 🚶🐾♿♿♿♿

ANCIENT & SACRED

5 MITCHELL'S FOLD STONE CIRCLE

large Bronze Age circle of 15 stones – it thought there were once 30 – high up n Stapeley Common. At 330m it affords lorious views over the hillside. Local walks nd a great picnic spot.

▶ Signed from A488, dir Priest Weston. ollow 1¼ miles, past SY5 0JJ, to track on end, follow track to parking at end. Path

straight on to circle.
5 mins, 52.5784, -3.0282 🚴🚶🚻

26 HEATH CHAPEL, BOULDON

Simply charming 12th-century Norman chapel, which has kept many of its original features with remarkably little alteration despite its continued use. Wall paintings are emerging through the later whitewash.

➔ From The Tally Ho Inn at Bouldon (SY7 9DP, see listing), turn L and follow signs to Heath. Chapel visible on L after 1 mile, shortly before SY7 9DS. Pull over by iron gate.
1 min, 52.4666, -2.6531 ✝

27 ST MILBURGA'S WELL

Crystal-clear water flows out of the spout of this holy well dedicated to St Milburga, who was said to have powers to cure blindness and protect crops from birds.

➔ In Stoke St Milborough (SY8 2EJ) well is at N, uphill end of village (Stoke Bank, but unsigned) on L if heading N. Pull onto verge at small, wooden gate into wooded area for old well basin, with a convenient dispensing standpipe outside.
1 min, 52.4370, -2.6372 ✝

28 CHECKERS PANTRY, MONTGOMERY

Formerly a Michelin-starred restaurant. The family have kept the same standards and dedication to high-quality, local ingredients to offer delicious breakfasts and lunches. The cheese soufflé is sublime! Rooms available. Tues–Sat.

→ Broad Street, Montgomery, SY15 6PN, 01686 669822.
52.5605, -3.1499

29 KERRY VALE VINEYARD

A new, award-winning vineyard planted on the site of an old Roman fort. Tours, tastings, café and shop.

→ Pentreheyling, SY15 6HU, 01588 620627.
52.5311, -3.1111

30 THE NAG'S HEAD, GARTHMYL

Modernised, award-winning coaching inn serving good-quality food. Rooms available.

→ Garthmyl, SY15 6RS, 01686 640600.
52.5828, -3.1913

31 THE CROWN COUNTRY INN, MUNSLOW

Traditional country inn dating back to Tudor times. The kitchen has a 'local to Ludlow' policy, ensuring the best local produce makes it onto the menu. Higgledy-piggledy rooms on multiple levels lead to a garden with great views of the Shropshire hills.

→ Munslow, nr Craven Arms, SY7 9ET, 01584 841205.
52.4821, -2.7065

32 THREE TUNS INN, BISHOPS CASTLE

Charming, oak-framed, rambling rooms provide the perfect setting to sup one of the many ales from the adjoining brewery. From here it's a short walk to the Old Castle Land 52.4953, -29989 where you can see the old castle ruins.

→ Salop Street, Bishops Castle, SY9 5BW, 01588 638797.
52.4945, -2.9968

33 THE ROYAL OAK, CARDINGTON

Relax with a pint or eat the famous cider-infused 'fidget pie' beside the vast inglenook fireplace. Rambling 15th-century pub with low-beamed rooms.

→ Cardington, Church Stretton, SY6 7JZ, 01694 771266.
52.5520, -2.7288

34 THE BRIDGES, RATLINGHOPE

Traditional home-made food, reasonably priced, and a good range of local ales from one of the UK's oldest licensed breweries, The Three Tuns (see listing). Served by friendly bar staff in a setting of oak beams, red quarry tiles and wood-burners.

→ Ratlinghope, Shrewsbury, SY5 0ST, 01588 650260.
52.5623, -2.8962

35 SUN INN, MARTON

A laid-back village pub serving delicious, home-made food.

→ B4386, Marton, SY21 8JP, 01938 561211
52.6149, -3.0550

36 MONTY'S BREWERY

A warm and friendly welcome awaits you when you visit. Tastings and tours arranged for larger groups, or simply call in to buy some beer and have a chat. Check website for opening times.

→ Cottage Inn, Pool Road, Montgomery, SY15 6QT, 01686 668933.
52.5649, -3.1480

37 THE STABLES INN, HOPESGATE

A genuine rural drovers' inn, dating back to 1680, selling hearty, home-cooked food and great ales. Friendly staff, great views over the hillside, rooms and a shepherds' hut available.

→ Hopesgate, Minsterley, SY5 0EP, 01743 891344.
52.6113, -2.9730

38 THE TALLY HO INN

Delightful, tucked-away 19th-century pub boasting the warmest of welcomes, with traditional food, ales and surroundings. A total joy.

→ Bouldon, Craven Arms, SY7 9DP, 01584 841811.
52.4623, -2.6729

39 THE HOUSE-BOX, KINTON QUARRY

A converted horse box nestled in a secluded quarry. Stargaze, relax, forget the world!

→ Kinton, SY15 6BU, canopyandstars.co.uk
52.5879, -3.0509

40 WALCOT HALL

You will be spoilt for choice with these superb glamping options: from yurts and showman's caravans to fire trucks and a

sublime chapel. Each one secluded, full of rustic charm and quirky individualism.
→ Walcot Hall, Lydbury, SY7 8AZ, 01588 680570, canopyandstars.co.uk
52.4588, -2.9600

41 ST ANDREW'S CHURCH, WROXETER
Make this church on the site of the Roman city of Viroconium your own for the night. The Saxon architecture and alabaster tombs make for an interesting and unusual stay, and 'champing' helps fund the upkeep. April–Sept.
→ St Andrew's Church, Wroxeter, SY5 6PH, champing.co.uk
52.6701, -2.6472

42 UPPER SHADYMOOR FARM
Wonderful, secluded location on a working farm with game. Hot, fresh bread from Kevan delivered to your safari tents helps make this a special place to stay. Part of the Feather Down glamping group.
→ Upper Shadymoor Farm, Stapleton, SY5 7AL, 01743 718670, featherdown.co.uk
52.6139, -2.8069

43 TREE HOUSE BARN, PITCHFORD
A stylish barn conversion on the Pitchford estate with views to the 17th-century tree house, reportedly the oldest in the world.
→ Pitchford, Shrewsbury, SY5 7DN, cottages.com
52.6329, -2.7038

44 WALCOT HALL CAMPING
Tranquil little campsite just inside the gates of the Walcot Estate, behind the friendly Powis Arms pub, which manages it.
→ Lydbury North, SY7 8AU, 01588 680254.
52.4666, -2.9597

45 MIDDLE WOODBATCH FARM CAMPING
Stargaze and wake to the wonderful backdrop of the Shropshire Hills at this fabulous site. Excellent facilities, and fire pits upcycled from washing machine drums. Pod and B&B also available.
→ Woodbatch Road, Bishops Castle, SY9 5JS 01588 630141.
52.4872, -3.0363

46 FOXHOLES CASTLE CAMPING
Family-run, friendly eco-site open all year round. Tents, campers and caravans all welcome or choose one of the wooden cabins or the bunk house. The Greedy Fox Catering trailer is open weekends during peak season
→ Montgomery Road, Bishops Castle, SY9 5HA. 01588 638924.
52.5015, -2.9976

47 THE WITHIES CAMPSITE
A fantastic, spacious camping and glamping site perfect for families with children and dogs. Glorious views along Wenlock Edge.
→ Stretton Road, Much Wenlock TF13 6DD, 07789 003459.
52.5916, -2.5785

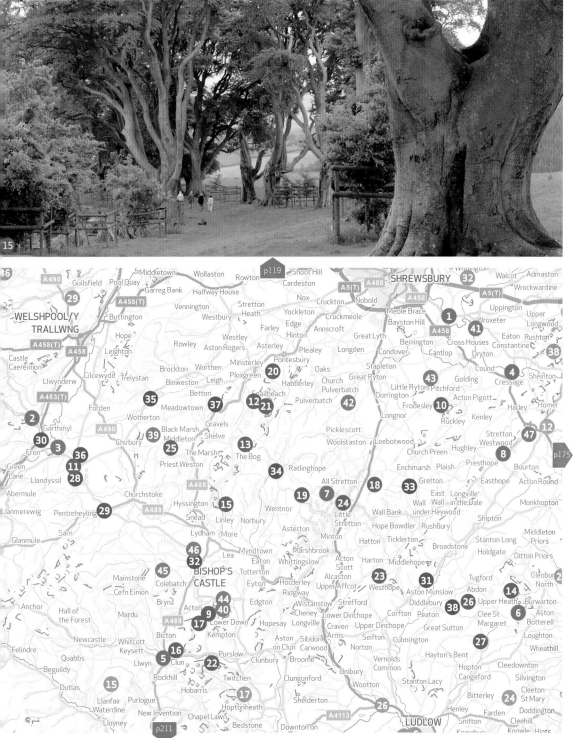

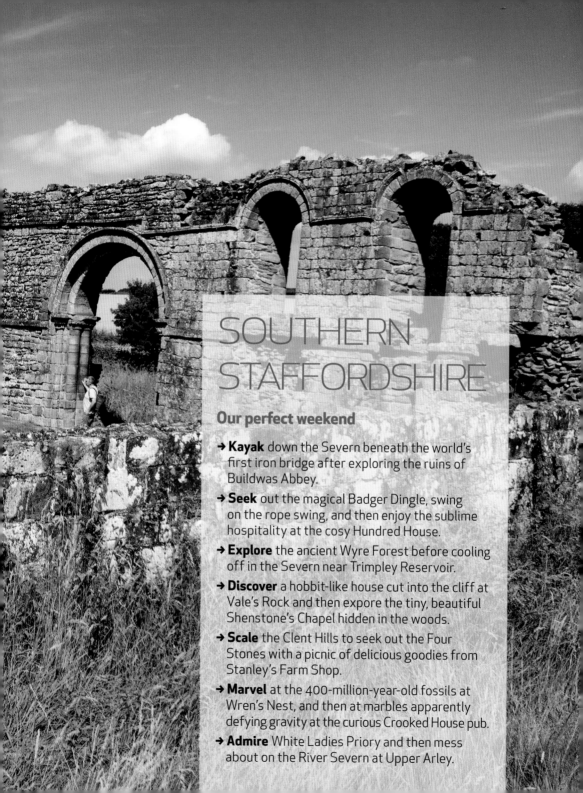

SOUTHERN STAFFORDSHIRE

Our perfect weekend

→ **Kayak** down the Severn beneath the world's first iron bridge after exploring the ruins of Buildwas Abbey.

→ **Seek** out the magical Badger Dingle, swing on the rope swing, and then enjoy the sublime hospitality at the cosy Hundred House.

→ **Explore** the ancient Wyre Forest before cooling off in the Severn near Trimpley Reservoir.

→ **Discover** a hobbit-like house cut into the cliff at Vale's Rock and then expore the tiny, beautiful Shenstone's Chapel hidden in the woods.

→ **Scale** the Clent Hills to seek out the Four Stones with a picnic of delicious goodies from Stanley's Farm Shop.

→ **Marvel** at the 400-million-year-old fossils at Wren's Nest, and then at marbles apparently defying gravity at the curious Crooked House pub.

→ **Admire** White Ladies Priory and then mess about on the River Severn at Upper Arley.

Nestled into a little space in between the vast conurbation of Birmingham and the delightful Shropshire Hills is quiet and little-visited South Shropshire: a land of sweeping vistas, quiet bridleways, walks on old railways and ancient packhorse trails, and pretty bluebell woods.

The Romans settled to the north around Penkridge with the building of the Watling Street, but until the 12th-century construction of many abbeys and priories along the Shropshire border, this was, and is again now, very much a land forgotten. Lilleshall Abbey and White Ladies Priory, tucked away in their rural idylls, are still well preserved and both offer a secluded spot for a romantic picnic. To the south-west, the better-known Buildwas and Wenlock Priories have interesting historical tales, the latter being the final resting place for the royal Benedictine abbess, St Milburga.

The countryside is very much ancient and unspoilt, and visiting places such as Wren's Nest with its fossil-rich landscape or ancient Chance Wood with its delightful riverside walk reminds you of what the landscape was like before the sprawling towns. The Wyre Forest, with its steep, wooded valleys, bubbling streams and miles of cycling and walking trails, is a popular destination for families and wildlife enthusiasts. There are many places to start from but we suggest exploring the deserted Knowles Mill and the historic Whitty Pear Tree.

The River Severn runs along the western border here and offers many exciting opportunities for swimming, kayaking and paddleboarding. To the south near Trimpley Reservoir is a perfect spot for a swim over to the little island, whilst further north, Ironbridge offers the chance for a glorious swim or paddleboard under the iconic bridge designed by Thomas Farnolls Pritchard.

The area is not short of cosy pubs or tempting restaurants to round out your day. For a quirky pint of ale head to The Crooked House near Dudley, where pennies appear to roll uphill and giddy slopes make you feel a little tipsy before you've even sipped an inch of ale. Or for a fantastic meal, head to The Hundred House at Norton, a higgledy-piggledy inn offering cosy log fires and an incredibly high standard of food. The name is a curious relic of ancient customs in this part of England. Over a thousand years ago, it was divided into 'hundreds', administrative areas of about 100 families, each looked after by a 'hundred court' administering local justice and taxes. Hundred houses were the bases for these courts, largely extinguished in 1867, but still remembered in the names of inns and pubs.

MAGNIFICENT SEVERN

1 TRIMPLEY, RIVER SEVERN

A tranquil walk through dappled sun-lit woods down to the reservoir and river. Various entry points to the river and an island to swim to and explore. No Swimming policy on the deep, man-made reservoir, which has a pumped-in supply.

→ Head in N out of Trimpley, turn L signed Trimpley Reservoir, dir DY12 1PH. Reservoir car park L after 1¼ miles. Walk down through woods to river. Turn L and find river entry point just outside reservoir border.

5 mins, 52.4047, -2.3325 🏊🚶🅿

2 THE OLD FOOT FERRY, RIVER SEVERN

A delightful swim in the River Severn where the old chain ferry used to cross. A great place to launch a kayak to Upper Arley (see listing).

→ From E of the River Severn, head S from Bridgnorth on A422. After 4.5 miles, turn R at signs for Hampton Loade and parking for River Severn. Car park at end of road, next to river. NT pay car park. A great longer kayak to Upper Arley (see listing).

1 min, 52.476418, -2.374549 🏊🚶

3 IRONBRIDGE, RIVER SEVERN

A glorious gorge swim under the iconic Ironbridge. Enter the water under the cooling towers at Dale End car park and swim down under the bridge to easy exit point at Severnside.

→ Head NW out of Ironbridge along river on Wharfage to Dale End car park on L (TF8 7NJ). Short walk to river. Exit at Severn Side path to L: 52.627095, -2.482523.

3 mins, 52.6272, -2.4853 🏊🚶🅿🚻🌲🚌🛶

4 UPPER ARLEY, RIVER SEVERN

A wide and tranquil section of the Severn, perfect for a swim or launching a kayak or paddleboard. The Riverside Tearoom serves delicious, home-made refreshments and lunches. This is also a stop on the Severn Valley Railway with walks along the Severn Way.

→ From E of the River Severn, head onto Arley Lane from A442 N of Kidderminster. Park in riverside pay car park. From W head to Arley car park (DY12 3NF) from B4194 N of Bewdley. Footbridge across river. A good exit point for a longer kayak down from The Old Foot Ferry (see listing).

2 mins, 52.4191, -2.3467 🏊🚶🅿🚻🚌🍴

5 ASTLEY ABBOTTS, RIVER SEVERN

A delightful dip in the Severn from a secluded section of riverbank.

→ From B4373 N out of Bridgnorth turn R onto Stanley Lane. Follow 1¼ miles, past golf club, to WV16 4SR and here turn R house to park on L before gated road. Path to river is at corner of road to R.

5 mins, 52.5562, -2.4072 🏊

POOLS & LAKES

6 COMER WOODS, DUDMASTON

A lovely woodland walk and cycle route past the secluded Brim Pool. A great picnic spot on the grassy banks.

→ Head S on A442 from Bridgnorth. Just after Quatford (WV15 6QL) NT Comer Woods pay car park signed L for easy cycle access to extensive paths. Or 1½ miles after Quatford, opp entrance to Dudmaston Estate (NT), turn L signed Claverley and park in Old Sawmill car park R after ⅓ mile. Walk back to signed footpath opp just before farm building. Follow path to woods and turn L. Brim Pool is furthest.

15 mins, 52.5012, -2.3725 🏊🚴🐕🚩

7 SHENSTONE'S CHAPEL, POTTER'S CROSS

Hidden in a yew tree grove at the edge of Priest's Wood lies this Gothic, fairy tale folly, built in 1763 as a memorial to the poet who helped design the Enville Estate.

→ On A458 N out of Potter's Cross turn L onto Wigley Bank Rd signed Compton. After 1 mile at bend turn R onto Sheepwalks Lane signed Romsley. Pull off to R (very limited space), after kinks at DY7 5LX (⅓ mile). Enter through gate, follow fence line straight ahead to gate into wood and head R, downhill to yews.

15 mins, 52.4648, -2.2656 ✝ ⊠

8 WREN'S NEST RESERVE, DUDLEY

Towering above the industrial setting of Dudley is this dramatic 420 million-year-old geological site, formed in warm tropical seas, then shaped by glaciers and limestone quarrying. World-famous for its abundance of fossils, with 86 types unique to this area.

→ On A457 NW from Tipton turn L onto Parkes Hall Rd, L onto Wren's Nest Rd, L at roundabout onto Hillside Rd, and L again onto Wren's Hill Rd. Signed path next to Caves Bar & Grill (DY1 3SB, 07405 131013).

5 mins, 52.5245, -2.0963 ♿ 🏕 🚶

9 FOUR STONES, CLENT HILLS

These megaliths aligned with the setting sun are not ancient, but were erected in 1763. They afford glorious panoramic views across the Worcestershire countryside, perfect picnic sites, cycle trails and woods for exploring.

→ Clent Hills signed S from A456 roundabout SW of Halesowen (past DY9 9JR). Follow 1 mile to T-junction, turn R signed Clent St Kenelm's Pass. Park at St Kenelm's Pass parking R after 200m and follow footpath to summit.

15 mins, 52.4209, -2.0988 🔲 ✝ 🏕 🏰 ♿ 🚶

10 LILLESHALL ABBEY

Dramatic remains of a 12th-century Augustinian abbey, fortified and then badly damaged during the Civil War. Perfect for a romantic evening picnic or an afternoon running around with the kids.

→ Signed from A518 about 2⅓ miles SW of Newport. Follow road ½ mile then take signed L on bend. Signed driveway L after 1 mile, opp TF10 9HW.

5 mins, 52.7247, -2.3898 ♿ ✝ 🦇 🏕 ⊞

11 WHITE LADIES PRIORY

Hidden away from the public eye, the enchanting remains of this 12th-century

church are all that remains of the Augustinian nunnery that hid Charles II after his defeat at the Battle of Worcester.

→ On A5 about 7 miles E from Telford, turn signed Bocobel Hs at crossroads (dir ST19 9AR). Follow 1½ miles to turn R to Boscobel House R. Park in car park (EH house and garden open to visit) and walk on ¾ mile to footpath R, or take a chance and drive on lane to very limited pulling-off space at footpath. Follow path to priory.
2 mins, 52.6656, -2.2582 ✝ ⅏ ↩ 🎋 ⚶

12 WENLOCK PRIORY

Founded on the site of a 7th-century monastery, believed to be the final resting place of the Benedictine abbess St Milburga, these still-imposing ruins are now host to some fantastical topiary.

→ Head E out of Much Wenlock on Bull Ring, past TF13 6HS. Parking L on bend of road. Follow signs to the priory opp. English Heritage, small fee.
2 mins, 52.5972, -2.55538 ⅏ 🎋 ↩ ⊞

13 BUILDWAS ABBEY

The remains of this Cistercian abbey, built in 1135, are surprisingly intact. Wonder at the story of the 14th-century monk accused of murdering the abbot during a most ungodly power struggle in the order.

→ Signed off A4169 just S of the river at Buildwas, TF8 7BW. English Heritage, free.
3 mins, 52.6353, -2.5284 ✝ ⅏ 🎋 ↩

WOODS & WILDLIFE

14 HIMLEY STATION PLANTATION

This 18th-century oak and sycamore wood is rich with bluebells and daffodils in spring. Part of South Staffordshire Railway Walk; head 2 miles N into Wombourne for cafés.

→ On B4176 bypassing Himley, turn onto Himley Ln dir DY3 4PW, signed S Staffordshire Railway Walk. Car park R just after bridge, 9am-dusk. If closed, space beside entrance.
5 mins, 52.5182, -2.1875 🅿 🧍 🚴

15 BAGGERIDGE COUNTRY PARK

A great place for a family outing. Wander through the woods, picnic in the meadow and relax by the lake.

→ Signed from A463/Wodehouse Lane in Gospel End, dir DY3 4HB. Follow road to furthest pay car park, past busy café. Walk down through woods to lake and meadow.
10 mins, 52.5342, -2.1488 🚴 ↩ 🧍 ❓

20

17

18

16 CHANCE WOOD

These tranquil woods offer a delightful walk near the River Stour in any season, starting off the year with a succession of snowdrops, daffodils and bluebells. Varied wildlife and a pet cemetery.

→ Take A458 out of Stourbridge. Footpath into woods at DY7 5BQ if you can pull off near here (tricky). Or take next L signed The Hyde (DY7 6LS) and follow to park near old mill and equestrian centre at end.
5 mins, 52.4603, -2.2180 🚶🎠

17 VALE'S ROCK, KINVER EDGE

Various houses cut into the sandstone were inhabited until the 1960s and some claim they inspired Tolkien's Hobbit homes. The famous Holy Austin houses have been restored, but further in, hidden amongst trees, are Vale's Rock (not accessible) and Nanny's Rock cavern (52.4406, -2.2526) on a beautiful circular walk around the ridge and up to hillfort.

→ Head N from Kingsford on Kingsford Lane ½ mile to Kingsford Forest car park signed L (near DY11 5SB). Follow path through gate opp. Holy Austin is N, beyond hillfort.
10 mins, 52.4368, -2.2556 🚵🎠🐕🎠

18 BADGER DINGLE

Magical, hidden dingle where a waterfall, beautiful woodland and caves surround an old, ornamental lake.

→ Park carefully in lane by St Giles Church in Badger (WV6 7JR). Walk 300m S on lane to to path into woods L. Follow path down to lake and waterfall. Rope swing at 52.5910, -2.3367.
15 mins, 52.5908, -2.3445 🚶🏕🏊🎠

19 SALTWELLS WOOD RESERVE

With gorse-clad hills and bluebell-filled woods, this is a super place to run around with the kids, build dens, cycle, follow the sculpture trail and climb trees. The country's largest urban nature reserve.

→ Head N from Cradley Heath on B4173 and turn L onto Saltwells Rd. Follow ½ mile past DY2 0BL, reserve signed R down Saltwells Lane, car park at end. Follow path to woods.
3 mins, 52.4803, -2.0995 🎠🚶🐕🏕🚴

20 THE WREKIN & THE ERCALL

Spectacular views reward visitors to these 500 million-year-old sister hills, cloaked in ancient oak woodland. Spring brings swathes of bluebells, whilst summer welcomes speckled wood and green hairstreak butterflies.

➜ From A5/M54 junction (J7) W of Telford, take unclassified continuation of B5061 S signed The Wrekin. Parking in extended lay-by on L after ¾ mile (200m past turning to TF6 5AW) or turn R at T-junction just after for Wrekin car park on L. Various signed paths up Ercall to L or Wrekin to R.

5 mins, 52.6828, -2.5294 🅿🚶🔺♿

21 CHADDESLEY WOODS

Truly an ancient forest: parts of it may have been woodland since the ice age ended, and the Domesday Book records a wood roughly here. It offers glorious walks and open glades.

➜ Take A448 NW from Bromsgrove 2 miles, turn R onto Woodcote Lane and after ½ mile L onto Woodcote Green Lane past B61 9EF. Lay-by R just beyond entrance after ⅛ mile.

2 mins, 52.3588, -2.1255 🚶♿🌳

22 WYRE FOREST

Straddling the border of Worcestershire and Shropshire, this extensive forest offers a great day out discovering the waterfall, lake, abandoned buildings and the 'Whitty Pear' tree (actually a relative of rowan), a descendant of the original burned by a poacher in 1862.

➜ Head W from Bewdley on A456 for 1⅛ miles

from roundabout with B4190 to signed forest entrance and car park R at DY14 9XQ. Tree near 52.3733, -2.3701.

5 mins, 52.3856, -2.3667 🚶♿🔺🌳🅿

INDUSTRIAL HERITAGE

23 TAR TUNNEL & HAY INCLINED PLANE

Remarkable miners' tunnel that oozes bitumen through the walls. Nearby is an inclined plane for shifting cargo between the canal and Severn boats.

➜ Tunnel can be viewed (Weds only) a part of the China Museum site tour, off Coalport High St, Coalport (TF8 7HU, 01952 433424)

1 min, 52.6202, -2.4530 🏞♿£

24 NETHERTON TUNNEL

A fascinating 1¾-mile walk or cycle along the last canal tunnel to be built in Britain. Set within Warrens Hall Nature Reserve which also plays host to Cobb's Engine House, which once pumped water from the coal mines. Trails and ponds to explore.

➜ On B4171 heading S from Dudley, reserve parking signed on R ¼ mile after passing L to DY2 8AN. Follow main path 500m into reserve towards engine house and canal.

6 mins, 52.4927, -2.0691 🚶🔺♿🏞

25 KNOWLES MILL

A beautiful walk along a bubbling stream in the Wyre Forest leads to this disused but picturesque 18th-century mill and waterwheel, preserved by the NT but free.

➜ Take B4190 W out of Bewdley, turn R onto The Lakes (DY12 2PH) then L onto Dry Mill Lane at crossroads (dir DY12 2LT). Follow ½ mile to Dry Mill Lane car park L. Follow Cycle Route 45 W along old railway line to mill.

20 mins, 52.3866, -2.3508 🏞♿🚶🅿♿🌳

swimming (see listing). Delicious homemade food and cakes.

→ Arley Lane, Upper Arley, DY12 1XA, 01299 861945.
52.4190, -2.3459

31 STANLEY'S FARM SHOP, PYO
Family-run farm shop with 25 acres of PYO fruit and veg. Local meat, bread, honey and other produce also sold.

→ Fishers Castle Farm, Sandy Lane, Harvington, DY10 4NF, 01562 700985.
52.3893, -2.1671

32 STABLES TEA ROOM
Lovely little tearoom in a former stables. Home-made food and delightful outdoor seating area. Open Tues–Sat.

→ Broad Acre Stables, Broad Lanes, Six Ashes, WV15 6EG, 01746 781019.
52.4950, -2.3281

33 ESSINGTON FARM
A great farm shop selling local produce, freshly picked from the fields. Butchery, deli, bakery and café. Well worth a visit.

→ Bognop Road, Essington, WV11 2AZ, 01902 735724.
52.6319, -2.0692

34 THE INN, SHIPLEY
Friendly, 18th-century pub with inglenooks, wood-burning stoves and leather armchairs. Great, locally sourced food, ale and cider.

→ Bridgnorth Road, Shipley, WV6 7EQ, 01902 701639.
52.5598, -2.2844

35 THE CROOKED HOUSE, DUDLEY
Higgledy-piggledy old pub built in 1765, serving ales in a traditional chop house ambience. Full of giddy slopes and strange angles, and optical illusions where marbles appear to roll uphill!

→ Coppice Mill, Himley, DY3 4DA, 01384 238583.
52.5150, -2.1524

36 THE FOUNTAIN INN, CLENT
Oak-beamed country inn serving real ale and home-cooked food, with a lovely outside seating area.

→ Adam's Hill, Clent, DY9 9PU, 01562 883286.
52.4151, -2.1133

SLOW FOOD

26 THE HUNDRED HOUSE HOTEL, NORTON
Captivating and quirky period property with roaring log fires and friendly staff. Renowned for its high-end food and ales. Secret garden is a must-see!

→ Bridgnorth Road, Norton, TF11 9EE, 01952 580240.
52.6003, -2.4025

27 APLEY FARM SHOP
Great range of local, seasonal food in a shopping courtyard: butchery, deli, bakery, farm produce and café. Seasonal events.

→ Norton, TF11 9EF, 01952 581002.
52.5945, -2.3962

28 WOODBRIDGE INN, COALPORT
Perfect riverside setting, quality food and a wide range of ales.

→ Coalport, TF8 7JF, 01952 882054.
52.6150, -2.4417

29 THE PHEASANT AT NEENTON
A cosy, award-winning dining pub, run by the local community. Fantastic food and a warm welcome to everyone. Rooms available.

→ Neenton, WV16 6RJ, 01746 787955.
52.4858, -2.5354

30 RIVERSIDE TEAROOM, UPPER ARLEY
A delightful little tearoom with a terrace overlooking the river, which is also good for

7 RAILWAYMAN'S ARMS, BRIDGNORTH

popular, converted waiting room right
n the Severn Valley Railway platform.
ake a step back in time and revel in the
emorabilia as you sup a pint of local real
e. Start of Severn Valley Pub Crawl on the
eritage trains.
→ Hollybush Rd, Bridgnorth, WV16 5DT,
1746 760902.
2.5303, -2.4204 🚻

RUSTIC HAVENS

8 MORRELLS WOOD FARM

ustic, self-catering cottages and three
hepherds' huts set on a working farm in a
ranquil woody valley with wonderful views
f The Wrekin.
→ Leighton, SY5 6RU. 1952 510273.
2.6533, -2.5480 🏕️🔆

9 THE ROCKHOUSE RETREAT

nique, hand-sculpted cave house with
nderfloor heating and concealed lighting.
he ultimate romantic retreat for two.
→ Honey Brook, Easthams Farm, Low
labberley, DY11 5RQ, 07789 160356.
2.4066, -2.2902 🏕️🔆🏕️

CAMP & SLEEP

0 AMBER'S BELL TENT CAMPING

estled into the edge of the Shropshire Hills
re these 6 stylish bell tents, hidden away in
he woods of the Hopton Court Estate,

→ Hopton Court Estate, Hopton Ct, Cleobury
Mortimer, DY14 0EF, 07580 072861.
52.3994, -2.5239

41 IRONBRIDGE COALPORT YHA

High-quality youth hostel housed in part
of a 19th-century red-brick china factory
with a café onsite. Step outside and you are
straight onto the banks of the River Severn.
Nearby are the mining and industrials ruins
of the Tar Tunnel and Hay Inclined Plane (see
listing) approached along the old canal or
along the Silkin Way.
→ John Rose Building, High Street, Coalport,
TF8 7HT, 03453 719325.
52.6188, -2.4503 🏕️

42 TEDS AT HUNGER HILL

A friendly, spacious rural campsite with
disabled-friendly facilities and big views of
the AONB countryside.
→ Hungerhill Farm, Sheriffhales, TF11 8SA,
0780 7798288.
52.7080, -2.3420 🏕️🔆

43 IRONGORGE CAMPING

A tranquil, caravan-free site up a private
road, with fantastic views over the
countryside. Fire pits, pods and a shepherds'
hut, too.
→ Coach House, Strethill Road, Coalbrookdale,
TF8 7EY, 01952 433047.
52.6372, -2.4999 🏕️🔆

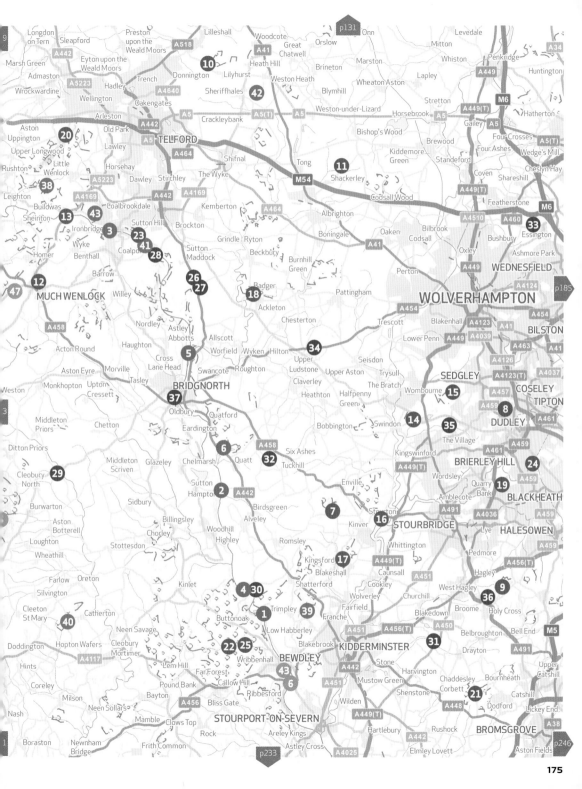

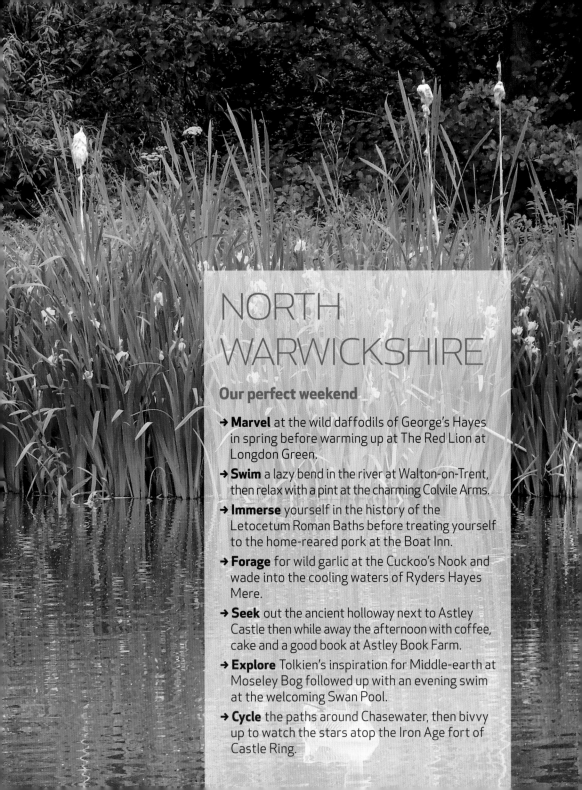

NORTH WARWICKSHIRE

Our perfect weekend

→ **Marvel** at the wild daffodils of George's Hayes in spring before warming up at The Red Lion at Longdon Green.

→ **Swim** a lazy bend in the river at Walton-on-Trent, then relax with a pint at the charming Colvile Arms.

→ **Immerse** yourself in the history of the Letocetum Roman Baths before treating yourself to the home-reared pork at the Boat Inn.

→ **Forage** for wild garlic at the Cuckoo's Nook and wade into the cooling waters of Ryders Hayes Mere.

→ **Seek** out the ancient holloway next to Astley Castle then while away the afternoon with coffee, cake and a good book at Astley Book Farm.

→ **Explore** Tolkien's inspiration for Middle-earth at Moseley Bog followed up with an evening swim at the welcoming Swan Pool.

→ **Cycle** the paths around Chasewater, then bivvy up to watch the stars atop the Iron Age fort of Castle Ring.

North Warwickshire is a patchwork of green rural fields, concealing ancient battle sites where wars have been lost and won. Scratch the surface and the landscape here is dotted with remnants from significant historical periods that left their traces when events moved on.

The Iron Age hillfort at Castle Ring is one of the earliest testaments to the significance of the area, and later hosted a medieval settlement. The Romans colonised a great deal of this county, leaving wisps of their occupation visible in the place names, the straight roads and the ruins scattered around the countryside. Boudica is believed to have fought her last battle in the village of Mancetter in AD 60, and Wall was an important strategic village for the Romans. Both are along the military Watling Street which dissects the county. Visitors to the beautiful Letocetum ruins in Wall can wander round the site, marvel at the complexity of the engineering of Roman baths, and enjoy a picnic.

Moated Astley Castle manor has a history you would not guess to look at the idyllic village today, and it can stand for many such forgotten stories. It was largely built in 1555 by the Grey family, who produced three Queens, the last of them Lady Jane Grey; after her ill-fated, nine-day reign it was slighted and forfeit to the Crown. Later it became a noted Parliamentary stronghold when the Civil War raged here. After that its life was more peaceful, until it burned down in 1978. Memories of a larger life lie around it, including a once-busy holloway lane that now leads to nowhere.

The Industrial Revolution saw a number of extensive mining and textiles communities develop, and the many coal and gravel pits that played an important role then have now been returned to nature and offer quiet, tranquil green spaces, cycle paths and shady glades. George's Hayes with its wild daffodils and melodious dawn chorus is the perfect spot for some mindful walking. Moseley Bog, near where JRR Tolkien grew up and an acknowledged inspiration in his writing, is a vibrant, green wonderland of ancient, gnarled trees and wetland walkways. Middleton Lakes offer miles of tracks to soak up the wildlife sights of herons, kingfishers and lapwings.

The River Tame snakes through the green countryside, making its way to the River Trent. At Kingsbury, it slows and widens slightly as it passes the lakes of the Water Park offering a pleasant paddle or swim in its depths. The river at Walton-on-Trent is a delightful place to explore, especially if you swim across to the island with the rope swing. Ryders Hayes Mere is loved by locals, and has a majestic backdrop when the sun sets, while clear and clean Albert Village Lake is frequented by Iron Man competitors.

LAKES & POOLS

KINGSBURY WATER PARK

Beautiful woodland walks and spacious meadows border the River Tame in this little country park oasis snuggled next to the M42. Smaller lakes make an ideal base for family fun; anglers and jet skis use the larger ones.

→ Signed from J9 of M42, on A4097 to Kingsbury. After ½ mile follow signs L at roundabout to entrance ½ mile on R (B76 0EA). 10 mins, 52.5627, -1.6948 🏊🚲🧍‍♂️🚻

SALTERSFORD BROOK, OAKTHORPE

A remnant from the mining era, the pools along this waterway lend themselves to a short dip, picnic or even some star-gazing. Use discretion.

→ Take Ashby Rd E out of Donisthorpe, Oakthorpe Picnic Site signed 1/2 mile on R. Alternative parking along road in lay-by on R 160m further: 52.7259, -1.5124. Follow footpath into grass clearing, take R fork down to little cove.
10 mins, 52.7239, -1.5099 🏊❓🪧🧍‍♂️🍴

CHASEWATER

Gravel-based, clear lake ideal for a secluded evening picnic. Great place to watch birds or

enjoy a cycle, too. No Swimming signs, but there is NOWCA-organised swimming from the Watersports Centre (52.6630, -1.9520) in summer. Use discretion.

→ Take no through road Church St from roundabout at Uxbridge Arms in Chasetown (WS7 3QL, 01543 677852). Park at the end of the road. Take footbridge over A1495, follow path down to lake, and walk along the bank to find a quiet spot.
15 mins, 52.6712, -1.9518 🏊🧍‍♂️🪧❓

4 SWAN POOL, SANDWELL VALLEY

A surprisingly welcoming place for a cooling swim in clear water. Signs encourage swimmers to assess their own risk rather than prohibiting them. Be mindful of anglers. Mountain bike trails in the woods.

→ Signed from A41/Holyhead road up Park Lane (B21 8LE). Follow 1½ miles N, past cemetery, to car park L after pedestrian crossing, with path down to lake.
4 mins, 52.5247, -1.9661 🏊🪧🚻🧍‍♂️🚲

5 RYDERS HAYES MERE

A lovely, wild spot, idyllic for a paddle with the wildlife: it is very deep and cold further out, so stay in the shallow ends well inshore of the islands.

→ In NE end of Pelsall travel N to end of St Johns Road (WS3 4EZ) where it turns to become Fairburn Crescent and park by sign for cycle path. Follow path to R, through gate and horse field, over stile and down to lake. Footpath from Ryders Hayes Lane (WS3 4EQ) leads to other end.
15 mins, 52.6371, -1.9547 🏊🔽🪧🚲🧍‍♂️🐕⛲

6 ALVECOTE POOLS

The River Anker pools alongside sweeping meadows and grazing cattle. Perfect for a quick dip or punt around in a kayak. Nearby, Pooley Country Park offers visitors another lake, beautiful, wooded walks and wetlands, and the remains of Alvecote Priory nestled under the chestnut trees alongside the canal.

→ Just NE of Tamworth follow Shuttington Rd NE from The Pretty Pigs pub, (B79 0ED, 01827 63129) for 1 mile as it becomes Polesworth Rd and bends right. ½ mile after bend pull off by gate R (room for 1 car) and walk through to river, or park by bridleway at bend and walk.
2 mins, 52.6395, -1.6266 🏊🧍‍♂️🐕

7 ALBERT VILLAGE LAKE

Large expanse of open water in a flooded pit, perfect for a paddle or dip next to a pretty, young woodland. Take a stroll or cycle and

spot a menagerie of birdlife. No-swimming rules here, except when supervised sessions are running.

→ Car park SW end of Occupation Rd, on the edge of Albert Village (DE11 8HD) and follow path to lake.

10 mins, 52.7526, -1.5510

RIVER SWIMMING

8 KINGSBURY, RIVER TAME

A gentle section of the Tame ideal for a paddle or swim. Crystal-clear lake adjacent used by jet bikes.

→ From A5 at S end of Kingsbury on A51, just N of roundabout with A4097 turn into dead end stub of Kingsbury Rd (B78 2DG) and park R before footbridge. Path to river on R. Lake over footbridge.

4 mins, 52.5592, -1.6833

9 WALTON-ON-TRENT

Rare serene section of the Trent offering seclusion and a rope swing, next to one of the country's newest nature reserves, a wetland in an old quarry where you may yet hear a bittern boom.

→ From crossroads in the centre of Walton-on-Trent head W on Station Lane (dir DE13

8EN), cross river and continue ½ mile to park in Tucklesholme Nature Reserve on R. Follow path around wetland to gate on R near elbow in the river.

15 mins, 52.7651, -1.6851

WETLAND MOSAICS

10 MOSELEY BOG

A last remnant of the landscape that inspired the forests in Tolkein's books, with gnarled trees, ancient burnt mounds and wetlands. A magical place to escape urban life.

→ Heading S through Moseley on Yardley Wood Road, car park signed L just after B13 9JX. Follow path into reserve.

5 mins, 52.4365, -1.8670

11 WHITACRE HEATH RESERVE

Beautifully wild and tangled Tame Valley wetland nature reserve. Home to thousands of migrating birds, kingfishers and otters. There are even Second World War pillboxes to discover.

→ From Whitacre Heath take Birmingham Rd W opp The Swan Inn (B46 2JA, 01675 462181 on Birmingham Rd, parking on L after ½ mile. Several waymarked trails from car park.

3 mins, 52.5335, -1.6933

16

12 MIDDLETON LAKES

This SSSI is a mosaic of woodland, meadows and wetland areas providing sanctuary to a wide range of wildlife, including herons, lapwings and kingfishers. Well-placed tracks provide miles of delightful and peaceful walks and plentiful picnic opportunities.

→ Signed along on A491 to Tamworth at roundabout at M6 Toll/M42 interchange. Follow 1 mile dir B78 2BA, follow signs R onto Bodymoor Heath Lane then L after 400m, follow to end and turn R near Middleton Hall to car park R (small fee). Signed from car park.
3 mins, 52.5829, -1.7146 🚴🦆🚶🅿🚻🎒

WOODS & WILDLIFE

13 CUCKOO'S NOOK & THE DINGLE

Forage for wild garlic in these peaceful woodlands with babbling brooks and carpets of bluebells.

→ Head E out of Walsall on Sutton Rd and at WS5 3AX turn R up fork and park. Walk back down and across road to brown sign and follow footpath to reserve. Alternatively walk in from Hayhead Wood car park (52.5891, -1.9402).
15 mins, 52.5865, -1.9222 🚶🎒🅿🚻🎒

14 GEORGE'S HAYES

A simply stunning little dingle with carpets of daffodils, wild garlic and bluebells. Early risers may be lucky enough to see red deer and hear a melodious dawn chorus.

→ From Longdon follow Borough Lane SW, turn L towards Thorley Hill at T-junction (WS15 4LW), car park ¼ mile on R (unsigned).
5 mins, 52.7157, -1.9020 🚶🎒🅿🚻🎒

15 HARTSHILL HAYES COUNTRY PARK

Peaceful country park featuring hilltop views across Anker Valley. Large enough to lose yourselves exploring and spotting the plentiful wildlife. Bluebells carpet much of the park in spring.

→ In Hartshill, signed from Church Rd along Oldbury Rd from memorial cross (past CV10 0TD). Car park on R after ½ mile with paths into woods.
2 min, 52.5458, -1.5326 🚗🚶🚴🎒🅿🐕🚻🎒

16 TOCIL WOOD & NATURE RESERVE

Designed to develop a rich and diverse habitat, these ancient woods, open areas, streams and pools team with flora and fauna. Follow the paths, bring a picnic and the bikes. Come for violets and wood anemones in early spring, bluebells in May, and autumn colours.

12

15

→ Roadside parking off Gibbet Hill Road, Coventry, CV4 7AJ. Reserve is south of the University of Warwick Campus.
5 mins, 52.3765, -1.5665

FORTIFICATIONS

17 CASTLE RING, CANNOCK

The highest point in Cannock Chase, this Iron Age hillfort was occupied 2,000 years ago, and also has low remains of a medieval building. Walk the ancient embankment and enjoy great views over the surrounding county.
→ Car park is at N of Cannock Wood on Holly Hill Rd, at the end of Park Gate Rd (WS15 4RN). Medieval remains 52.7138, -1.9371.
5 mins, 52.7124, -1.9350

18 ASTLEY CASTLE

A ruinous, moated 16th-century manor house, with the lake, church and a beautifully dappled medieval holloway lined with venerable trees, all accessible. A truly unique place to picnic, play or even book a stay in the unique renovation (see listing).
→ Follow B4102 from Fillongley just over 2 miles to Astley, turn L at crossroads onto Nuthurst Lane, dir CV10 7QN. Little parking in Astley, but gravel area R by barn. Walk up

Castle Dr to holloway R and castle ahead, follow around L to church.
4 mins, 52.5009, -1.5409

19 SECKINGTON CASTLE

Motte and bailey remains of an 11th-century castle surrounded by traces of ridge and furrow cultivation. Particularly pretty in late spring, when the trees are in blossom.
→ From junction 11 of M42 take B5493 dir Tamworth 4 miles. Just after crossroads for Seckington (B79 0BJ) pull into separated lay-by L. Walk on to kissing gate in hedge L, past driveway gate.
1 min, 52.6651, -1.6183

ANCIENT & SACRED

20 ROWTON'S WELL, SUTTON COLDFIELD

An ancient spring valued enough to have been "quined round with stone" by 1763. Still in great condition with cold, crystal-clear water, in one of the nation's largest urban parks. Old peatlands, so boots advisable.
→ Car park at Banners Gate entrance to Sutton Park, off Monmouth Drive by B73 6JX. Follow path N for 15 mins out of car park, using GPS to find exact location.
15 mins, 52.5661, -1.8646

21

21 LETOCETUM ROMAN BATHS

Once a significant staging post on Watling Street, the major military road to North Wales, all that remains is the ruins of a bathhouse and mansio (Roman inn). NT/EH, free.

→ Just off the A5/Watling St SW of Lichfield, 1 mile E from Muckley Cross roundabout take L with slip lane into Wall, dir WS14 0AW and park immediately in car park L. Walk on to end of houses on L and entrance signed 'Wall Roman Site'.

4 mins, 52.6568, -1.8568 🐾🏞🏕🎿⊞

SLOW FOOD

22 ASTLEY BOOK FARM

Gorgeous, extensive second-hand book shop housed in a network of converted farm buildings. Charming onsite café selling sublime cakes. A great place to lose yourself for a few hours if the weather is bad.

→ Astley Lane, Astley, CV12 0NE, 02476 490235.

52.4888, -1.5243 🍴

23 THE BOAT INN, LICHFIELD

Michelin Guide-recognised, high-end modern dishes with a focus on first-class organic produce, including home-reared pigs and chickens, all served with finesse.

→ Walsall Road, Muckley Corner, WS14 0BU, 01543 361692.

52.6518, -1.8895 🍴

24 THE SWAN, WALTON-ON-TRENT

Quirky and vibrant gastropub with eclectic, rustic and industrial decor. Wood-fired pizzas and Japanese yakitori sticks the speciality.

→ Main Street, Walton-on-Trent, DE12 8LZ, 01283 712378.

52.7604, -1.6802 🛏🍴

25 THE MALT SHOVEL AT BARSTON

Enjoy well-prepared dishes from seasonal and local produce on the patio overlooking the lovely garden or in the converted barn.

→ Barston Lane, Barston, B92 0JP, 01675 443223.

52.4070, -1.7109 🛏🍴

26 THE FOUR SHIRES FARM SHOP

A friendly, family-run, traditional farm shop selling a fantastic range of local produce, fresh fruit and veg, meat and sweet treats.

→ The Green, Seckington, Tamworth, B79 0LB, 01827 839171.

52.6634, -1.6138 🍴

24

26

27 COTTAGE VINTAGE TEA ROOM

A lovely coffee shop with a delightful little garden to the rear, situated opposite the village church. Central to many footpaths and cycle routes. B&B available.

→ Duffield Lane Burton-on-Trent DE13 8SH
52.8259, -1.7996 🍴 ⛺

28 THE SMITHY FARM SHOP

A super farm shop selling great fresh, local produce and a wide range of cheese. Great tearoom for an extra treat.

→ Warton Lane, Grendon, CV9 3DU, 01827 714216.
52.6042, -1.5664 🍴

29 BODNETTS FARM SHOP

An authentic, no-frills farm shop, well stocked with fresh produce. Well worth a visit.

→ Plantation Lane, Tamworth, B78 3AU, 01827 64937.
52.6312, -1.7391 🍴

30 THE VICTORIAN TEAROOMS

Victorian Café situated on the platform of the Battlefield Line Railway serving a range of delicious, home-made refreshments and light lunches. Plenty of walks in the area and along the Ashby Canal.

→ Shakerstone Railway, Station Road, Shakerstone, CV13 6NW, 07950 512587. Pedestrian access only via station road along the side of Ashby Canal, use sat nav postcode: CV13 0BS for station car park.
52.6556, -1.4413 🍴

COSY PUBS

31 COLVILE ARMS, LULLINGTON

Neil & Rebecca welcome guests to this charmingly traditional pub. Red-brick with sprawling rooms and a large garden with pétanque pitches. Food is hearty and local ales are well kept.

→ Main Street, Swadlincote, DE12 8EG, 07510 870980.
52.7146, -1.6318 🛏 🍴 ⛺

32 THE RED LION, LONGDON GREEN

A classic country pub that just gets everything right! Delicious, locally sourced food, friendly staff, a good range of ales and a lovely beer garden for sunnier days.

→ Hay Lane, Longdon Green, WS15 4QF, 01543 490410.
52.7194, -1.8764 🛏 🍴

CAMP & SLEEP

33 ASTLEY CASTLE

A quirky, prize-winning project built inside the old walls, giving up to eight guests the unique experience of life in a ruined castle whilst not scrimping on luxury. Great surroundings for exploring, particularly the ancient holloway (see Astley Castle entry).

→ Astley, CV10 7QN, landmarktrust.org.uk
52.5022, -1.5423 ⛺

34 ETTIE'S FIELD

Very cool, boho glamping site where those with vintage or alternative camping set-ups are welcome – or rent one of their vintage airstreams. Small tents may be accepted, but not larger, standard campers and tents.

→ Sibson Road, Ratcliffe Culey, CV9 3PH, 01827 712512.
52.5970, -1.4953 ⛺

35 SEALWOOD COTTAGE VINEYARD

Camping by a vineyard in the beautiful National Forest. Delightful!

→ Sealwood Lane, Linton,, DE12 6PA, 01283 761371.
52.7380, -1.5848 ⛺ ⛺ ☕

36 THE HEDGEHOG, LICHFIELD

Rustic, restored lodge set in its own grounds. Seasonal food, real ales, and well-appointed, modern rooms.

→ Stafford Road, Lichfield, WS13 8JB, 01543 415789.
52.6924, -1.8496 🍴 🛏

37 COSY NOOK AT THE OLD BEERHOUSE

Family-run, adults-only, back-to-nature camping in a flat, two-acre field that backs onto a large woodland reserve, off-grid (no electric hook-ups or showers) but camper vans are welcome.

→ 112 Woodhouses Road, Burntwood, WS7 9EJ, 07544 135421
52.6814, -1.8827

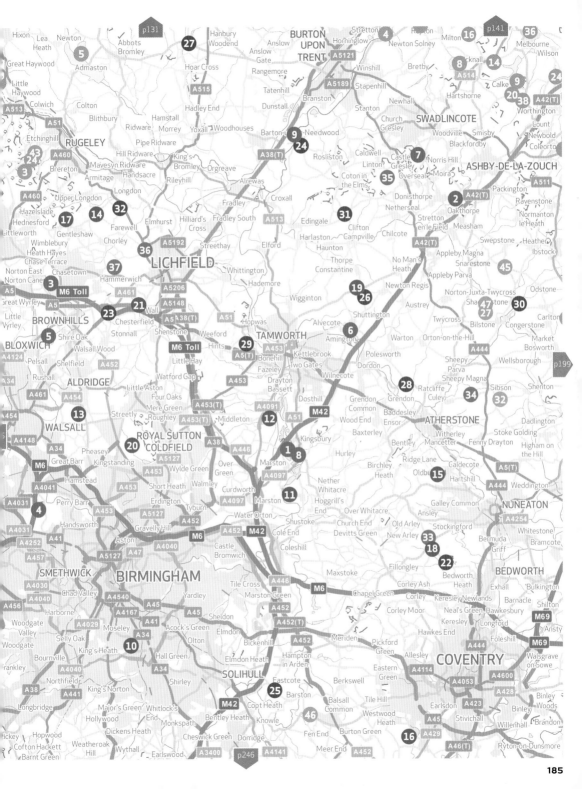

LEICESTERSHIRE

Our perfect weekend

→ **Scramble** up the ancient oaks and rocks of Bradgate Park then climb Old John to take in the breathtaking views from the tower.

→ **Launch** yourself off the cliff at Swithland Wood to bask in the crystal-clear quarry waters before munching a home-made pork pie at the bustling Griffin Inn.

→ **Feast** on a ploughman's lunch made from award-winning cheeses at Sparkenhoe Dairy then seek out the romantic remains of Gopsall Temple.

→ **Paddle** down the Grand Union Canal to camp wild in the tranquil Fieldside Covert Woodland.

→ **Join** the Burger Club at Leicester's most welcoming red-brick local, The Black Horse in Aylestone, before wandering around the moat at Kirby Muxloe Castle.

→ **Celebrate** Easter Monday with the quintessentially English Hare Pie Scramble followed by the annual Bottle Kicking match between the villagers of Hallaton and Medbourne.

→ **Soak** up the history amongst Leicester's oldest trees, clamber over volcanic rock forms and wander among the bluebells at The Outwoods.

A jaunt into the beautiful Leicestershire countryside presents rolling hills and pretty, flower-lined lanes of the east contrasting dramatically with rocky crags and heathlands of the north. Discover a flourishing National Forest, stunning wild flower displays, glorious hilltop views and an intimate array of Roman and Saxon settlements and medieval abbeys.

Violent volcanoes and magma flows deep underground are the hidden story told by the dramatic outcrops and stunning topography around the Charnwood Forest, home of Leicestershire's jewel, Bradgate Park. Each visit here offers something different, especially with the changing seasons. Colourful local legend has it that the mug-shaped appearance of the folly tower, Old John, was a tribute to a beer-loving miller, tragically killed during Bonfire Day celebrations. There are ancient trees and rugged rocks perfect for climbing, the deep red ruins of Bradgate House and a maze of paths winding through the deer and bracken.

The landscape appears even more rugged at Beacon Hill, where the energetic are rewarded with an unrivalled panorama across three counties. Nearby, ancient woodlands recall a different pace of life at The Outwoods and Burroughs Wood. A walk in Swithland Wood is a joy at any time of year, with or without a swim in the quarry, and it is the perfect place to build a den and forage for blackberries.

Wild swimmers in search of rivers need look no further than the waters north of Barrow upon Soar feeding into the River Trent, where there are also plenty of opportunities to explore with a kayak or paddleboard. Hidden clear-water coves and sandy beaches where quiet woodlands lap at the shores of picturesque reservoirs such as Foremark and Thornton are perfect to wile away a summer's day.

The discovery of Richard III in a city centre car park has fully occupied local historians recently, but the rich heritage extends elsewhere. This area was not disputed enough to be rich in Norman remains – the wooden castle that stood on the motte at Brinklow never needed to be replaced with stone – but the striking ruins of the Grace Dieu Priory offer tranquillity and beauty.

Generations of tradition and experience have produced some excellent local foods, several known worldwide. Leicester cheese carries the county name beyond these shores, and the finest can be sought at the Sparkenhoe Dairy, site of the Handmade Cheese. Malt Kiln Farm Shop and Manor Farm Shop showcase some of the best regional produce, or head to Melton Mowbray for iconic pork pies from Ye Olde Pork Pie Shoppe, in business since 1851.

SECRET SOAR

BARROW UPON SOAR

lovely swim or kayak on a gentle meander
f the grand River Soar. Follow it with great
ood at The Moorings pub, where you can
lso launch your kayak.

In Barrow-upon-Soar park at The Moorings
ub (LE12 8PN, 01509 768560), cross bridge
nd turn R along towpath ⅓ mile. Grassy banks
nd some beach areas for entry.
mins, 52.7534, -1.1574

STANFORD, RIVER SOAR

quiet stretch of river with many access
oints, including a metal footbridge that
akes you across to a secret island where you
an wild camp and paddle the loop or swim
hen the water is high.

Take Meadow Lane N out of Loughborough,
r LE12 5PY. Just after crossing the river,
ark L under railway bridge and follow track
long river. For island, continue to bend, turn
and park in small lay-by L after 180m by
ootpath sign. Path through gate opp to river:
2.7892, -1.1951.
mins, 52.7934, -1.2011

3 1860 BRIDGE, MOUNTSORREL

A beautiful, arched, red-brick bridge,
formerly used to carry slate from the local
quarry, provides a stunning backdrop for a
cooling evening swim.

→ Park at The Waterside inn (LE12 7BB, 0116
2302758), cross road and follow footpath
along river to bridge.
5 mins, 52.7330, -1.1428

BLUE POOLS

4 STONEY COVE, STONEY STANTON

Large, flooded, granite quarry which attracts
divers from across the country thanks to
its vast range of underwater attractions,
including a tugboat, helicopter and double-
decker bus. Supervised sessions: swimmers
pay a small fee, no single swimmers.

→ From B581 through Stoney Stanton (LE9
4DQ) follow Sapcote Rd S ⅓ mile, turn L
through stone gateway to parking.
5 mins, 52.5420, -1.2738

5 SWITHLAND WOOD QUARRY

The most flora-rich woodland in
Leicestershire spreads a sumptuous carpet
of bluebells each spring. 300-year-old
trees provide habitats for varied wildlife,

whilst volcanic outcrops lure young limbs
to clamber. The jewel, though, is the old
slate quarry with beautifully clear water
and prominent jumping locations for the
brave. Swimming permission is granted by
request, though the locals simply wait until
after 6pm.

→ From Swithland folly (see entry) follow
Swithland Rd, signed Newton ¾ mile to
crossroads, turn L on Roecliffe Rd signed
Swithland Wood, car park ½ mile on the L
(past LE12 8TN). Follow R fork path, quarry
fence 500m on L.
10 mins, 52.7046, -1.2033

6 SHAWELL POOL, LUTTERWORTH

Azure blue pool with a footpath around it, in
a quiet location, perfect for a gentle stroll
on a warm summer's evening. Follow on
with a fantastic gourmet dinner including a
vegetarian tasting menu at The White Swan,
in nearby Shawell.

→ Follow A5 N from Crick 5 miles. Immediately
after L to Newton (at CV23 0TB) pull off L by
green road sign. Cross road, walk back 50m to
find small gate in hedge, and follow footpath
sign for 100m, pool on R. The White Swan;
Main St, Shawell LE17 6AG, 01788 860357.
7 mins, 52.4134, -1.2163

8

7

9

RESERVOIRS & LAKES

7 SWITHLAND RESERVOIR

Remote, mirror-like reservoir in the SSSI wooded valley of Charnwood. A quiet, narrow lane runs alongside, leading to the waterworks, with the shore fenced. Some Deep Water and No Swimming signs, but secluded.

→ At S end of Woodhouse take School Lane fork at church (LE12 8UZ), follow for ¾ mile (becomes Brand Lane at national speed limit signs) and turn L on Rushey Lane signed unsuitable for motors. Follow 1 mile to park R at sharp L bend. Waterworks beyond.
8 mins, 52.7283, -1.1767 🚶🏊

8 THORNTON RESERVOIR FLY FISHING

Picturesque roadside reservoir in the National Forest, renowned for its trout fishery and fly fishing. Day tickets, boats and lessons available. A range of ales and good food available at the nearby Reservoir Inn.

→ Follow Main St S through Thornton and shortly after LE67 1AJ take L fork onto Reservoir Rd, car park L after 100m. Follow path around reservoir. 01530 230807, www.flyfishthornton.co.uk
15 mins, 52.6655, -1.2994 🚶🚲🍴

9 BLACKBROOK RESERVOIR

Constructed in 1796 to feed the Charnwood Forest Canal, which has long since vanished. A bridleway leads up to an old viaduct bridge from which it is possible to explore the deeply wooded shores. The old quarry before the bridge is sometimes used by climbers, though the land above is private.

→ On A512 at crossroads SW of Shepshed, turn onto Charley Rd signed Oaks in Charnwood. Follow ¾ mile (past LE12 9EW) and park in lay-by L across from gravel track (One Barrow Lane). Cross rd and follow track 500m to bridge, quarry to R.
5 mins, 52.7488, -1.3149 🛶❓🚶🚲🍴

10 WELFORD & SULBY RESERVOIR

Built to feed the canal, with open, grassy shores, locals often swim or kayak here in the summer. Enjoy a tranquil walk across the causeway to find the earthworks of lost Old Sulby village, lying either side of the path, perfect for a picnic.

→ Entering Welford from the N on A5199 after passing The Wharf Inn (NN6 6JQ, 01858 575075) take L at the bend, cross over the bridge, to car park L after 300m. Old Sulby 52.4278, -1.0383.
4 mins, 52.4247, -1.0424 🚶🏕🚲🛶🍴❓

KING LEAR LAKE, WATERMEAD PARK

rmer gravel pit used by the local triathlon
b, with a namesake statue by the western
nk. Beautiful, clear water, but check for
ue-green algae and anglers.

From Syston follow Wanlip Rd and just
er roundabout and the Hope & Anchor (LE7
'D, 0116 2601963) turn L into pay car park
fore road joins A46.

nins, 52.6868, -1.1059 🏊‍♀️❓🚶‍♀️🚴‍♀️🏕️

WOODLANDS & WILDLIFE

FIELDSIDE COVERT, YELVERSTOFT

is delightful hidden woodland next to the
and Union Canal can be reached by canal
th, but for an adventure, arrive by kayak
d camp out. The higher side of the wood,
rpeted with primroses in spring, offers
acious clearings perfect for hanging a
mmock or building a den.

If walking, take Elkington Rd NE out of
lvertoft past NN6 6LU, park in the lay-by
Elkington Bridge after 2 miles. Follow path
wn to canal and turn R, walk to the next
dge and cross water to woods R. If kayaking,
ke High St SE out of Yelvertoft for ½ mile
d park in large lay-by L before road crosses
nal (NN6 6LA). Kayak E for 3 miles. Hire from

www.outdoorhire.co.uk for delivery straight
to your door.

15 mins, 52.3783, -1.0973 🏊‍♀️🚣‍♀️🚶‍♀️🏕️🅿️

13 NARBOROUGH BOG

A little gem nestling in a corner of
Leicester's urban sprawl, next to the River
Soar. There is a substantial reed bed on the
only significant peat deposits in the county,
while herb-rich meadows and wet woodland
support many forms of wildlife and have
earned it SSSI status. Look out for the
beautiful orchids.

→ Approach on B4114 heading S from B583
roundabout, to NE of Narborough. Just
after LE19 2AZ take small L turn just before
motorway bridge signed Recreation Ground.
Park at end of track and follow path R from
there past allotments to reserve L.

7 mins, 52.5756, -1.1933 🚶‍♀️🚗

14 OUTWOODS, NANPANTAN

One of the oldest surviving woodland sites
in Charnwood and an SSSI, the stunning
Outwoods offer circular walks for all
abilities. Huge, gnarled trees and granite
outcrops provide a natural playground,
whilst the vast swathes of bluebells in spring
are renowned in the area.

16

17

17

→ From Beacon Hill car park (see entry) continue N 1 mile to pay car park R. Follow R fork trail for bluebells.
3 mins, 52.7387, -1.2371 🐾🚶🅿️🏞️👁️🐄

15 STOKE WOOD, DESBOROUGH

Catch a glimpse of muntjac and fallow deer in this unspoilt and quiet woodland. A series of footpaths radiate outwards from the centre, leading to secluded benches and bubbling streams. One of the few habitats left for Britain's rare dormice.

→ Take B669 S from Stoke Albany ¾ mile (past LE16 8PT) and park in lay-by L at end of trees. Cross road back to field entrance and follow path along hedge L to gate into SE corner of woods.
10 mins, 52.4684, -0.8238 ❀🚶🚲🏞️👁️

16 BURROUGHS WOOD, RATBY

A wood of two halves either side of a public right of way. The ancient woodland to the north is awash with bluebells and anemones in the spring, and the newly planted deciduous wood to the south offers gentle, undulating paths for exploring this peaceful part of the National Forest.

→ Take Burroughs Rd W out of Ratby dir LE6 0XZ, car park R after 1 mile. Follow footpath

from car park N for bluebells.
5 mins, 52.6525, -1.2691 🚶🏞️🚲👁️

17 HERBERT'S MEADOW

Hidden away behind the woods, this tranqu[i] wild flower meadow (best in spring and summer) is the perfect antidote to modern life. Bring a picnic and a book, maybe even sleep out under the stars. Part of the Ulverscroft Nature Reserve, there are ancient forest and heathland to explore.

→ From Copt Oak follow B591 N, dir Loughborough. After 300m, turn R onto unsigned Whitecrofts Lane, dir LE67 9QE. Park in lay-by L by gate after ½ mile. Follow path through gate up over heathland and int[o] Poultney Wood to T-junction with track, turn then R into meadow.
20 mins, 52.7158, -1.2692 🚶🏞️🏞️❀👁️

SUNSET HILLTOPS

18 BEACON HILL COUNTRY PARK

The 700 million-year-old rocky outcrops, woodlands, wildlife and carved sculptures offer a wonderful family walk and lead out to magnificent views over the Leicestershir[e] countryside. The remains of a hillfort skirt the eastern slope and Bronze Age finds sho[w]

19

19

21

eople have been drawn to this spot for over
,000 years.

→ From N end of Woodhouse Eaves (LE12
RU) follow Beacon Rd W ⅓ mile and turn R on
reakback Rd signed Nanpantan. Car park L
ter 300m, follow footpath uphill.

0 mins, 52.7282, -1.2458 🚶🏊🏕📷🪨👥

9 THE BOMB ROCKS, CHARNWOOD LODGE

beautifully rugged area of moorland
ontaining the fascinating volcanic outcrop
f the 'bomb rocks', formed 600 million years
the Ediacaran Period – the very beginning
f multicellular life.

→ From Coalville, take Broom Leys Rd/
eadow Lane E past Castle Rock High School
E67 4BR. Straight on at dog-leg crossroads
nto Abbey Rd for 300m, park in lay-by R and
llow path through gate.

5 mins, 52.7295, -1.3194 🚶🏕🪨🧭

0 CROFT HILL

riginally part of a mountain range in the
rdovician Era, Croft Hill now offers a
eautiful circular walk around the quarry
ith panoramic views of the surrounding
untryside next to a vast red granite
uarry. A woodland trail, a scramble to the
mmit, a roll down the other side and a

paddle in the Soar make this an entertaining
walk for all ages.

→ Take Station Rd N in Croft and park on road
where it bends right at The Heathcote Arms
(LE9 3EG, 01455 699107). Walk back to bend
and follow Huncoat Rd 350m to footpath R
through wooden gate in stone gateway. Follow
L 400m then turn R up hill. Paths around N of
quarry and down to Soar.

15 mins, 52.5655, -1.2489 🚶🏊📷🏕

21 BRINKLOW CASTLE

A delightful example of a 12th-century
Norman fortification, with a 12m motte, deep
moat and rare double bailey. Beautiful views
of the surrounding countryside.

→ In Brinklow park outside St John the Baptist
Church (CV23 0LR) and follow the signed path
through the field to the R of the church.

5 mins, 52.4124, -1.3570 🏊🏕📷🪨

22 OLD JOHN, BRADGATE PARK

Extraordinarily beautiful country estate
great for walks, scrambles, views, tree and
rock climbing. The mock-ruin tower on Old
John hill is a prominent landmark.

→ Follow Main St NW out of Newtown Linford
and ¾ mile after end of town, past LE6 0AH,
to Hunts Hill car park signed on R. Follow

20

22

footpath out of car park leading to a choice of
routes with hill straight ahead.
5 mins, 52.6964, -1.2235 🌊🏃🏊🚴🏇🐄🚃🖼

RUINS & FOLLIES

23 KIRBY MUXLOE CASTLE
Impressive English Heritage castle complete
with moat, beautiful gatehouse and
complete corner tower.
➔ Take Oakcroft Ave off Main St in Kirby
Muxloe, follow signs down driveway for 2
mins, castle on R. EH: small fee to enter castle,
alternatively take the circular path around
the moat.
5 mins, 52.6367, -1.2275 🌊⊞🐌

24 PERCY PILCHER MONUMENT
A memorial to Percy Pilcher, the pioneer of
unpowered aviation, who managed a record-
breaking 250m before crashing and dying
at this spot in 1899. In the next field to the
south the undulations of a lost village are
still clearly visible.
➔ From Stanford on Avon (NN6 6JR), take
road next to church signed South Kilworth.
Monument visible to R in field after 200m.
7 mins, 52.4087, -1.1300 🖼

25 GREAT OXENDON TUNNEL
This 418m tunnel is a highlight of the 14-mi
Brampton Valley Way trail following the old
Northampton to Market Harborough railwa
line. Perfect for walking or cycling – bring a
torch and watch out for puddles.
➔ Take A508 S from Great Oxendon. After
½ mile, just past LE16 8NL, turn L onto small
unsigned road and park before gate. Follow
path L to tunnel.
15 mins, 52.4409, -0.9160 🌊🏃🚴🚲

26 GRACE DIEU PRIORY
The self-titled White Nuns of St Augustine
lived confined to this priory from the 13th t
the 16th century. Today, visitors are treated
to a substantial array of ruins best viewed
as the sun begins to set, casting dramatic
shadows through the archways.
➔ From Shepshed take A512/Ashby Rd W fo
2 miles to LE67 5UG. With priory visible L, tu
R on Gracedieu Lane signed Belton, park in la
by R. Walk back over road and take path R to
of ruins, stepping stones over brook into site
4 mins, 52.7610, -1.3564 🌊🏃🌳🖼🚻✝

27 GOPSALL HALL TEMPLE
Elegant pillars rising from the undergrowth
are all that remains of the once-mighty

26

...opsall Hall and Estate. Handel was a regular visitor, and romantic belief holds that this ...emple inspired his 'Messiah', but alas, it was ...uilt 23 years too late.

▶ Head N out of Congerstone and take L on ...end before school (CV13 6NH) onto Gopsall ...d. Follow to crossroads and over, lay-by ...00m on L. Follow footpath L to woods, in ...oods keep to R, temple 200m.
...0 mins, 52.6499, -1.4777 🚶🏻 🚲 🚗

...8 THE BRAND FOLLY

...idden just below the road, across from ...withland Wood, lies a beautiful circular ...ower serving as a lookout across a ...erdigris-coloured, flooded quarry. On ...rivate land, please be respectful and view ...rom the roadside.

▶ From Woodhouse Eaves follow Church ...ill/Brand Hill SE and turn R at end signed ...withland. Just around bend, turn R onto ...nd Rd signed Newton, dir LE12 8TN, ...nd park in Swithland Wood North car park ...n L. Follow road back downhill. Folly can be ...iewed over low wall on L.
... min, 52.7133, -1.2041 🚗

SLOW FOOD

29 MALT KILN FARM SHOP, STRETTON

Family-run farm shop, butcher's, bakery, PYO and coffee shop serving a delicious range of seasonal meals, snacks and cakes.

➔ Main Street, Stretton under Fosse, CV23 0PE, 01788 832640.
52.4286, -1.3314 🍴

30 WATERLOO COTTAGE FARM SHOP

Farm shop, café and community garden with yurts backing onto the old railway footpath. Run by people with a real passion for great food and local produce.

➔ 34 Harborough Road, Great Oxendon, LE16 8NA, 01858 467158.
52.4458, -0.9181 🍴🛏

31 YE OLDE PORK PIE SHOPPE

Award-winning Dickinson & Morris are the oldest bakers of the authentic and protected pork pie in Melton Mowbray. Try the fruit-laden Melton Hunt Cake from an 1854 recipe.

➔ 10 Nottingham Street, Melton Mowbray, LE13 1NW, 01664 482068.
52.7653, -0.8875 🍴

27

28

32 LEICESTERSHIRE HANDMADE CHEESE CO.

Homely, converted barn houses a tearoom serving cheese-themed light lunches. Adjacent is the dairy shop selling a range of award-winning cheeses, including their world-renowned vintage Red Leicester.

→ Sparkenhoe Farm, Main Road, Nuneaton, CV13 6JX, 01455 213863.
52.5937, -1.4629 🍴

33 CAFÉ VENTOUX, TUGBY

Destination cycling café (though bikes are optional) housed in a converted barn. Gorge on their renowned pancakes to replenish your energy levels whilst enjoying the stylishly themed interior and extensive cyclist's facilities.

→ Tugby Orchards, Wood Lane, Tugby, LE7 9WE, 0116 2598063.
52.6032, -0.8733 🍴

34 MANOR FARM SHOP & KITCHEN

Award-winning farm shop and tearoom packed full of the finest home-grown and home-made produce, ranging from rare-breed meats to fresh local vegetables, cheese, pies, chutney and delicious cakes. Book a table for Sunday lunch.

→ Main Street, Catthorpe, LE17 6DB, 01788 869002.
52.3982, -1.1915 🍴

35 LANE'S DELI & FINE FOODS

Fantastic deli-cafe serving home-cooked food, sandwiches and coffee. Shop stocks a range of fine foods, cheeses and continenta meats. Stays open late on Friday evenings t serve a glass of wine and a deli platter.

→ 12 High Street, Lutterworth, LE17 4AD, 01455 697060.
52.4550, -1.2002 🍴🍷

36 FARNDON FIELDS FARM SHOP

An award-winning farm shop born out of Kevin and Milly selling potatoes from the farmhouse door! Butchery, bakery, deli and cafe serving top-notch, home-cooked food and delicious afternoon tea.

→ Farndon Road, Market Harborough, LE16 9NP, 01858 464838.
52.4703, -0.9332 🍴

COSY PUBS

37 THE BLACK HORSE, AYLESTONE

Alan and Sarah welcome you to this thriving backstreet local adjacent to Aylestone Meadows. Serving a varied, good-value men including The Gourmet Burger Club. A wide, ever-changing range of real ales and ciders.

→ 65 Narrow Lane, Aylestone, LE2 8NA, 0116 2837225.
52.6029, -1.1595 🍴

38 THE GATE HANGS WELL, SYSTON

A great traditional pub with a secret beer garden alongside a beautiful stretch of the River Wreake. Swimming possible if you can find an entry point!

39

Fosse Way, Syston, LE7 1NH,
16 2609242.
2.7102, -1.0799 🏷️🔲

9 THE NEW INN, PEGGS GREEN

ccentric, friendly, family-run pub,
kuding charm and crammed full of equine
emorabilia. Excellent range of real ales and
large garden.

Peggs Green, Clay Lane, Coleorton,
E67 8JE, 01530 222293.
2.7551, -1.3908 🔲🔲

0 THE REAL ALE CLASSROOM

ormer teacher Ian keeps an extensive
nge of local real ales, ciders and gins in
is characterful micropub with beer garden.
ld school-style chalkboards and other
araphernalia you may remember from your
rmative years set the atmosphere. In town
ut worth leaving the wilds for.

4 Station Road, Lutterworth, LE17 4AP,
116 3196998.
2.4552, -1.1991 🔲🔲

1 THE GRIFFIN INN, SWITHLAND

riendly and bustling country inn, full of
haracter. Honest and well-priced food.
ecret garden out the back, and the
xcellent Odd John's Café.

174 Main Street, Swithland, LE12 8TJ,
1509 890535.
2.7115, -1.1838 🔲

42 THE FOX INN, HALLATON

Friendly, lively traditional pub with picnic
tables by the village pond. Every Easter
Monday, the bruising Bottle Kicking game
between neighbouring villages Hallaton and
Medbourne – claimed to be the country's
oldest sport – starts here.

→ 30 North End, Hallaton, LE16 8UJ,
01858 555278.
52.5630, -0.8359 🔲

43 NEVILL ARMS, MEDBOURNE

Impressive, stone-built Victorian inn, with
fine foods, real ales and a courtyard cafe. A
stream runs along outside seating.

→ 12 Waterfall Way, Medbourne, LE16 8EE,
01858 565288.
52.5282, -0.8244 🔲🔲

44 THE STAR INN, THRUSSINGTON

Stylish country inn offering mouth-watering
home-made food and its very own real ale in
the Viking-founded village of Thrussington.

→ 37 The Green, Thrussington, LE7 4UH,
01664 424220.
52.7373, -1.0419 🔲🔲🔲

45 THE BELPER ARMS

Oldest pub in Leicestershire,
sympathetically refurbished to embrace its
heritage. Extensive coffee menu.

→ Main Street, Newton Burgoland, LE67 2SE,
01530 587519.
52.6793, -1.4562 🔲🔲

38

40

44

46

46

CAMP & SLEEP

46 THE DANDELION HIDEAWAY, OSBASTON

High-end, sumptuous glamping in canvas cottages, complete with roll-top baths and wood-burning stoves, set on a beautiful working farm. Indulgence doesn't get better than this.

→ Osbaston House Farm, Lount Road, Osbaston, CV13 0HR, 01455 292888.
52.6457, -1.3891

47 GOPSALL PARK TIPIS

Five traditional American Indian-style tipis, beautifully furnished with mats, rugs and beds, and completed with fairy lights and a fire pit for that relaxing countryside feel.

→ Gopsall Hall Farm, Twycross, CV9 3QJ, 07816 605677.
52.6542, -1.4777

48 KNOTTING HILL, BARN HOUSE

Leap into the lake for a midnight dip and then warm up in the wood-fired hot tub whilst staying in your very own cabin in the woods. Sleeps eight.

→ Ashby Pastures Wood, Great Dalby Road, LE14 2TU, 07771 713071, canopyandstars.co.uk
52.7168, -0.9337

49 FOXTON LOCKS LODGES

Tucked away in the quaint village, away from the crowds at the nearby Foxton Locks canal staircase, lie these wonderful log cabins.

Immaculately presented with full amenities, including hot tubs, set on a beautifully tended site.

→ North Lane, Foxton, Market Harborough, LE16 7RF, 01858 545273.
52.5069, -0.9709

50 BROOK MEADOW CAMPSITE

Peaceful lakeside setting with generous plots and good facilities. Luxury lodges and bell tents also available.

→ Welford Road, Sibbertoft, LE16 9UJ, 01858 880886.
52.4430, -1.0219

51 LET'S GET LOST LEICESTER

Small company offering kayak tours around the waters of north Leicestershire with overnight wild camps.

→ 20 The Newarke, LE2 7BY, 07875 683396, letsgetlostleicester.com
52.6307, -1.1419

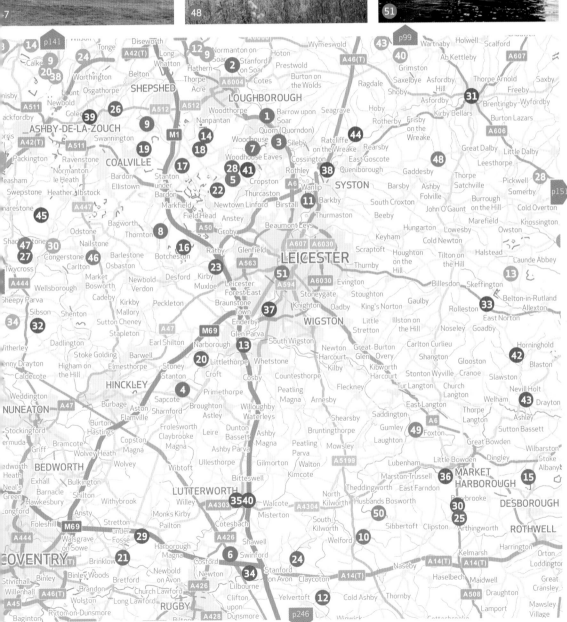

NORTH HEREFORDSHIRE

Our perfect weekend

→ **Conquer** Hergest Ridge before enjoying a pint and the stunning views at the traditional Harp Inn at Old Radnor.

→ **Spend** the day exploring the river at Bredwardine before taking a bath under the stars at one of Daphne's unique stays in Brilley.

→ **Skinny-dip** in the deep pools of the River Lugg at Mortimer's Cross then feast on some cheese goodies from Monkland Dairy.

→ **Climb** a tree in Mortimer's ancient forest or scramble around Richard's Castle with the goats.

→ **Descend** into Downton Gorge to discover the remnants of an old mill weir and mess about on the river for a few hours.

→ **Enjoy** a pint at the traditional parlour pub, The Sun Inn at Leintwardine, then stroll along the River Teme with its tempting rope swing and crystal-clear pools.

→ **Fly** a kite atop Titterstone Clee Hill with a scrumptious picnic of local produce from the Ludlow Farmshop.

→ **Bathe** in the warm waters of Bodenham Lake then 'honk for cider' at Newton Court.

→ **Treat** yourself to lunch at CSONS at the Green Cafe in Ludlow before cosying up by the wood-burner at The Bivvy.

North Herefordshire is a delightful patchwork of gently rolling hillsides and golden, arable lands. It is studded with important historical landmarks and stitched together by small, thriving, rural communities.

In a place almost forgotten in the ebb and flow of modernisation, there are ancient landscapes, customs and ruins seemingly around every twist and turn of the leafy country lanes. The black and white Tudor villages in this area have stood the test of time, with hundreds of them clustered along a 40-mile circular route to the east of Leominster. Yarpole village is a fine example of a thriving community, where you will find a friendly pub, the oldest free-standing bell tower in Britain, and a community shop and fantastic café in the local church.

A number of glorious rivers flow through this area, most notably the Wye, Teme and Arrow. For a long, deep, swim, try the Teme at Ludlow, swimming below the majestic ruins of its castle. Further to the west, the Wye meanders across the south of the area, and Bredwardine is a great spot for a family adventure; picnic on the bank or pebble beach, splash in the shallows or swim out to the bridge and jump from the supports. Lugg Meadows or the Wars of the Roses battle site at Mortimer's Cross both offer seclusion for a bit of skinny-dipping, should you be feeling brave.

The Welsh Marches have a tumultuous history of power struggles, religious unrest and medieval discord, especially right at the borderland. Past battles are well attested by many ruins, like the castles at Hopton and Wigmore, the Iron Age fort at Wapley Hill and the ultimate in border defences: Offa's Dyke. There are many walks long this scheduled monument, with Offa's Dyke Path running for 177 miles largely along the English/Welsh border. Take in the best of the local scenery on circular walks, or drive up to an incredibly intact part of the dyke between Llanfair Waterdine and Newcastle.

No trip to Herefordshire would be complete without sampling the local specialties: apple orchards, hopyards and carefully farmed lands produce tantalising local fare. Dunkertons Cider have a beautifully restored barn offering delicious, home-made food to accompany its product, while at Newton Court Cider, you take the more rustic approach of driving into the farmyard and honking your horn to sample the delights straight from the barrel.

RIVER LUGG

MORTIMER'S CROSS, RIVER LUGG

antastic, discreet spot to spend a sunny fternoon with the family and a picnic. Deep ools on a lazy, meandering loop with jumps d shallows to paddle in.

→ Take B4362 E from Mortimer's Cross dir R6 9PE. Park on R in lay-by just before idge. Cross bridge and take footpath to R ong riverside to beaches.

5 mins, 52.2661, -2.8386 ⛱🍴🏃🏕🐟⚘

RIVER LUGG & BODENHAM LAKE

ake a dip in the deep pools of the eandering River Lugg with a long, sandy tretch of beach at this point. The river here orders Bodenham Lake Nature Reserve here there are orchards, gravel lakes and eadows to explore. Look out for otters!

→ In Bodenham park at Church Walk, HR1 3JU. ollow path through church over footbridge nd follow footpath W along the river. Best ccess to Bodenham Lakes is from the eserve entrance and car park 52.1547, .6959, signed from the village.

5 mins, 52.1533, -2.6939 ⛱🏃🐟⚘

3 LUGG MEADOWS, HEREFORD

Secluded beach at the point where two tributaries of the River Lugg meet on meadows near the outskirts of Hereford. Tall banks and trees make this the perfect spot for paddling, a picnic or even a skinny-dip in the deeper pools either side of the beach.

→ Follow A465 N out of Hereford dir Worcester, to car park L just after passing HR1 1JJ and 40 mph signs. Cross road, walk back to gated track and follow path 500m straight over meadows to river.

10 mins, 52.0701, -2.6858 ⛱🐚⚘🏕🏃⚘

RIVER TEME

4 DOWNTON GORGE, RIVER TEME

Dramatic swim in a deep gorge hidden among trees. Remnants of old mill, weir and caves to explore. Deep pools in beautiful surroundings.

→ Downton signed from A413 W of Ludlow, near SY8 2LB. Follow road 2 miles S past Downton Castle. Park carefully by gate R after passing red-brick estate offices (52.3592, -2.8325). Take track across road and follow the tree line downhill until steep track on L takes you to river. Cross bridge and follow footpath to weir.

25 mins, 52.3577, -2.8264 ⛱🏛💧🏊🏕🐟⚘

5 LEINTWARDINE, RIVER TEME

Rope swing, beaches and a weir all with easy access near the bridge: ideal for an afternoon in the sunshine. Follow the river upstream for secluded, deep pools and beaches for paddling.

→ Park on Rosemary Lane, opp Lion Hotel (SY7 0JZ, 01547 540203). Walk upstream from bridge to rope swing and beach. Also, secret weir and pool further upstream at 52.3523, -2.9190.

8 mins, 52.3595, -2.8777 ⛱🌀🍴⚘🏃🚻🏕

6 LUDLOW CASTLE, RIVER TEME

The imposing castle ruins provide a historic backdrop to a gentle swim in the river meanders below, away from the tourists in the town.

→ Pay car park for Linney Riverside Park near SY8 1EG. Various entry points along bank.

2 mins, 52.3660, -2.7257 ⛱🏃🌀🚻🏕

RIVER WYE

7 BREDWARDINE BRIDGE, RIVER WYE

A pebble beach alongside the elegant bridge when flows are low provides a beautiful setting for a swim or jumps from the base of the bridge.

→ From Bredwardine, turn R opposite Red Lion (HR3 6BU, 01981 500303) signed Hereford and follow ½ mile, over river to lay-by L 100m up hill beyond. Walk back down over river, turn L over stile onto footpath to shingle.
5 mins, 52.0967, -2.9697

8 BREINTON SPRING, RIVER WYE
A delightful spot on the River Wye for a picnic and a swim. See also the fresh water spring and the pretty St Michael's Church.
→ Park in car park in Lower Breinton, HR4 7PG. Head down sloping path to riverside walk, and spring. Church in orchard to L. Earthworks to R are remains of Breinton Camp, an old moated house.
5 mins, 52.0498, -2.7691

9 FISHPOOL VALLEY, CROFT CASTLE
Crystal-clear water in a quiet pool, part of the picturesque styling of the valley, which is currently being restored to its 18th-century glory by the National Trust. Lovely walks around the area.
→ Croft Castle is signed just off B4362 up no through road at Cock Gate crossroads, HR6 0BL. Fishpool Valley is signed 200m on R along castle driveway. NT fee payable for entrance to castle.
5 mins, 52.2863, -2.7953

10 PEMBRIDGE, RIVER ARROW
A delightful bend of the river by the bridge with a pebble beach perfect for paddling. Deeper swims possible for ½ mile downstream. Shop and tearoom in village.
→ On A44 through Pembridge, turn R by New Inn (HR6 9DZ, 01544 388427). Follow 400m to parking L just over river.
2 mins, 52.2212, -2.8935

11 STAUNTON ON ARROW, RIVER ARROW
Secluded, deep swims above and below weir in a quiet corner of a Herefordshire field.
→ From Staunton on Arrow (HR6 9HR) take road W for Titley. After ½ mile, park carefully L by gate (one car space). Enter field over stile and follow footpath signs to river.
5 mins, 52.2368, -2.9374

ANCIENT & SACRED

12 LAUGH LADY WELL, BRAMPTON BRYAN
Holy well with a brick surround and lid, into which young people would drop a pin and

wait the gurgle to tell them their wish was
[gr]anted! Ruined castle open Sundays, estate
[p]ark worth exploring with magnificent trees.
→ Park in Brampton Bryan, just off A4113
[S]Y7 0DH). Take L fork at village green,
[o]pposite historic yew hedge. Follow private
[ro]ad/bridleway into estate, straight on to well
[o]R at base of hill.
[ ] mins, 52.3401, -2.9409 ⛪🚶🏕️

[1]3 YEW TREE & GROTTO, HOPE BAGOT

[A] brooding ancient yew overhangs a small
[gr]otto housing a quaint holy well. For full
[e]ffect enter through back of churchyard.
→ Park at Hope Bagot village hall (SY8 3AF) and
[c]ut through churchyard to far side of church.
[ ] mins, 52.3632, -2.6055 ⛪

[1]4 THE ARCHES, SHOBDON

[A]rched remains of a fine Romanesque
[c]hurch of the famed Herefordshire School,
[r]elocated to the top of an old tree-lined
[a]venue as a folly in the 18th century.
→ From B4362 W of Shobdon, turn signed
[U]phampton, dir HR6 9NJ. Follow 1¼ miles to
[p]ark opposite triple gates at Uphampton Farm
[a]nd follow footpath sign R just beyond.
[ ] mins, 52.2641, -2.8796 📷⛪

15 OFFA'S DYKE, KNIGHTON

Stroll along this glorious section of the
spectacular 117-mile long earthwork,
constructed by the 8th-century Anglo-Saxon
King of Mercia.
→ Heading W into Newcastle on B4368, take
first small, unsigned L at SY7 8PB. Follow
1¾ miles, over crossroads at Spoad, to park
L where Offa's Dyke Path forks L (52.4096,
-3.1030) and walk S.
10 mins, 52.4019, -3.0994 🚴🚶

CRUMBLING CASTLES

16 WIGMORE CASTLE

An extensive and interesting ruin built
shortly after the Norman conquest and a
ruin since the Civil War. Climb up to the top
of the keep.
→ In Wigmore, turn off A4110 at The Oak (see
listing) and to castle parking near HR6 9UN.
Walk back, across road, up no through road
signed to castle. EH, free entry.
15 mins, 52.3178, -2.8686 🚶🐕🏕️🚴♿

17 HOPTON CASTLE

Lovingly preserved Norman castle with a
dark history of a likely massacre after a
siege during the Civil War.

21

18

20

→ Park in the village of Hopton Castle, SY7 0QF, and walk to castle at SE end of village.
3 mins, 52.3957, -2.9318 ⛵📷♿

18 RICHARD'S CASTLE & CHURCH

This pre-conquest but Norman-style castle lies hidden behind the equally impressive Norman church, with many walls and the keep still standing. Close the gate so the goats don't escape!

→ Leave B4361 at Richard's Castle village following road to St Bartholomew's Church (SY8 4ET) and park at church. Path from church through gap in wall to newer graveyard leads up to castle R.
5 mins, 52.3278, -2.7601 ⛵📷♿

TREES & WOODLANDS

19 WAPLEY HILL WOOD

A historic site now dominated by graceful beeches, with paths for walking and cycling around the Iron Age hillfort and through the peaceful woodland.

→ Wapley Hill Fort is signed S from B4362 at Coombes Moor. Follow ¾ mile, passing LD8 2HU, to Forestry Commission car park R. The fort is at 52.2564, -2.9580.
4 mins, 52.2551, -2.9460 🌳🚶🏃♿

20 CREDENHILL PARK

Follow the well-marked paths uphill through the elder, oak and yew woodland and clamber over the rock sculpture in the shape of the Iron Age hillfort. Sling a hammock between trees and while away an hour or two in total tranquillity. Boots advisable for some paths.

→ On A480 heading E through Credenhill take L just after HR4 7DJ, signed Credenhill Park Wood. Car park 250m on L.
5 mins, 52.0920, -2.7980 ❇🚶🏕♿

21 GREAT OAK, EARDISLEY

A magnificent old oak at the side of the road named after it. Allegedly 800 years old, and with a girth of nine metres, it has a hollow space to hide in. In a quiet village. The nearby black and white Tram Inn serves local cider and cheeses.

→ In Eardisley turn off A4111 beside The Tram Inn (HR3 6LX, 01544 327 521) and follow ¾ mile. Great oak signed R just off road, with space for one car by it.
1 min, 52.1406, -3.0246 ♿

MEADOWS & WILDLIFE

22 THE STURTS SOUTH

This nature reserve and meadow, made up

seven fields, lies on the floodplains of the
ye and is flooded in winter. The pond and
ld flowers form an important habitat for
rdlife, small mammals and insects. Lovely
late spring and summer.

→ Take A438 NW from Staunton on Wye for
mile, reserve signed R on road to Kinnersley
 HR3 6DH. Park carefully by gate R after ½
ile (52.1202, -2.9652) and walk on 50m to
e gate on L.

 mins, 52.1220, -2.9726 🚶🐕♿

TITLEY POOL

his pool is one of the largest natural, open-
ater areas in Herefordshire and provides
e ideal habitat for crested grebe, teal,
ochard and goosander. Follow the trails
nder the tree canopy to the bird hide, then
omplete a loop around the pond.

→ Park at 52.2303, -2.9939 just off Eywood
ane, Titley (turning to HR5 3RU). Cross the
eld to the gate to R of the pond. Follow path
 the cottage and turn left down the narrow
ack to the bird hide. The Herefordshire Trail
rom the Stagg Inn (see listing) also passes
e far side of the pool.

 mins, 52.2288, -2.9902 🚶 X 🌲🐕

SUNSET HILLTOPS

24 TITTERSTONE CLEE HILL

At 533m, Titterstone Clee Hill is one of
the highest Shropshire Hills and wonderful
views abound, but the most fun can be had
exploring the remnants left from industrial
quarrying. Mined for its dark Carboniferous
dolerite, you can enter the empty ruins
and search for the remnants of the ancient
hillfort.

→ On A4117 from Cleehill dir Ludlow.
Titterstone Clee summit is signed R through
Dhustone. Turn onto Dhustone Lane and follow
½ mile, passing SY8 3PQ, to car park near top
of hill.

4 mins, 52.3952, -2.6005 🅿🚶🚻👁🐕🌲

25 MORTIMER FOREST

Extensive ancient hunting forest. Views
across Shropshire, Herefordshire and Wales
reward those who summit High Vinnalls.

→ From B4361 just S of Ludlow, turn L on
Whitcliffe Rd, becoming Killhorse Lane, signed
Burrington and Forestry Commission. Follow
2½ miles to signed Vinnalls car park L, just
beyond SY8 2HF.

30 mins, 52.3465, -2.7661 🅿🌲🚶♿

31

26

28

33

30 THE RIVERSIDE AT AYMESTREY

A traditional 16th-century black and white building serving innovative, locally sourced food with tables right on the river bank.

→ Aymestrey, HR6 9ST, 01568 708440.
52.2839, -2.8443

31 EARDISLAND COMMUNITY SHOP

Quaint, little shop in old dovecote, alongside river with memorabilia stored upstairs for a small entry fee.

→ The Dovecote, Eardisland, HR6 9BN, 01544 388984.
52.2231, -2.8512

32 DUNKERTONS CIDER BARN

Grade II listed barn at Dunkerton's Cider, celebrating the best of the county's local produce: high-quality food and, of course, cider on tap.

→ Pembridge, HR6 9ED, 01544 388161.
52.2033, -2.8867

33 CSONS AT THE GREEN CAFE

Modern British dishes and light refreshments all served with a twist of creativity. Absolutely delicious food with a beautiful riverside setting.

→ The Mill on the Green, Linney, Ludlow, SY8 1EG, 01584 879872.
52.3663, -2.7250

34 STOCKTON BURY GARDENS CAFÉ

Delightful cafe in a converted tithe barn offering delicious, home-made treats, light lunches and afternoon tea with ingredients grown on the estate or locally sourced.

→ Kimbolton, HR6 0HB, 07880 712649.
52.2454, -2.7084

35 MAHORALL FARM CIDER

A cider company run by a family with passion, enthusiasm and natural wild yeasts

→ Nash, Ludlow, SY8 3AH, 01584 890296.
52.3513, -2.6013

COSY PUBS

36 DUKE OF YORK, LEYSTERS

Great historic, traditional pub interior with curious curved settle, and small hatch serving keg beers. The friendly landlady is from the family who have run it since 1910. No food.

→ 1910 A4112, Leysters, HR6 0HW, 01568 750230.
52.2689, -2.6519

SLOW FOOD

26 LUDLOW FARMSHOP

Part of the Earl of Plymouth's Oakly Park Estate. Half the products are produced onsite in kitchen units visible around the shop, and 80 percent of the produce locally sourced.

→ Bromfield, SY8 2JR, 01584 856000.
52.3886, -2.7598

27 NEWTON COURT CIDER

Drive up into the farmyard and honk your horn for cider! Real people making real craft cider on a farm surrounded by orchards. It doesn't get more authentic than this.

→ Newton, HR6 0PF, 07971 886138.
52.1819, -2.7198

28 THE STAGG INN, TITLEY

A warm welcome to all visitors at this elegant pub-restaurant. Sit outside in the sunshine and sample the delicious, hand-made salted crisps with foamed vinegar dip, or dine in the elegant dining room. Weds–Sunday only.

→ Titley, HR5 3RL, 01544 230221.
52.2321, -2.9830

29 MONKLAND DAIRY

A working dairy producing and selling artisan cheeses from around the country. Award-winning tearoom and dairy tours available.

→ 9 Baker Lea, Monkland, HR6 9DB, 01568 720307.
52.2133, -2.7993

SUN INN, LEINTWARDINE

[Ex]ceedingly rare historic 'parlour pub' with [tw]o very traditional front rooms, now with additional rear bar and garden. Range of [loc]al ales and ciders. Bring your fish supper in [fro]m the chippy next door!

10 Rosemary Lane, Leintwardine, SY7 0LP,
[015]47 540705.
[52.]3597, -2.8742 🔲

ENGLAND'S GATE INN, BODENHAM

[16]th-century coaching inn with wooden [be]ams and large, well-maintained gardens. [Enj]oy a great selection of local beers, ciders [an]d good-quality food.

England's Gate Inn, Bodenham, HR1 3HU,
[01]568 797286.
[52.]1579, -2.6688 🔲🍴🖼

THE SWAN, HUNTINGTON

[Ec]centric, warm and welcoming village pub [th]at hasn't changed in decades. Bottled [be]ers, and a fascinating 'museum' room.

Huntington, HR5 3PY, 01544 370656.
[52.]1762, -3.0993 🔲🏔

YE OLDE TAVERN, KINGTON

[Ol]d-fashioned pub with a parlour and a range [of] well-kept ales.

22 Victoria Road, Kington, HR5 3BX,
[01]544 231945.
[52.]2057, -3.0228 🔲

THE HARP INN, OLD RADNOR

[Am]azing pub with amazing views, amazing [sta]ff and amazing ales! You can even stay in [on]e of their amazing rooms.

Old Radnor, Presteigne, LD8 2RH, 01544
[37]0655.
[52.]2253, -3.0988 🔲🖼🍴

THE BELL, YARPOLE

[T]hriving community pub in a friendly [vil]lage with the oldest bell tower in Britain [an]d a community shop and café in the [ch]urch. All well worth a visit.

Green Lane, Yarpole, HR6 0BD,
[01]568 780515.
[52.]2797, -2.7812 🔲

THE OAK, WIGMORE

[B]eautifully restored 16th-century coaching [inn] serving fresh seasonal food and a range [of l]ocal ales, with a couple of smart rooms [to] stay.

Ford St, Wigmore, HR6 9UJ, 01568 770424.
[52.]3164, -2.8610 🍴🔲🖼

45

44 NEW INN, PEMBRIDGE

Ancient, three-room inn with antique settles, beams, worn flagstones and impressive inglenook. Serves well-kept, changing ales, traditional cider and good-value food – the game pie is recommended.

➔ Market Square, Pembridge, HR6 9DZ,
01544 388427.
52.2179, -2.8938 🔲🍴

RUSTIC HAVENS

45 THE BIVVY

Rustic charm oozes from this upcycled cabin set in beautiful Shropshire countryside. The fire pit offers the perfect place to watch the sun set and the stars come out. There's an outside shower and a loo with a view. Secluded, yet within walking distance of Ludlow, you really do feel off-grid.

➔ Whitcliffe Farm, Ludlow, SY8 2HB,
canopyandstars.co.uk
52.3588, -2.7228 🖼🛏

46 CRUCKBARN, WIGMORE

The perfect place to stay with family or friends: cosy yet spacious with wood-burners and impressive views over the countryside.

➔ Wigmore, HR6 9UG, 01568 770036
52.3149, -2.8764 🖼🛏

47 NEW INN, BRILLEY

Go and stay at Daphne's for the most peaceful, relaxing stay in one of her

41

44

46

quirky, bohemian creations. Choose from a tabernacle for two, a roundhouse with a glass portal in the roof, or a gypsy wagon with an outside bathtub. Daphne is friendly, hospitable and interesting and you can be assured of a truly unique and dreamy stay.
→ Brilley, HR3 6HE, canopyandstars.co.uk
52.1257, -3.0883

CAMP & SLEEP

48 ROWDEN MILL STATION
Unusual opportunity to stay in a former station. Dine outside on the platform and explore the old Worcester, Bromyard and Leominster line railway cutting.
→ Bredenbury, Bromyard, HR7 4TG, railwaystationcottages.co.uk
52.2056, -2.5468

49 WALKERS COTTAGE CAMPSITE
A special little place for some back-to-nature escapism. Preserves from home-grown orchard fruits, honey and fresh eggs all available in the shop. Bell tents also available to hire.
→ Parks Road, Clifford, HR3 5HQ, 01497 831684.
52.1051, -3.0833

50 RIVERSIDE ORCHARD, BYFORD GLAMPIN
The most idyllic of glamping locations, wit a gypsy wagon and tipi under the old cider apple trees by the River Wye. Off-grid and wifi-free!
→ Garnons, Byford, HR4 7JU, 01793 76540
52.0782, -2.8755

51 THE BUZZARDS
An idyllic, basic rural campsite set on a 2,000-acre organic estate, ideal for exploring the Welsh Marches. Campfire are and farm produce available. Self-catering cottages also available.
→ Kingsland, HR6 9QE, 01568 708941
52.2617, -2.8500

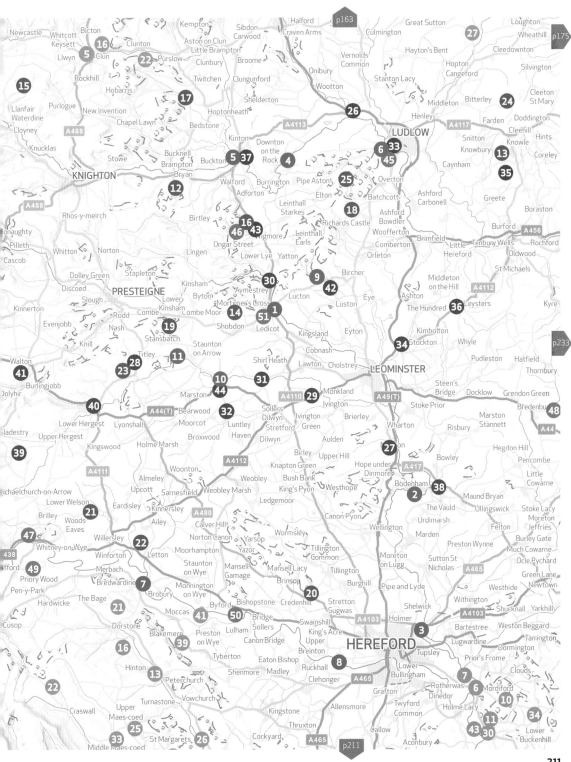

p233

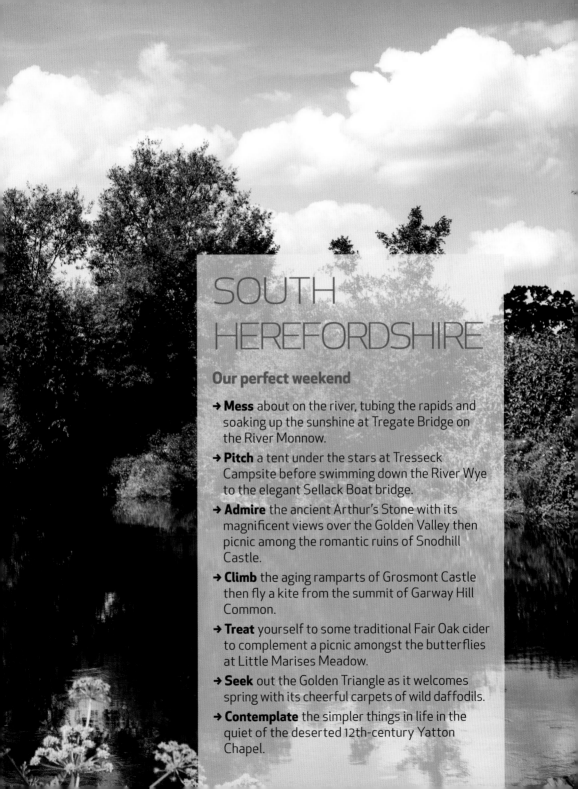

SOUTH HEREFORDSHIRE

Our perfect weekend

→ **Mess** about on the river, tubing the rapids and soaking up the sunshine at Tregate Bridge on the River Monnow.

→ **Pitch** a tent under the stars at Tresseck Campsite before swimming down the River Wye to the elegant Sellack Boat bridge.

→ **Admire** the ancient Arthur's Stone with its magnificent views over the Golden Valley then picnic among the romantic ruins of Snodhill Castle.

→ **Climb** the aging ramparts of Grosmont Castle then fly a kite from the summit of Garway Hill Common.

→ **Treat** yourself to some traditional Fair Oak cider to complement a picnic amongst the butterflies at Little Marises Meadow.

→ **Seek** out the Golden Triangle as it welcomes spring with its cheerful carpets of wild daffodils.

→ **Contemplate** the simpler things in life in the quiet of the deserted 12th-century Yatton Chapel.

The breathtaking countryside of South Herefordshire is sheltered by the Black Mountains to the west, flowing gently into the Golden Valley with rolling hills and wide floodplains. It is an ancient land, still sparsely populated and vastly unspoilt by modern progress. This is one of the last places in the country where you will find ancient woodlands, agricultural fields, wild flower meadows and traditional orchards all in the same area, interwoven with streams and rivers of crystal-clear water.

Much of the boundary line between England and Wales follows the famous Wye River as it winds its way from Wales to the Severn Estuary. Rural, quiet and secluded, it affords many pleasurable destinations where you can really experience the wild, relax and cut yourself adrift. Its tributaries are the idyllic Rivers Lugg and Monnow, meandering, mostly shallow waters with intermittent deep pools, perfect for swimming.

The brooding presence of numerous 11th-century Norman castle ruins haunts the border between England and Wales, most notably at Grosmont, Longtown and Snodhill. These battle-scarred remains tell the tale of the clashes where these countries met and fought over two centuries. Legend and fable are also an important part of the tapestry of Herefordshire and many great stories, such as the grumpy owner of Higgin's Well and a giant slaying at Neolithic Arthur's Stone, give colour to the local history.

The lands south-east of Hereford have a more peaceful past than the border region, and the limestone hills of the Woolhope Dome are covered in a mosaic of ancient woods. Haugh and Nupend Woods both offer atmospheric and peaceful places to yomp with the kids, build dens and feast on picnics. Haugh is famous for its bluebells in spring and butterflies in summer, whilst Nupend offers the addition of some ancient yews, unique in the area.

Food is an important legacy in this rural community, where farms, orchards and producers have been working alongside each other for centuries, taking advantage of their rich, fertile lands to produce superb-quality cider, meats and cheese. Many pubs and restaurants boast of their locally sourced food and The Bridge Inn at Michaelchurch has not only a great reputation for food but also a small campsite, rooms and glamping options, as well as their own gin. For famous Herefordshire cider, head to Gwatkin, where you couldn't meet anyone who looks more like a cider maker than Mr Gwatkin himself. Hilary at Fair Oak cider has restored a 17th-century horse-driven apple press believed to be the only one working commercially in the country. Visits are by appointment, but very much worth it. She is so honestly passionate about reviving a lost tradition – and her cider tastes sublime!

MARVELLOUS MONNOW

TREGATE BRIDGE, RIVER MONNOW

tranquil spot with dappled shade, shallows,
pids and deep pools, all perfect for a day
essing about on the river.

Turn off B4374 past NP25 5PW and
ntinue 1½ miles, following signs to Maypole,
en R signed St Maugham's Green, and R
gned Tregate Bridge. Pull off just over bridge
eyond gate. Swim spots for a mile up and
wn stream.

mins, 51.8515, -2.7602 🏊🐕🏕

SKENFRITH CASTLE

ollow the path through the beautiful ruins
f the 13th-century castle to the riverbank
find a number of perfect spots for a dip or
dive. Great community shop and pub across
e lane.

Signed just off the B4521 at Skenfrith, NP7
UH, with grass parking outside the castle.
mins, 51.8787, -2.7898 🏊🏕🍴🍺🛏ℹ️

LLANGUA BRIDGE, MONNOW GAP

deep pool on the border next to the road
idge, with ledges for jumping. The perfect
ot for a hot day cool-down.

→ On A465 just S of Pontrilas, right on the
England/Wales border. Park in lay-by 50m
down fork dir NP7 8HD and walk to bridge and
signed footpath down, L on English side.
2 mins, 51.9340, -2.8809 🏊🏕

WILD WYE

4 BACKNEY COMMON, RIVER WYE

Ancient common land and pasture border
a tight meander of the Wye with a large
shingle and sand beach shelving to a
generous pool.

→ From A49 just W of Ross-on-Wye, turn
signed Backney at crossroads. After 2 miles
(passing HR9 6PZ), follow no through road R
to Foy and car park R after 300m. Adjacent is
a track to meadows, continue ⅓ mile upstream
for beach.
15 mins, 51.9390, -2.6009 🏊🏃🐚🛶

5 SELLACK BOAT, RIVER WYE

Perfect for a family day out, a shingle beach
shelves to a deeper swim on the far bank.
Walk upstream to take a longer swim back
down under the beautiful suspension bridge,
named for the ferry service it replaced.

→ From Kings Caple (HR1 4TY), head S at
crossroads signed Sellack Boat and park on

R as road turns sharp L after ½ mile. Follow
footpath over bridge and L to shingle beach.
8 mins, 51.9485, -2.6327 🏊🏊🐚🏕🐕🏃

LUSCIOUS LUGG

6 MORDIFORD BRIDGE, RIVER LUGG

A relaxing swim under the old bridge
towards some gentle rapids. Explore upriver
following the Wye Valley Way or down river
to join the confluence with the Wye.

→ From Mordiford (HR1 4LN) follow
Wallflower Row/B4224 W just over bridge and
park in lay-by L beyond parapets. Cross road
and follow path N down to pebble beach.
2 mins, 52.0349, -2.6288 🏊🏕🐕

7 HAMPTON BISHOP, RIVER LUGG

An ideal spot for a skinny-dip in a secluded
stretch of the gentle River Lugg. At this
point a deep, wide pool graduates down from
pebble beach.

→ In Hampton Bishop (HR1 4JY) take unsigned
Church Lane N from bend in Rectory Rd 150m
and park at end. Follow track R for 200m.
3 mins, 52.0423, -2.6406 🏊🍴🏕👤🐕

WOODS & WILDLIFE

8 DYMOCK WOODS

A pretty and extensive ancient woodland noted for its spectacular spring flowers, especially its wild daffodils, but flora- and fauna-rich all year round. Miles of peaceful trails to discover.

→ Leave B1425 at Dymock (GL18 2AZ), signed Kempley on Kempley Rd, turn L after bridge, signed Oxenhall, past Western Way Chapel, then R at fork signed Normansland. Follow this 1½ miles, passing GL18 2BE, to woods. Various lay-bys and wide turnings, park carefully (51.9573, -2.4548).

2 mins, 51.9570, -2.4550

9 KETFORD BANK, GOLDEN TRIANGLE

The Golden Triangle is an enchanted landscape when the cheery wild daffodils flower each spring. Hedgerows, verges, woods and embankments are carpeted in yellow sunshine. The best examples are the reserves at Ketford Bank, Vell Mill Meadow (51.9807, -2.4229) and Gwen and Vera's Fields (51.9467, -2.4426).

→ Head S out of Bromesberrow Heath signed Botloes Green (past HR8 1PG). After 1½ miles, just before GL18 2BL, pull onto grass L at

bend before bridge (51.9750, -2.3946). Walk over bridge to bridleway R (Poet's Path No 1) and follow ⅓ mile. Daffodils on R.

10 mins, 51.9754, -2.4039

10 HAUGH WOOD, MORDIFORD

A peaceful wood alive with bluebells in spring, butterflies in summer and birdsong all year round. One of the top ten woods in the country for insects, and an SSSI.

→ Signed from B4224 at Mordiford (HR1 4LW). Car park signed L after 1½ miles.
2 mins, 52.0276, -2.5973

11 NUPEND WOOD

An atmospheric, ancient woodland mostly of ash and oak, with the special addition of some mystical old yews.

→ Follow Woolhope Rd NE from B4224 at Fownhope. After ½ mile, passing HR1 4PD, turn L by bridleway sign and park just before or just over bridge. Wood through gate.
10 mins, 52.0155, -2.6131

TERRIFIC TREES

12 MUCH MARCLE YEW & CHURCH

Thought to be at least 1,500 years old, this

hollow yew tree has a bench inside to sit on. Set in the grounds of the 13th-century St Bartholomew's church, which has beautiful carved tombs from several centuries, including one of wood.

→ In Much Marcle (HR8 2LY) follow B4024 S for ⅓ mile from A449, church signed R.
1 min, 51.9918, -2.5008 🗺

13 ST PETER'S YEW

A beautiful, ancient yew with a girth of 7.24m, estimated to be one of the oldest in the country at over 2,000 years. Hub Café inside church offers delicious, home-made cake.

→ On B4348 heading N through Peterchurch (HR2 0RS) church is signed L down turning by Boughton Arms (closed at time of writing).
1 min, 52.0414, -2.9564 🗺

CRUMBLING CASTLES

14 KILPECK CASTLE

With earthworks dating from 1090 and fragments of a 13th-century stone keep, the motte and bailey Kilpeck Castle stands proudly next to a 12th-century church, one of the best examples of the Romanesque 'Herefordshire School'.

→ In front of The Kilpeck Inn (HR2 9DN, 01981 570464) turn N and park in front of church at bend in lane. Head L around churchyard to motte and ruins behind.
5 mins, 51.9699, -2.8105 🗺🏃🎣🍺

15 LONGTOWN CASTLE

This well-preserved, peaceful and interesting little castle was built on a Roman fort, still visible as a much larger square embankment straddling the road. EH, free.

→ Signed off road through Longtown, HR2 0LE. Parking 100m N and opp.
3 mins, 51.9569, -2.9898 🏃🗺🖼🎴

16 SNODHILL CASTLE

Surprisingly little is known of the mysterious early Norman castle, although it was one of the largest and most elaborate in Britain. Its unusual, 12-sided keep, unique designs and glorious views give it a tantalisingly romantic air.

→ From SE end of Dorstone (HR3 6BE) follow signs to Snodhill and there turn L at crossroads by barn, signed Peterchurch. Pull off where road bends L after 230m. Access through gate on R ahead.
1 min, 52.0575, -2.9894 🖼🗺

17 GROSMONT CASTLE

Climb the ramparts of this remarkably complete 13th-century castle, a sister to Skenfrith (see entry) raised on an earlier motte.

→ Park where possible on the road in Grosmont (NP7 8EP) and follow signed lane between houses opp post office to castle.

5 mins, 51.9152, -2.8659 🚲🚇🎪🛶

ANCIENT & SACRED

18 HIGGIN'S WELL

Legend tells of a landowner who was fed up of locals trespassing, so filled in his well – only for it to spring up into his front room, compelling him to reopen it. Take a look in the pretty Victorian church, too, with its decorative ironwork and Norman font.

→ From Kingsthorne head SE to Little Birch Church on Mesne Lane, past HR2 8AS, turning R at bend L, to park at church (51.9771, -2.7128). Walk N on track opp turning into church, well at bend over stream.

3 mins, 51.9789, -2.7124 🚇🚶

19 YATTON CHAPEL

An enchantingly simple little early Norman chapel with an earth floor and a 12th-century arched tympanum over the door, hidden deep in the countryside.

→ Turn off B4224 for Yatton and Much Marcle at HR1 4TE, and follow ½ mile. Take R signed Yatton on bend and follow ½ mile to track R (no vehicle access). Pull off carefully here or L beyond, and walk ⅛ mile on track to chapel R.

2 mins, 51.9707, -2.5442 🏔️✝️

20 ST MARY'S CHURCH, KEMPLEY

An exceptional Norman church showcasing some of the best preserved medieval paintings in Britain and the oldest timber roof of any building in Britain. Stunning in spring with swathes of wild daffodils in summer. English Heritage, free entry. Also explore nearby Dymock Woods (see listing).

→ Signed L off B4215, 1 mile N of Dymock, GL18 2AT.

1 min, 51.9788, -2.4819 🚲✝️

21 ARTHUR'S STONE

A 5,000-year-old Neolithic chambered tomb with magnificent views across the Golden and Wye Valleys. According to legend, King Arthur slew a giant here, whose elbow left an imprint in the rock as he fell.

→ Signed from B4348 just NE of Dorstone, on lane passing HR3 6AU. After ¾ mile turn L on

arrow, unsigned lane uphill. Tomb L after ¾
ile, with space to pull off.
min, 52.0822, -2.9952 ⛪🏕️⊞

2 CRASWALL PRIORY

he highest of all English monastic sites,
nce home to monks of the austere and
ilent Grandmontine Order. These overgrown
uins are superb for scrambling over (bring
our boots) and provide wonderful views up
o Offa's Dyke. Landowners permit access,
e respectful.

→ From Hay-on-Wye take Forest R (HR3 5DX)
or Capel-y-ffin 3 miles to fork, then L signed
raswall 1¼ miles, to farm track L to HR2 0PX.
ollow track down hill to park on hard standing
next to ruins.

mins, 52.0327, -3.0616 💚⛰️🏕️⛪

HILLS & MEADOWS

3 THE PARKS NATURE RESERVE

loping down to the Dulas Brook, this
eaceful expanse of grassland is home to
diverse range of flora and fauna. Water
oles, otters and peregrines are all spotted
egularly.

→ Follow Longtown Rd N signed Dulas from
4347 at Ewyas Harold 1½ miles, stop in the
gateway of the first field on the right after
HR2 0NW.
1 min, 51.9602, -2.9199 🚶🏇🐕

24 GARWAY HILL COMMON

Enjoy the wonderful, ever-changing,
360-degree panoramas over five counties of
England and Wales from the summit.

→ Signed N from W of Garway. Follow 1¾
miles past HR2 8HA. Immediately after
bend with fork back right to St Weonards,
take bumpy lane uphill L and follow down to
common entrance with car park at end. This
may not be one for very low-slung cars.
20 mins, 51.9213, -2.8203 🚶🏕️⛱️📷

25 LITTLE MARISES MEADOW

A glorious meadow filled with a variety of
pretty flowers and butterflies from spring to
early summer.

→ From B4348 S of Peterchurch, turn R
signed Vowchurch follow 3 miles, then L
at crossroads signed Michaelchurch and
Longtown. Parking by gate L after ⅓ mile.
Alternatively, walk in from the W along a
green-lane bridleway from neighbouring
Canon Tump reserve.
2 mins, 52.0078, -2.9760 🌼🚗🚶🐕

SLOW FOOD & CIDER

26 GWATKIN CIDER
Close your eyes to picture a cider maker and what you'll see is the amiable Denis Gwatkin. Take time to visit the rustic bar and enjoy your drink on the veranda – if you love cider, this is a must-visit.
→ Moorhampton Park Farm, Abbey Dore, HR2 0AL, 01981 551906.
52.0015, -2.9083 🅿️

27 FAIR OAK CIDER
Hilary has worked some magic to restore her 17th-century horse-driven apple press – there still may be over 2,000 of these abandoned around the barns and farms of Herefordshire. The ciders are delectable, all the better for being made in the traditional way. Visit by appointment.
→ Fair Oak, Bacton, HR2 0AT, 01981 510250.
51.9910, -2.9371 🚶🗺️

28 TY GWYN CIDER
A small craft cider with a shop and bar in the stone barn and views of the surrounding Black Mountains.
→ Pen Y Lan Farm, Pontrilas HR2 0DL
51.937526, -2.889562 🅿️

29 ROWLESTONE FARM ICE CREAM
Indulge in award-winning, farmhouse-made ice-cream at this idyllic farm at the foot of the Black Mountains. Wildlife walks and a Camping & Caravan Club campsite onsite and a pretty Norman church just up the lane.
→ Rowlestone Court Farm, Rowlestone, HR2 0DW, 01981 240322
51.9394, -2.9100

30 GREENMAN INN, FOWNHOPE
A picturesque, family-run pub with a traditional bar and more contemporary restaurant inside a wonderful black-and-white-and-stone building. Rooms and cottages for overnight stays.
→ Fownhope, HR1 4PE, 01432 860243.
52.0071, -2.6154 🍺🍴🛏️

31 KILCOT INN, NEWENT
Award-winning country pub with a great atmosphere and locally sourced food, ale and ciders. Bike shelters, playground and rooms available.
→ Ross Road, Newent, GL18 1NA, 01989 720707.
51.9285, -2.4380 🍺🍴🅿️🛏️

COSY PUBS

32 CORNEWALL ARMS, CLODOCK
A delightful survivor of a bygone era: comfy chairs, open fires, pub games, photos of village life, and knick-knacks everywhere. Gorgeous views of the Black Mountains and a warm welcome from the landlady. Bottle-conditioned beers served from the hatch, occasional casks, no food or credit cards. Open all day weekends, weekday evenings.
→ Hunthouse Lane, Clodock, HR2 0PD, 01873 860677.
51.9415, -2.9813 🍺🍴

33 THE BRIDGE INN, MICHAELCHURCH ESCLE
A picturesque setting, highly rated food, camping pitches, B&B in that farmhouse, self-catering accommodation and romantic yurts. They even distil their own gin.
→ Michaelchurch Escley, HR2 0JW, 01981 510646.
52.0011, -2.9948 🍺🍴🅿️

34 THE CROWN INN, WOOLHOPE
Fantastic, locally sourced food served with finesse in a lovely old pub with garden. Extensive cider menu championed by the owne
→ Woolhope, HR1 4QP, 01432 860468.
52.0185, -2.5675 🍺🍴🅿️

35 CARPENTER'S ARMS, WALTERSTONE
Known locally as the Glue Pot (you won't want to leave!). Unspoilt character pub with great food, cask ale and charming decor.
→ Walterstone, HR2 0DX, 01873 890353.
51.9195, -2.9604 🍺🍴

36 THE COTTAGE OF CONTENT, CAREY
A lovely 15th-century traditional pub serving great home-made food and a range of ales. Delightful garden and accommodation.
→ Carey, HR2 6NG, 01432 840242.
51.9758, -2.6371 🍺🍴🛏️

RUSTIC HAVENS

37 WRIGGLES BROOK GYPSY CARAVAN
Quirky gypsy caravan B&B in a beautiful Herefordshire valley.
→ 2 Brookside, Hoarwithy, HR2 6QJ, 01432 840873.
51.9657, -2.6692 🛏️🐾

38 TAWNY OWL, CLODOCK
Escape the world and let the gurgling stream send you to sleep in these beautifully rustic

oden wagons, set on a woodland edge in the
onderful Black Mountains. Wood-fired hot
b and compost loo, yoga classes available.
Lower Hunthouse, Clodock, HR2 0PD,
nopyandstars.co.uk
..9355, -2.9760 🏕️

FRIDA, THE MOON AND I
lax amid a kaleidoscope of soft
rnishings in this tranquil, stargazing Lotus
elle tent with clear roof. Amazing open-air
ashroom with roll-top bath.
The Plough, Blakemere, HR2 9PY,
nopyandstars.co.uk
.0607, -2.9293 🏕️

AMP & SLEEP

TAN HOUSE CAMPING
e perfect base for access to the local
untryside and Offa's Dyke. Surrounded by
acres of sheep farm with the River Monnow
nning through the grounds. B&B available.
Longtown, HR2 0LT, 01873 860221.
..9492, -2.9811 🏕️

41 BYECROSS FARM CAMPING
Camp in an apple orchard next to the Wye.
A quiet family site with two furnished yurts,
fire pit and canoe hire onsite.
→ Preston on Wye, HR2 9LJ, 0981 500284
52.0776, -2.911

42 TRESSECK CAMPSITE, HOARWITHY
A peaceful, back-to-basics campsite in a
stunning location right on the River Wye,
with the local pub right by the entrance.
Closed in winter.
→ Hoarwithy, HR2 6QH, 01432 840492.
51.9593, -2.6592 🏕️

43 ST CUTHBERT'S, HOLME LACY
Near a pretty bend of the River Wye
with easy access points to the water,
this delightful church offers quirky
accommodation in a stunning historic
building. A 'champing' favourite.
→ Church Road, Holme Lacy, HR2 6LX,
champing.co.uk
52.0093, -2.6302 ⛪

39

42

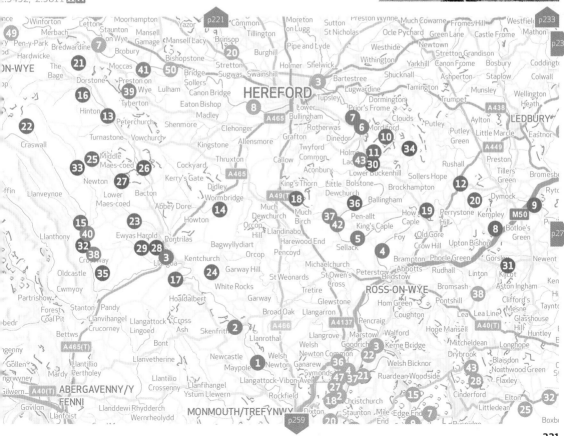

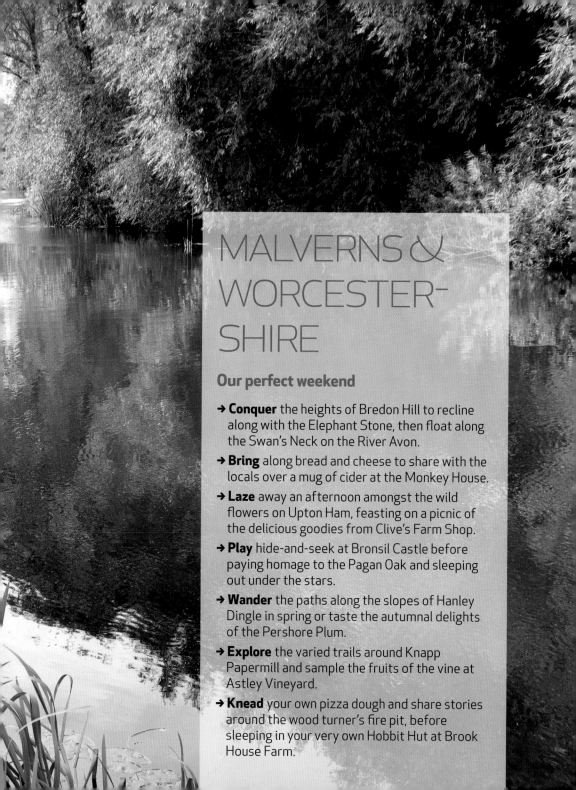

MALVERNS & WORCESTER-SHIRE

Our perfect weekend

→ **Conquer** the heights of Bredon Hill to recline along with the Elephant Stone, then float along the Swan's Neck on the River Avon.

→ **Bring** along bread and cheese to share with the locals over a mug of cider at the Monkey House.

→ **Laze** away an afternoon amongst the wild flowers on Upton Ham, feasting on a picnic of the delicious goodies from Clive's Farm Shop.

→ **Play** hide-and-seek at Bronsil Castle before paying homage to the Pagan Oak and sleeping out under the stars.

→ **Wander** the paths along the slopes of Hanley Dingle in spring or taste the autumnal delights of the Pershore Plum.

→ **Explore** the varied trails around Knapp Papermill and sample the fruits of the vine at Astley Vineyard.

→ **Knead** your own pizza dough and share stories around the wood turner's fire pit, before sleeping in your very own Hobbit Hut at Brook House Farm.

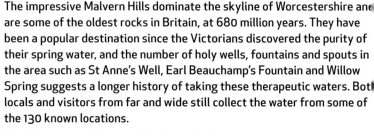

The impressive Malvern Hills dominate the skyline of Worcestershire and are some of the oldest rocks in Britain, at 680 million years. They have been a popular destination since the Victorians discovered the purity of their spring water, and the number of holy wells, fountains and spouts in the area such as St Anne's Well, Earl Beauchamp's Fountain and Willow Spring suggests a longer history of taking these therapeutic waters. Both locals and visitors from far and wide still collect the water from some of the 130 known locations.

The Abberley and Malvern Hills Geopark offers many opportunites to explore and learn more about the fascinating geology of the area, the history of which covers 700 million years. Its rich biodiversity spans over five counties, showcasing hillforts, unique landscapes, hills, valleys and walks all available to discover and explore. Recognised by UNESCO as having global significance, the 110-mile Geopark Way is a great way to explore the area.

Move on to the Severn Valley, and hints of the agricultural past are apparent. The undulating hills and farmland have produced fruit and hops for centuries, and cider houses such as the quirky Monkey House were once commonplace. Many traditional inns still flourish in this county – the Three Kings being an extraordinary example, a captured memory of a bygone era impervious to corporate whitewashing. Locals will welcome you with open arms, fiercely proud of their history, done their way, by their rules.

Bubbling springs, trickling streams and meandering rivers make for exciting exploration by many means – the tranquil pools upstream of the medieval Eckington Bridge on the River Avon and the deep meander of the Teme at Bransford are perfect for swings, jumps and swimming with a picnic. The River Teme at Stanford Bridge or Kingswood Common both yield a stunning dip in beautiful surroundings with a secret stretch of river beach and pools that make it the perfect destination for an afternoon of paddling, tubing and swimming.

The fertile floodplains and dense forests here proffer spectacular carpets of spring flowers and wild garlic at Hanley Dingle and meadows like Upton Ham. All this is studded with relics of the past, like the whimsical Dunstall Castle or the intriguing fragments of Bronsil Castle near Eastnor. As a rural county, the deep green landscape offers plenty to explore. Most people probably couldn't pinpoint this area on a map and, perhaps for this reason, it has remained largely unspoilt. For some it holds a spiritual resonance, full of mysticism, pilgrimages and ancient magic; discovering the iconic Pagan Oak or the curious Elephant Stone atop Bredon Hill can be a spine-tingling experience for explorers willing to veer off the well-beaten trail.

TERRIFIC TEME

KINGSWOOD COMMON, RIVER TEME

secret stretch of riverside with old stone
eir, beach and pools. Ideal for a paddle or
wim upstream.

» On the B4204, steep hill from Martley
 own to Ham Bridge (WR6 6QT) park halfway
 own hill in lay-by on R (52.2419, -2.3696) and
 llow signed footpath from other side of road
 river.

 5 mins, 52.2405, -2.3752 🏊🌳👪⛰

BRANSFORD, RIVER TEME

 deep meander with tree swings and jumps
 om high earth embankments. Perfect for a
 cnic with the kids.

 Park at The Fold Café (WR6 5JB, see listing),
 llow nature trail out the back and L path to
 ver.

) mins, 52.1772, -2.2984 🏊🌳🍴🎪⛰🚶🏃

STANFORD BRIDGE, RIVER TEME

entle section of the Teme with beaches and
eper pools on the bend downstream. A
eat secluded stretch on which to spend a
zy afternoon.

» In Stanford on B4203 park at The Den Café

Bar at Mill Farm (WR6 6SP, 01886 853800)
opp footbridge. Walk over bridge and follow
footpath back around the river to the L under
the trees.

5 mins, 52.2896, -2.4199 🐚🌳🎪⛰🚶

RIVERS AVON & SEVERN

4 ECKINGTON BRIDGE, RIVER AVON

This roadside picnic area by the medieval
bridge gives easy access to a lovely river
swim.

→ Signed off A4104 just before bridge ½ mile
N of Eckington, WR10 3DD. For more secluded
swim walk over bridge and head R, across field
to Swan's Neck (52.0794, -2.1028).

1 min, 52.0786, -2.1144 🏊🚣🚶⛰🌳

5 PERSHORE OLD BRIDGE, RIVER AVON

Now closed to vehicles, this bridge was built
about 1413 by monks, supposedly after
the abbot drowned when he fell from the
stepping stones. A delightfully tranquil
stretch of river for a swim.

→ Head S out of Pershore on B4084 past
WR10 1AX over river and park in Bridges Car
Park L. Head through gate to R and follow river
upstream for 100m.

10 mins, 52.1044, -2.0708 🏊🚣🌳

6 DEVIL'S SPITTLEFUL, RIVER SEVERN

One of the largest heathland habitats in the
county, dominated by bell heather and at
its best in late summer. A chance for a swim
or kayak launch, and an impressive rock
outcrop (the spade- or spittleful) and cave
give panoramic views.

→ Heading S from Bewdley on B4194, dir
DY12 2TQ, pass under A456 bridge and
after 100m turn L into Blackstone Riverside
car park. Easy entry point for swim or kayak
on bend of river. Kayaks available further
upstream from Bewdley Canoe Hire, 07397
005355.

10 mins, 52.3643, -2.3063 🚶🎪🏞🏊🚣

BLUE POOLS

7 GULLET QUARRY, EASTNOR

Stunning, spring-fed quarry lake in great
natural amphitheatre of Malverns. Swimming
is now prohibited. Beautiful walks amongst
the wooded hills and along the ridge line.

→ Heading E out of Hollybush on A438 turn
L at unsigned crossroads just after HR8 1ET.
Continue 1 mile to Swinyard pay-and-display
car park R around bend. Walk L up road
blocked with bollards 500m.

5 mins, 52.0406, -2.3483 🏊❓🔻

8 SHAVERS END QUARRY

Just off the Worcestershire Way, dramatic cliffs make the perfect backdrop to these steep-sided, azure-blue lagoons formed from stone quarrying. Part of the Abberley and Malvern Hills Geopark. Walk the ridge line footpath for stunning views. Popular with summer swimmers but private - keep out.

→ Head NE from Yarhampton on A451, take first L, past DY13 0UU, L again at fork. Layby L after ½ mile and path to the L side of old quarry entrance.

5 mins, 52.3099, -2.3391 🏊 ❓ 🅥 🚶

WOODS & WILD FLOWERS

9 HOLLYBED FARM MEADOWS RESERVE

Stunning wild flower meadow alive with plants and wildlife. The Victorian perry pear orchard and bubbling stream make it the perfect destination at any time, but especially for a summer's picnic amongst the meadow flowers.

→ Take B4208 SW from Welland 1½ miles, turn R onto New Road opposite Robin Hood pub (WR13 6BS, 01684 833212), dir WR13 6BU. Meadow on L after ½ mile. Space for one car by gate.

2 mins, 52.0421, -2.3237 ✚ 🎪 ➤

10 KNAPP & PAPERMILL NATURE RESERV⬛

Tucked away in the Leigh Brook Valley, this pretty little reserve boasts a profusion of butterflies, orchids, wild flower meadows and wooded glades.

→ Head E out of Alfrick Pound on Stocks Rd. After ½ mile, just after WR6 5HR, car park R entrance to reserve.

10 mins, 52.1670, -2.3659 ✚ ➤ 🚶

11 BROMYARD DOWNS COMMON

A delightful place at all times of the year: ancient wood, heathland and wild flower meadows swimming with yellow rattle. There even a World War II bunker hidden in the woods, and stunning views across the valley.

→ Signed off the B4203 1¼ miles NE of Bromyard, dir HR7 4QP. Car park L after ¼ mile, with two footpaths out of the car park for a circular walk.

5 mins, 52.1997, -2.4838 ✚ ➤ 🎪 ⬇

12 TRENCH WOOD

This peaceful ancient woodland, currently being restored, has entrancing displays of woodland butterflies and orchids.

→ From Droitwich Spa WR9 7GD follow Tegwell Rd under motorway and take next

13

14

16

nsigned L, then turn R at end on Trench Lane
gned Dunhampstead. Follow 1⅓ miles to car
ark R.

mins, 52.2277, -2.1046 🅿️🚶

3 UPTON HAM

his beautiful, species-rich wild flower
eadow on the fertile floodplain banks of
e River Severn is haunted by the wild calls
f curlews.

Heading S through Upton-upon-Severn on
d St/A4104, turn L onto Minge Lane at WR8
NW. Park before bend into Gardens Walk
nd follow track straight on between houses
50m down to reserve.

mins, 52.0621, -2.2046 🔆🏊

4 HANLEY DINGLE

aptivating dingle blanketed in wild garlic
spring. The views from the ridge line
re spectacular and well worth the climb.
eserve is permit-only beyond public
otpaths, to protect the rare plants.

At Stanford on Teme turn off the B4203
gned Orleton, past WR6 6ST. Park R after
rm and houses, 52.2978, -2.4517. Follow
ad to stile on edge of wood on R; OS map
commended for footpaths.

mins, 52.2983, -2.4555 🚶🅰️🅿️🚗🅱️

15 DUNSTALL CASTLE

Unexpectedly posturing at the side of the
road, this whimsical folly was built in 1766 to
look like a ruined castle.

→ Follow A4104 W from Defford. After
1¾ miles turn R at bend (WR8 9BP), signed
Dunstall. Castle on L after ½ mile with lay-by.

1 min, 52.0841, -2.1684 📷

16 BRONSIL CASTLE

Intriguing fragmentary remains of a 15th-
century moated castle. Legend has it that
Lord Beauchamp buried his fortune here so
that his family wouldn't spend it unwisely
whilst he was away at war, and it was never
found.

→ From Eastnor follow A438 E for 1 mile, turn
L for HR8 1EP, and park in lay-by after ¼ mile.
Short walk up to castle on R.

10 mins, 52.0327, -2.3666 📷

17 ROBERT'S HILL OLD CIDER MILL

Atmospheric old ruins set beside the river,
perfect for a picnic and a paddle.

→ Take B4203 NW from Bromyard 1¾ miles
and turn L signed Edvin Loach just before HR7

15

17

4PL. Park on L on sharp RH bend. Follow round bend, past ruins on R to gate. Paddle across the river.

5 mins, 52.2106, -2.4862

SACRED & ANCIENT

18 LEIGH COURT BARN

This magnificent barn was built in 1325 for Pershore Abbey. With 18 crucks, each from a single oak, it is the largest cruck-framed structure in Britain. EH, free entry.

→ From Bransford roundabout on A4103 follow signs for Leigh 1 mile to WR6 5LB and barn R.

1 min, 52.1793, -2.3180

19 EDVIN LOACH OLD CHURCH

Ruins within ruins: the interesting remains of an 11th-century church with unusual herringbone stonework lie inside the bailey of a Norman castle, with the motte beyond the new church.

→ Take B4203 NW from Bromyard 1¾ miles and turn L signed Edvin Loach just before HR7 4PL. Follow 1¾ miles and take signed L to church with parking 250m down lane (HR7 4PW).

1 min, 52.2231, -2.4953

20 PAGAN OAK

This legendary, gnarled old oak, growing remarkably atop the rocky edge of a deep hollow, is an important place of pilgrimage, especially at solstices. Adorned with ribbon feathers, pentagrams and other trinkets – climb inside to find more decorations and see if there is a new visitors' book hidden in the trunk. Perfect for a wild camp.

→ Heading E out of Hollybush on A438 turn R at unsigned crossroads just after HR8 1ET, past green corrugated-metal village hall. After ¾ mile, turn sharp R onto Whiteleaved Oak. Follow for ⅓ mile and park in lay-by L jus before sharp bend to L. Follow road/track, then footpath into field on L, continue throug to second field and oak in L corner.

15 mins, 52.0239, -2.3584

FANTASTIC FORTS

21 ELMLEY CASTLE

Rising impressively above a medieval deer park, the extensive earthworks of this once-important Norman castle dominate th skyline. By the 16th century its stone was robbed to mend Pershore Old Bridge (see entry). An energetic walk offers splendid, unobstructed views and a secluded picnic spo

In Elmley Castle village (WR10 3HS), take narrow lane between houses SE from end of Main St past the cricket ground to picnic area R opp playground. Park here and follow footpath around edge of field, parallel to road, then uphill towards castle.

10 mins, 52.0604, -2.0311 🚶🏼‍♀️🪧📷🐾🚲↩

22 BRITISH CAMP

The imposing tiered earthworks of this important hillfort are believed to have been first constructed in before 100 BC. Lots to explore, including the reservoir and man-made Clutter's Cave, cut into pillow lavas – their shapes can still be seen at the cave mouth.

Car park on A449 from Welland, opp B4234 junction to West Malvern and WR13 6DW. Follow footpath from car park for ½ mile. Reservoir to the L, Clutter's Cave is at 52.0522, -2.3485.

10 mins, 52.0580, -2.3521 🚶🏼‍♀️📷🐾🪧🚲🏊↩

23 ELEPHANT STONE, BREDON HILL

Upon cresting Bredon Hill above the imposing earthworks of Kemerton Camp, the most obvious landmark is the austere Parson's Folly at the summit – but the real gem is the delightfully shaped Elephant Stone or Bambury Rock just below. Magnificent views.

→ From Kemerton village, turn up unsigned lane beside the church and follow ¾ mile, passing GL20 7JP, to park in lay-by L before gate at end. Space for 3 cars. Follow path up through woods to summit.

35 mins, 52.0603, -2.0644 📷🚶🏼‍♀️🐾

SLOW FOOD

24 THE INN AT WELLAND

Exquisite, locally sourced food served in a stylishly renovated, family-run inn. Vast views over the Malverns and a genuinely warm welcome.

→ Hook Bank, Welland, WR13 6LN, 01684 592317.

52.0603, -2.2761 🍴🍷

25 ALFRICK & LULSLEY COMMUNITY SHOP

A heart-warming community shop, post office and café, beautifully crafted to serve the village and surrounding area.

→ Clay Green, Alfrick, WR6 5HJ, 01886 832862.

52.1763, -2.3694 🍴

26 ST ANN'S WELL CAFÉ

Renowned as far back as the 13th century, the pure mineral waters of the Malverns flow freely here from a beautifully carved Sicilian marble spout and basin. Climb the 99 steps from the town and then weave your way up the path for a well-earned coffee and cake!

→ St Ann's Road, Great Malvern, WR14 4RF, 01684 560285.

52.1099, -2.3340

27 THE FOLD CAFÉ & FARM SHOP

A stylish café in a beautiful 17th-century converted barn, serving delicious, organic home-made food from the farm.

→ A4103, Bransford, WR6 5JB, 01886 833 633.

52.1719, -2.2972

28 ROOTS FAMILY FARM SHOP

Great range of locally sourced organic vegetables, onsite bread oven and bakery. Good selection of cheeses, butters and gifts.

→ Bransford Road, Rushwick, WR2 5TD, 01905 421104.

52.1800, -2.2751

29 CLIVE'S FRUIT FARM

Friendly, family-run farm shop, café and fruit farm. Home-brew cider and fruit juices, PYO, farm produce, butcher's and delicious, home-made cakes.

→ Willingsworth, WR8 0SA, 01684 592664.

52.0650, -2.2328

30 CRUMPTON HILL FARM SHOP

Small farm shop, set in an extensive orchard, selling locally sourced fresh produce and a fine selection of craft ciders and beers.

→ Crumpton Hill Road, Crumpton Hill, WR13 5HP, 01886 880802.

52.1333, -2.3605

31 ASTLEY VINEYARD

Once the most northerly in the world, the vineyard produces a range of exceptional wines. Cellar door shop, and incredibly passionate owners offer tours.

→ Hampstall Lane, Stourport-on-Severn, DY13 0RU, 01299 822907.

52.3049, -2.2885

32 GREEN COW KITCHENS

Taster menu at the weekend and brasserie food Wednesdays and Thursdays showcase the farm's excellent produce. Accommodation available.

→ Crumplebury Farm, Whitbourne, WR6 5SG, 01886 821992.

52.2093, -2.4400

COSY PUBS

33 THE THREE KINGS INN, HANLEY CASTLE

The regulars of this beautifully unspoilt historic hostelry genuinely welcome visitors. Experience an extraordinary scene spilling into Nell's old lounge, where locals play their fiddles, flutes and guitars whilst sharing a platter of bread and cheese. Don't ask for a lager! Real ales rule here!

→ Church End, Hanley Castle, WR8 0BL, 01684 592686.

52.0761, -2.2370

34 THE MONKEY HOUSE, DEFFORD

A step back in time to one of only five such cider houses left in the country. Order from the hatch and drink in the garden or quaint old bakehouse. Locals bring bread and cheese, sharing food and conversation with old and new friends. Incredible place, too easily missed in passing! Closed Mon–Tues and evenings Fri and Sun.

→ Woodmancote, Defford, WR8 9BW, 01386 750234.

52.0813, -2.1405

35 THE MUG HOUSE, CLAINES

Lovely 700-year-old beamed pub tucked away behind the church, one of two known to be built on consecrated ground. Cosy, old snug with traditional stone floor and an open fire in the bar.

→ Claines Lane, Claines WR3 7RN, 01905 456649.

52.2271, -2.2193

36 THE LIVE & LET LIVE, BRINGSTY

This cosy 16th-century former cider house with its authentic timbered interior is one of the oldest buildings on Bringsty Common, and the only thatched pub in Herefordshire.

→ Bringsty Common, Bringsty, WR6 5UW, 01886 821462.

52.1911, -2.4402

37 THE NAG'S HEAD, MALVERN

Delightful old pub with beamed interior, flagstone floors, nooks and crannies to cosy up in, and old settles and open log fires dotted around. Good range of ciders, ales and food.

→ 19-21 Bank Street, Malvern, WR14 2JG, 01684 574373.

52.1200, -2.3276

38

RUSTIC HAVENS

8 BROOK HOUSE WOODS

Choose a handcrafted wooden cabin complete with a wood-burner and king-size bed in beautifully secluded woods – or pick a luxury tree cabin with an outdoor bath, a yurt or an exciting tree tent. Cook in the clay pizza oven or over the fire pit. There is a wood-fired hot tub, woodland yoga classes and woodworking courses. The perfect retreat!

→ Brook House Farm, Avenbury Lane, Bromyard, HR7 4LB, 07966 529815.
52.1694, -2.4954

9 LILLA STUGAN, MILLHAM FARM

The 'little cottage' is a quirky red and blue Scandinavian-inspired cabin set in its own apple, pear and plum orchard, with a cosy wood-burning stove and outdoor fire pit. A private gate leads out onto the beautiful Knapp and Papermill reserve (see listing).

→ Millham Farm, Millham Lane, Alfrick, WR6 5HS, canopyandstars.co.uk
52.1649, -2.3655

0 OCKERIDGE RURAL RETREATS

The perfect place to relax and unwind, with stunning views across the countryside. Two luxurious and well-equipped shepherds' huts and a cosy log cabin.

→ Ockeridge Lane, Wichenford, WR6 6YR, 07974 444412.
52.2590, -2.3192

CAMP & SLEEP

41 CAVES FOLLY NURSERIES CAMPING

Awake to the sound of the wild birds in Oak Meadow, or rent the Pleck holiday cottage and your own private flowering prairie for a group. The perfect tranquil getaway, with a fire area.

→ Evendine Lane, Colwall, WR13 6DX, 01684 540631.
52.0688, -2.3635

42 CAMP HOUSE INN, GRIMLEY

Unspoilt traditional pub with small campsite. Great food and a relaxed atmosphere on the banks of the River Severn.

→ Camp Lane, Grimley, WR2 6LX, 01905 640288.
52.2300, -2.2427

43 KATESHILL HOUSE, BEWDLEY

Elegant Georgian town house with views over the old town and a classic English garden, home to the vast and venerable Bewdley sweet chestnut.

→ Red Hill, Bewdley, DY12 2DR, 01299 401563.
52.3719, -2.3130

44 ANDREW'S FIELD CAMPING

A stunning, peaceful location on the banks of the River Avon. Walks and kayaking on your doorstep. Open during summer months.

→ Mill Lane, Pershore WR10 3BG, 07775 733506
52.0623, -2.1238

41

39

43

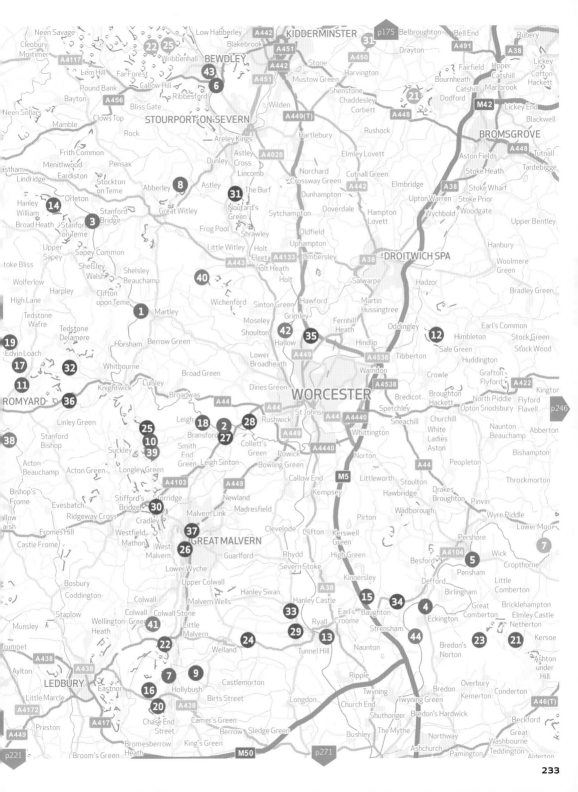

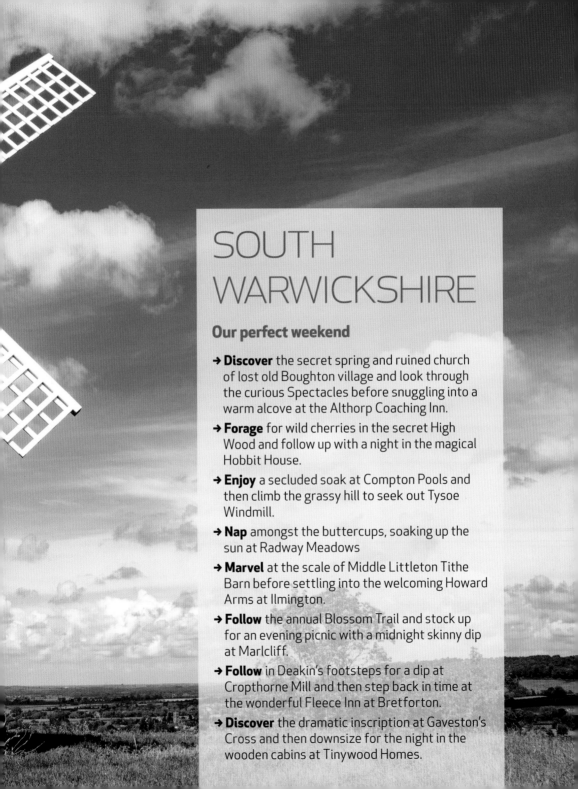

SOUTH WARWICKSHIRE

Our perfect weekend

→ **Discover** the secret spring and ruined church of lost old Boughton village and look through the curious Spectacles before snuggling into a warm alcove at the Althorp Coaching Inn.

→ **Forage** for wild cherries in the secret High Wood and follow up with a night in the magical Hobbit House.

→ **Enjoy** a secluded soak at Compton Pools and then climb the grassy hill to seek out Tysoe Windmill.

→ **Nap** amongst the buttercups, soaking up the sun at Radway Meadows

→ **Marvel** at the scale of Middle Littleton Tithe Barn before settling into the welcoming Howard Arms at Ilmington.

→ **Follow** the annual Blossom Trail and stock up for an evening picnic with a midnight skinny dip at Marlcliff.

→ **Follow** in Deakin's footsteps for a dip at Cropthorne Mill and then step back in time at the wonderful Fleece Inn at Bretforton.

→ **Discover** the dramatic inscription at Gaveston's Cross and then downsize for the night in the wooden cabins at Tinywood Homes.

Imagine a picturesque county, steeped in history, with buttercup meadows overflowing into the undulating countryside, windmills perched atop grassy hills, and an unspoilt sprinkling of thatch-and-stone Tudor cottages in much-loved villages. Welcome to South Warwickshire.

The pretty, sparsely populated county of Shakespeare's birth is the rural heart of England, so much so that the setting of the BBC's bucolic radio soap 'The Archers' is based on locations here. Pretty dells such as Snitterfield Bushes are carpeted in bluebells and snowdrops in spring and offer dappled shade for a summer stroll. Radway Meadows is a sea of buttercups from May to July and perfect for a romantic picnic or lazy summer nap.

The landed gentry built many country residences and estates, many still private or costly to visit. However, look a little further and you can often find examples of their frivolous nature in remote and forgotten places. On the Welcombe Hills just outside Stratford is a disused swimming pool built into the hillside, long past its sell-by date but fascinating nonetheless. On a grander scale are The Spectacles, a castellated arch designed purely as an 'eyecatcher' framing the views to a nearby church from the Boughton Park estate.

Local myths and legends still thrive here. Old St John's church and its sacred spring are all that is left of the medieval village that once thrived there, with a tale attached of a tragic bride, widowed on her wedding day, who delivers a deadly kiss. Further south in Kenilworth, the ruins of St Mary's Abbey stand in beautiful parkland, said to be protected by a curse of disaster befalling anyone who tries to take away the land from the church.

The Avon is a beautiful, serene river, which winds its way south through the county towards the River Severn. There are many great places to enjoy its clean, tranquil waters around the Stratford area. For quiet, secluded spots try Hampton Lucy or Alveston, where you can while away a few lazy hours on a summer's day; for a deep, wide meander try Marlcliff, above a pretty weir; for a swim with easy access and jumps near the bridge, Bidford is the place to go.

As the county unfurls south towards the Cotswolds, the landscape rolls over the Vale of Red Horse into the beautiful wolds so often associated with that area. Lanes narrow, village greens widen and scenic landscapes take on a quintessentially English hue. The Burton Dassett Hills and Tysoe Windmill offer majestic hilltops with stunning panoramas, perfect for some stargazing. Award-winning pubs and farm shops have built up a fantastic reputation for high-quality, local produce. Try Talton Mill farm shop, or the 15th-century Fleece Inn at Bretforton for inglenook fireplaces and top-quality food.

AWESOME AVON

HAMPTON LUCY, RIVER AVON

Swim tucked away on a gentle stretch of the Avon just above the mill and weir, or swim down from Wasperton!

Turn R off A429 S of Warwick signed NT Charlecote Park. Then R to park in Hampton Lucy. Walk back over both bridges and take bridleway on L, just after Charlecote Mill (flour for sale, 01789 842072). Halfway through second field, cross stream on L and head to river. Wasperton river path for fishermen from mill-in at 52.2295, -1.6079.

30 mins, 52.2151, -1.6205

THE OLD BATHING PLACE, STRATFORD

Large lawn for sunbathing and picnicking, and a gentle curve in the River Avon for swimming, where many learnt to swim.

Watch out for boats: it can get very busy with rowers, tourist cruisers, and hired motor boats. Head NE out of Stratford-upon-Avon on A439 past CV37 6YP. Dedicated car park R after ½ mile with path down to river.

5 mins, 52.1989, -1.6936

WELFORD-ON-AVON

Enjoy the walk down past quintessentially English thatched cottages to a lovely wide, tranquil section of the Avon, with a millpond and weir. Take your pick of places to swim. Retreat to the marvellous Bell Inn (01789 750353) for a cosy pint to follow your dip.

→ Signed from B439 4 miles W of Stratford. From Bell Inn (CV37 8EB) head past church to bottom of Boat Lane. Follow permissive path to R.

10 mins, 52.1688, -1.7922

4 BIDFORD BRIDGE

Swim from the medieval bridge against the current up to the church and then float back down and admire your surroundings.

→ Head out of Bidford-on-Avon S over the bridge on B4085, dir B50 4PG. The Big Meadow car park is R immediately after. Cross road and enter water beside bridge.

2 mins, 52.1635, -1.8566

5 ALVESTON, RIVER AVON

Down the old ferry steps lies a quiet stretch of the Avon bequeathed to villagers, with platforms for diving. For village use only?

→ Park in village or at The Ferry Inn (CV37 7QX, 01789 269883), head down Ferry Ln to descend to river. Steps just before last house.

10 mins, 52.2065, -1.6542

6 MARLCLIFF, BIDFORD-ON-AVON

Swim and jump into the deep water below the wooded slopes on this wide, slow-moving bend of the Avon.

→ A mile's walk downstream from Bidford Bridge (see entry), or signed Marlcliff off B4085, turning L down track where The Bank bends R to B50 4NT and parking by waterside.

1 min, 52.1531, -1.8657

7 CROPTHORNE MILL

One of Roger Deakin's favourite places, featured in 'Waterlog', with a variety of spots to get in above and below the weir.

→ Follow Mill Bank S out of Fladbury past WR10 2QA and park in lay-by R just after national speed limit signs. Cross road and follow path over stile down to mill pool.

5 mins, 52.1122, -2.0051

RIVERS & LAKES

8 COMPTON POOLS, COMBROOK

A delightful dip in a secluded location. Perfect for a picnic and a lazy summer afternoon with friends.

→ Combrook is signed off B4455/Fosse Way S about 1 mile N of CV35 9HS. Follow lane curving

through village, take fork L at church, park at end. Follow footpath L to and around shore L to swim entry through gate at end of trees.
5 mins, 52.1664, -1.5548

9 STUDLEY, RIVER ARROW

Great place to swim in a deep bowl at a bend in the river, overlooked by Studley Parish Church, and not far from the grand Gothic Revival castle (now a hotel).

→ Head E out of Studley on Church Rd to B80 7AB. Park L by the church or around bend by cemetery, walk on or back to kissing gate and follow footpath down to river. Road becomes footpath beyond bend for a view of the castle.
5 mins, 52.2713, -1.8835

10 KISLINGBURY MILL POOL, RIVER NENE

Charming, disused village mill pond, perfect for a splash around with the family, with deeper pools by the footbridge.

→ Kislingbury is signed from A4500 roundabout just W of Northampton. Follow road ¾ mile, turn R on Mill Lane, past NN7 4BD to bend L at end and park on road. River across road, footbridge L.
2 mins, 52.2288, -0.9845

11 MIDDLE LITTLETON TITHE BARN

Built for Evesham Abbey, this imposing 14th-century tithe barn is one of the largest remaining in the country, and Grade I listed. Mighty cruck frames support a vast stone roof.

→ Middle Littleton is signed from B4085 NE of Evesham. Turn off past WR11 8LJ, follow round bend to L and take signed L off bend R. Parking at barn.
1 min, 52.1217, -1.8849

12 ALL SAINTS, BURTON DASSETT

The 'cathedral in the hills' is a simple but lovely 12th-century parish church with a holy well nearby. Quirky beasts, both real and mythical, are carved on the pillars. The landscape above is curiously shaped by years of ironstone quarrying and topped by medieval beacon tower and panoramic views.

→ Country Park signed on B4451 heading W, after crossing M40. Follow 2 miles dir Gaydon, then L onto B4100 signed Country Park, opp CV47 2UD. Follow road into park and pay car park at summit. Follow road R down and over cattle grid to church. Well at 52.1607, -1.418.
1 min, 52.1599, -1.4189

HOLY WELL, SOUTHAM

[th]e crystal waters of possibly the oldest [ho]ly well in England, recorded in 998, [ca]scade from three carved stone faces [int]o a delightful pool before disappearing [un]derground. Part of the Holy Well Walk [ar]ound various historical remains at Southam.

→ From High St heading N through Southam, [tur]n L onto Park Lane, past CV47 0JA, then L [on]to Watton's Lane at end. At R bend with salt [bi]n, go straight on to small parking area L, or [pa]rk on street before bend. Walk on straight, [ro]ad becomes footpath, well is ¼ mile.

[ ] mins, 52.2534, -1.4007 ♿ 🚶

OLD ST JOHN'S CHURCH & WELL

[All] that remains of medieval Boughton village [are] these 12th-century church ruins and a [sa]cred spring. Legend says it is haunted by a [re]d-headed woman, who bestows a kiss that [br]ings death exactly a month later.

→ On A508 N out of Northampton turn R at [ro]undabout onto Vyse Road into Boughton, [fol]low 1½ miles in all, round bend to become [Ch]urch St then Moulton Lane out of village. [Pa]rk in large lay-by L shortly after NN2 8RE [an]d enter via creaky iron gates ahead.

[ ] mins, 52.2836, -0.8802 🚉 ♿

15 ST MARY'S ABBEY, KENILWORTH

Delightful 12th-century Augustinian abbey ruins in beautiful parkland to wander around. A ruined gatehouse, substantial barn, extensive cloister walls and pools, all next to St Nicholas Church with views across to Kenilworth Castle.

→ On A452/Bridge St in Kenilworth, car park is in corner of parkland, opp CV8 1BP. Ruins in cemetery beyond church.

2 mins, 52.3487, -1.5827 ♱ ⚓ 🚻 🍴

RUINS & FOLLIES

16 LEICESTER TOWER, EVESHAM

Hidden from view, this many-windowed octagonal folly was built in 1842 to commemorate Simon de Montfort, 13th-century Earl of Leicester and founder of the House of Commons. An obelisk nearby claims to mark where he fell in the Battle of Evesham; it overlooked the battlefield before the trees grew up.

→ On A4184/Greenhill heading N through Evesham turn L onto The Squires no through road opp WR11 4NT. Follow to end, park and cross stile beyond gate to tower in trees over field. Follow path around to 52.1078, -1.9520 for obelisk. Can be visited with other

memorials on a longer-looped Battlefield Walk from town.

5 mins, 52.1098, -1.9570

17 SWIMMING POOL, WELCOMBE HILLS

Mysterious Victorian pool with steps, set in a peaceful hillside nature reserve. Judging by the current clarity of water, swimming not advised! Below lies Margaret's Well, named for a woman spurned in love, said to have drowned herself there in 1580 and inspired the watery death of Shakespeare's Ophelia.

→ In Stratford on A4300/Birmingham Rd NW, turn N onto Clopton Rd at CV37 0TJ (opp A4390). Follow ¾ mile to park before cattle grid. Walk on along to end, into field, and up diagonally L to lower copse of trees. Well at 52.2105, -1.7056.

10 mins, 52.2096, -1.7048

18 GAVESTON CROSS

Hidden in the woods atop a hill stands this 200-year-old stone monument to the beheading in 1312 of England's own Rasputin-esqe figure, Piers Gaveston, by 'barons lawless as himself'.

→ From Kenilworth, take Warwick Road south through Leek Wootton, and after roundabout by golf club, take first R onto North Woodloes

no through road dir CV35 7QS (near A46/Warwick bypass roundabout). Park at end, climb over gate to R, walk up through field towards wood. Cross near middle of wood.

10 mins, 52.3050, -1.5772

19 THE SPECTACLES

Built around 1770, this castellated arch 'eyecatcher' was designed to frame a view from the estate, possibly of Moulton Church

→ Continue E from Old St John's Church (see entry) and take next L after ⅓ mile onto Spectacle Lane. Eyecatcher 250m on R.

1 min, 52.2870, -0.8763

WOODS & WILDLIFE

20 HAMPTON WOOD RESERVE

Charming and peaceful ancient woodland with an array of spring flowers, notably primroses and bluebells. Over 500 species beetles call this magical place home.

→ Sherbourne is signed from the A429 just S of M40. Follow Fulbrook Lane 1½ miles dir Hampton Lucy, past CV35 8AS to wildlife tru members' car park L at start of woods. Space for one car to pull off L at other end of woods with path in.

3 mins, 52.2380, -1.6287

HAY WOOD RESERVE

ncient woodland interspersed with trails.
uebells abound during the spring, and
ld garlic is plentiful later in the year.
ot muntjac deer and maybe throw up a
mmock and stargaze as night falls.

Turn off A4141 at (B93 0DH) onto Rising
ne signed Baddesley Clinton, turn L onto
ywood Lane after ½ mile following brown
gn, and pull off L by gated track after 1 mile.
llow track into woods.
mins, 52.3402, -1.6923 🔲👣⛰️🔥🔦🌳🐾🅿️

SNITTERFIELD BUSHES RESERVE

sea of bluebells bathed in dappled
nshine greet spring visitors to this
autiful, ancient woodland. Second World
ar bomb stores can be found in the centre
the woods.

From crossroads in Snitterfield (CV37 0LB)
llow Bearley Rd between school and church
or 1 mile. Park in lay-by L next to sign and
te. Follow path into woodland opposite.
min, 52.2410, -1.7085 🅿️🔀👣

HIGH WOOD & MEADOW

arming, secluded woodland filled with
ld cherry trees offering the perfect place

to read a book or take a romantic stroll.
Wonderful wild flower meadow adjacent.

→ From Farthingstone village head N on
Everdon Rd to R of church past NN12 8HB.
Take L at crossroads after 1 mile, continue
1 mile, park in lay-by R at end of woods on L.
Follow Knightley Way path L along wood edge
⅓ mile then turn R. Follow path to High Wood
(see wildlife trust sign).
15 mins, 52.1885, -1.1353 👣⛰️⛺🔥❄️🌳🍂🐾

24 UFTON FIELDS NATURE RESERVE

This tranquil, old limestone quarry offers
an abundance of wildlife: bluebells, orchids,
butterflies, dragonflies, birds, and toads.
The path meanders around the perimeter
where the diverse areas offer space for
picnics or den building and various crystal-
clear pools.

→ Ufton Fields signed of A425 W of Southam
at Ufton roundabout. Car park is ½ mile on L
with bar over entrance at 2.1m height. Pools
52.2481, -1.4452.
5 mins, 52.2497, -1.4464 🌳👣🐾🔀

25 HARBURY SPOIL BANK RESERVE

This tucked-away nature reserve is on
a bank of clay excavated in 1845 for
the construction of the Leamington to

Oxford railway line, which now runs next to it. A fantastic quiet spot to find wild strawberries, orchids and other wild flowers.

→ On the B4452 ½ mile SE from Harbury, dir Deppers Bridge and CV47 2TA, park in the small lay-by L just before waymarked footpath into reserve, 52.2353, -1.4380.
3 mins, 52.2354, -1.4354 🚂🐑🚶

WONDERFUL WINDMILLS

26 CHESTERTON WINDMILL
Elegantly crowning the hillside overlooking Chesterton village, this 380-year-old windmill offers stunning views across the local landscape from under its arches. Take a picnic for a romantic al fresco lunch.

→ From B4087 S out of Warwick through Whitnash, take R signed Leamington Football Club and Harbury past CV33 9QA. Follow 3 miles, crossing Fosse Way, and turn R onto Windmill Lane signed Chesterton at top of hill. Park in lay-by on either side, follow path through gate R to windmill on skyline.
5 mins, 52.2312, -1.4908 📷🚶🐑🅿️

27 TYSOE WINDMILL
Standing majestically atop Tysoe Hill, this curious 12-sided, 18th-century windmill

affords glorious views over the countryside. Annual fundraising run to the top in June. Lovely tea room in Village Stores (CV35 0S 01295 688333).

→ In Upper Tysoe follow Shipston Rd (CV35 0TR) SW out of village. As you leave village, pull off to L on bend just after national speed limit sign. Walk up road for 20m, turn L onto footpath and follow uphill through field.
20 mins, 52.0817, -1.5175 📷🐑🅿️🚶

WILD FLOWER MEADOWS

28 RADWAY MEADOWS RESERVE
Breathtaking swathes of buttercups, orchids and wild flowers adorn the hillside in this tucked away South Warwickshire vale. Forage for haws and crab apples in the ancient hedgerows in autumn.

→ From Radway village (CV35 0UE) follow Tysoe Rd around church and SW, then turn L onto King John's Lane no through road at ber R. Pull off R near footpath sign after 150m.
3 mins, 52.1232, -1.4672 🌸🐑🚶

29 TASKER'S MEADOW & STOCKTON CUTTING RESERVES
A delightful wild flower meadow beside the Grand Union Canal, alive with orchids and

29

...tterflies in summer. Relax with a picnic ...d listen to the grasshoppers. The railway ...tting alongside offers further walks.

Follow A426 2 miles NE from Southam, over ...nal and turn immediately L, opp CV23 8HG, ...d park L. Walk back over bridge and through ...gned gate opp into meadow.

...mins, 52.2826, -1.3576 🚶🪧♿

BLOSSOM TRAIL, EVESHAM

...wonderful display of apple, plum and pear ...ossoms is to be found in the many orchards ...attered around the pretty villages of the ...ale of Evesham. From mid-March to mid-...ay, and the trail changes each year, so pick ... a leaflet.

Ellenden Farm shop (WR11 8LU, 01386 ...70296) or Clive's of Cropthorne (WR10 3NE, ...7772 980912, 52.1005, -2.0156) are both ...ood places to pick up a leaflet and start.

...mins, 52.1395, -1.9289 ♿

SLOW FOOD

THE STAG, OFFCHURCH

...iendly 16th-century thatched pub serving ...cal ales and delicious food including local ...me and inventive vegetarian dishes. ...vely terrace and garden.

→ Welsh Road, Offchurch, CV33 9AQ, 01926 425801.
52.2896, -1.4740 🅿🍴

32 THE EBRINGTON ARMS

Award-winning inn dating back to the 15th-century, tucked away in a small Cotswolds village offering outstanding local food and drink. Sumptuous rooms for B&B. Booking recommended.

→ Ebrington, GL55 6NH, 01386 593223.
52.0578, -1.7318 🍴🛏

33 MILL WOODHOUSE CAFÉ, TALTON MILL

Feast on a fabulous full English breakfast made from their home-reared bacon and sausages whilst relaxing next to the millstream, then stock up at the artisan butchery. Open on Friday and Saturday.

→ Newbold on Stour, CV37 8UG, 01789 459140.
52.1218, -1.6485 🍴

34 HILL TOP FARM

Family-run farm shop stocking the best seasonal produce alongside delicious, home-made food in the café. Glamping also available, see Hilltop Hideaways listing.

31

32

→ Fosse Way, Hunningham, CV33 9EL, 01926 632978 (glamping 07966 797474).
52.3013, -1.4493

35 THE ROYAL OAK, WHATCOTE

Sympathetically renovated, stone-built village pub combining fine dining with classic pub touches and great local ales. High-quality food using local ingredients won it a Michelin star in the 2020 Guide.

→ 2 Upper Farm Barn, Whatcote, CV36 5EF, 01295 688100.
52.0992, -1.5631

36 THE BOOT INN, LAPWORTH

This charming village inn with a quirky country-chic interior combines high-class food with the finest wines and cask ales, all in a country pub atmosphere.

→ Old Warwick Rd, Lapworth, B94 6JU, 01564 782464.
52.3381, -1.7360

37 KING'S HEAD, ASTON CANTLOW

Brett Sandland is delighted to welcome guests to this traditional 15th-century village inn. Original oak beams and open fires along with exceptional food and drink create a wonderful experience.

→ 21 Bearley Road, Aston Cantlow, B95 6HY, 01789 488242.
52.2372, -1.7986

38 THE KITCHEN AT FARNBOROUGH

Jo and Anthony are obsessive about food, and you will find sumptuous seasonal dishes using locally supplied ingredients here. An elegant and welcoming listed 16th-century inn; in summer the terraced gardens are a real delight.

→ Main Street, Farnborough, OX17 1DZ, 01295 690615.
52.1440, -1.3669

COSY PUBS

39 THE FLEECE INN, BRETFORTON

Built around 1425, The Fleece is steeped in history and character and owned by the National Trust. Snugs, open fires, beams, nooks and crannies and protective witch marks on the hearths and doors, combined with excellent, home-made food and local ales, make for the perfect visit whatever the season.

→ The Cross, Bretforton, WR11 7JE, 01386 831173.
52.0920, -1.8652

40 THE CASE IS ALTERED, ROWINGTON

An unspoilt, drinks-only pub serving traditional cask ale. Brewery memorabilia and traditional interior is kept spotless by friendly, long-serving landlady, Jackie. No children or dogs, and a fine for using your mobile phone!

→ Case Lane, Five Ways, CV35 7JD, 01926 484206.
52.3280, -1.6718

41 THE RED LION, HUNNINGHAM

Delightful pub offering good food and a wonderful beer garden next to a river. Help yourself to one of the many blankets or deckchairs to while away a summer's afternoon and evening.

→ Main Street, Hunningham, CV33 9DY, 01926 632715.
52.3138, -1.4540

42 THE HOWARD ARMS, ILMINGTON

Heart-warming archetypal village pub, with stone floors, roaring open fires and relaxed friendly charm. Don't miss the local Grumpy Frog cider and Spirit of Ilmington apple brandy. Excellent rooms available.

→ Lower Green, Ilmington, CV36 4LT, 01608 682226.
52.0912, -1.6904

43 CASTLE INN

A pub in an 18th-century folly castle, with glorious (and appropriately military) views over the vale of the Civil War Battle of Edgehill. This is a perfect upmarket pub offering 4* accommodation, locally sourced food and Hook Norton ales.

→ Edge Hill, Oxfordshire, OX15 6DJ, 01295 670255.
52.1237, -1.4555

44 THE CHANDLERS ARMS, EPWELL

This 16th-century stone local is the hub of a pretty village. Relax with a fine selection of real ales in the delightful garden.

→ Sibford Road, Epwell, OX15 6LH, 01295 780153.
52.0595, -1.4856

45 THE OLD BULL, INKBERROW

Picture-perfect Tudor pub with high ceiling and bulging black and white walls. It may have served Shakespeare and is reputed to be the model for The Bull in 'The Archers', hence the collection of memorabilia on show. A fine selection of real ales and welcoming log fires.

Village Green, Inkberrow, WR7 4DZ,
386 792428.
.2136, -1.9793 [icons]

YE OLDE SARACEN'S HEAD
cosy, 16th-century village pub mixing
traditional and contemporary, with specialist
steak and wood-fired pizza menus. High-
quality food served in a home-from-home
atmosphere.
Balsall Street, Balsall Common, CV7 7AS,
676 533862.
.3911, -1.6729 [icons]

THE OLDE COACH HOUSE
rustic bar and contemporary restaurant
offering good quality food, with
accommodation available.
Main Street, Ashby St Ledgers, CV23 8UN,
788 890349.
.3087, -1.1690 [icons]

ALTHORP COACHING INN
everything you could want in an old coaching
inn: beams, snug alcoves, log fires, cobbled
courtyard and a charming garden, plus a
good selection of real ales and great food.
Main Street, Great Brington, NN7 4JA,
.604 770651.
.2782, -1.0244 [icons]

RUSTIC HAVENS

TINYWOOD HOMES
selection of unique tiny, handcrafted
cabins that pack a lot in, with hot tubs and
BBQs and some big enough for families.
online or email bookings only.
Snowford Grange, Southam, CV47 9QE,
tinywoodhomes.com
.2916, -1.4307 [icon]

JESTERS SHEPHERD HUT
enjoy the glorious Warwickshire countryside
from this well-appointed shepherds' hut set
on an eco-focused farm.
Hill Farm, Priors Hardwick, CV47 7SP,
canopyandstars.co.uk
.1969, -1.3203 [icons]

HOBBIT HOUSE, DODFORD
quaint, little space crafted out of local
reclaimed logs. The turf roof and wonky
lines make it the perfect quirky, romantic
getaway.
Honeymoon Cottage, Dodford, NN7 4SZ,
canopyandstars.co.uk
.2406, -1.0989 [icon]

CAMP & SLEEP

52 THE BATH HOUSE
Beautiful octagonal folly for two with shell
decorations and an unusual cold plunge pool
in the basement for the brave.
→ Bath Hill Wood, Walton, landmarktrust.org.uk.
52.1722, -1.5773 [icons]

53 MOUSLEY HOUSE FARM CAMPSITE
Quiet, family-friendly campsite with endless
views over the beautiful Warwickshire
countryside and glamping options available.
The Case is Altered pub (see listing) is a
short walk away.
→ Case Lane, Rowington, CV35 7JG,
07443 475434.
52.3242, -1.6815 [icons]

54 COTTAGE OF CONTENT, BARTON
Traditional English country pub with rooms
and a quiet camping field of 25 grass pitches.
Eat, drink, stay the night!
→ 15 Welford Road, Barton, Bidford-on-Avon,
B50 4NP, 01789 772279.
52.1590, -1.8448 [icons]

55 ST PETER'S CHURCH, WOLFHAMPCOTE
'Champ' with family and friends in this simple
and elegant, rural 14th-century church. Once
a village lay over the lane in front. Paths,
a canal, and dismantled railway lines to
explore nearby.
→ St Peter's Church, Wolfhampcote,
CV23 8AR, champing.co.uk.
52.2833, -1.2249 [icons]

56 THE GREEN MAN, LONG ITCHINGTON
An English cottage garden camping field with
only the most basic facilities – no showers! –
and warm welcome in the pub. Bob's fish and
chip van visits Friday nights.
→ Church Road, Long Itchington, CV47 9PW,
01926 812208.
52.2829, -1.4011 [icons]

57 HILLTOP HIDEAWAYS
Camping heaven on a working farm, with a
farm shop and café onsite (see Hill Top Farm
listing). Either bring your own tent or rent
one of their furnished bell tents, shepherds'
huts or wooden cabins, each with glorious
views of the rolling countryside. There's a
children's play area, farm animals and the
pretty River Leam runs through the farm.
→ Hilltop Farm, Fosse Way, Hunningham,
CV33 9EL, 07966 797474.
52.3013, -1.4503

50

51

52

53

55

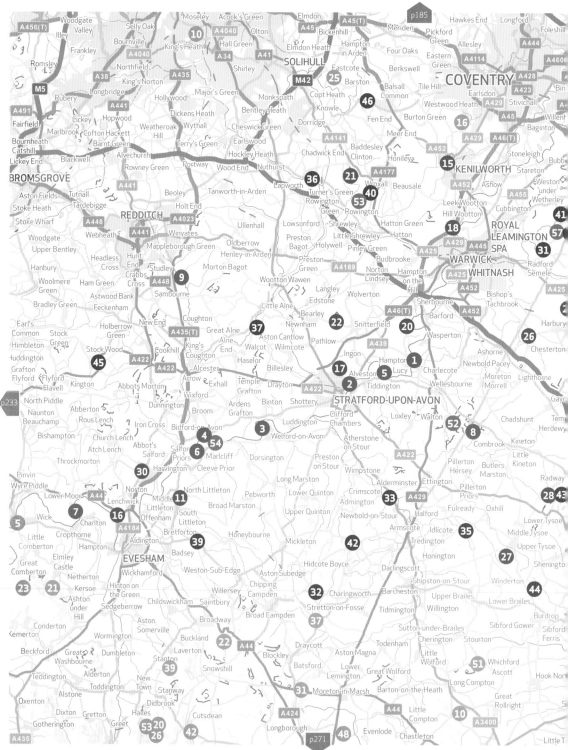

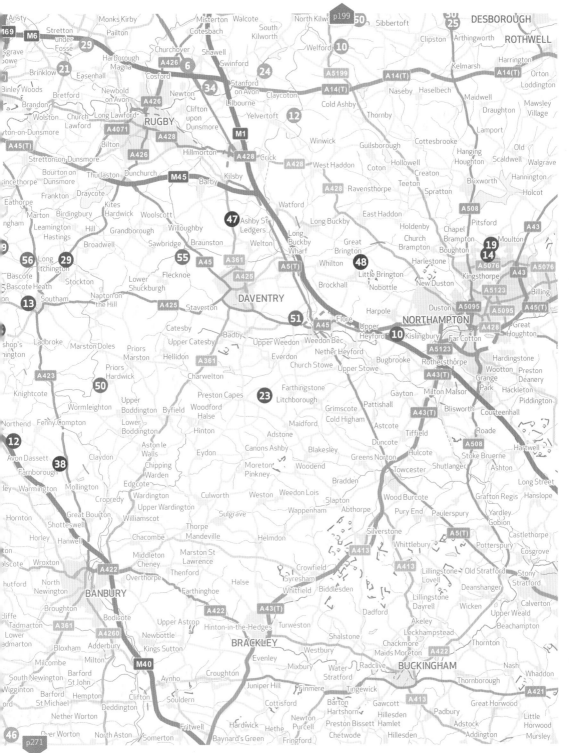

WYE VALLEY

Our perfect weekend

→ **Kayak** or swim down from Kerne Bridge to Symonds Yat and a warm welcome at the Saracen's Head, where a roaring log fire or a sunny veranda awaits.

→ **Refresh** yourself in the crystal-clear plunge pool of St Anthony's well and stroll around the Forest of Dean Sculpture Trail in search of wild works of art.

→ **Jump** into the cooling waters of the Wye beneath the bridge at Redbrook, then sup a beer or two at the Boat Inn at Penallt next door and admire the beautiful view from the terrace.

→ **Wander** through the woods to the majestic Hundred Trees, then pitch up at the Forest and Wye Valley Camping Site with its fascinating tufa waterfall.

→ **Source** amazing local produce from the Brockweir and Hewelsfield Village Shop and Kingstone Brewery for a picnic in the grounds of the beautiful St Mary's Church at Tintern.

→ **Hike** up to the Devil's Pulpit with its stunning views over the valley below, or hide away in the lost ruins of Lancaut church.

→ **Seek** out King Arthur's Cave high above the River Wye, then discover the location of the Suck Stone, where ledges and overhanging trees offer the perfect wild hideaway.

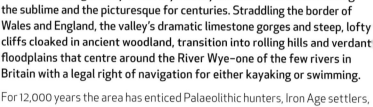

The breathtaking beauty of the Wye Valley has attracted those seeking the sublime and the picturesque for centuries. Straddling the border of Wales and England, the valley's dramatic limestone gorges and steep, lofty cliffs cloaked in ancient woodland, transition into rolling hills and verdant floodplains that centre around the River Wye—one of the few rivers in Britain with a legal right of navigation for either kayaking or swimming.

For 12,000 years the area has enticed Palaeolithic hunters, Iron Age settlers, Romans, Saxons and Victorian Industrialists, all drawn to the river, its geology and fertile plains, and leaving relics for us to discover and explore.

The UK's fifth-longest river, the meandering Wye offers endless hours of fun with many entry and exit points. Hire kayaks from one of the companies along its length, float downstream on inflatable rings, or just let the current guide you as you swim its silky depths. Kayak from Kerne Bridge or swim down to Lower Lydbrook and spend the day with a picnic, in and out of the water, splashing around in the rapids and discovering its deeper pools. For a longer canoe, carry on to Symonds Yat and the popular Saracen's Head pub. Other great swims in the area can be found at The Biblins with its old wooden suspension bridge and under the historic railway viaduct of Redbrook Bridge.

Symonds Yat has become synonymous with the Wye Valley, where rocks and overhangs such as King Arthur's Cave have provided shelter and wild camping spots for millennia. Natural hilltops and promontories afford vistas over the glorious countryside where sightings of peregrines, goshawks and the rare whitebeam are commonplace. Symonds Yat Rock, with its old miners' track up from the river, the Buck Stone and the Suck Stone all showcase the surrounding landscape at its best.

Further south are Lancaut church ruins, set in a nature reserve dotted with old limekiln remains, and the legendary Wintour's Leap, where Sir John is said to have survived a leap from the cliff whilst being pursued by Parliamentary forces. Over the border into Wales, the grand structure of Tintern Abbey dominates the valley and draws the crowds, but delve deeper and you will find overlooked gems and relics of bygone eras. Seek out the atmospheric remains of St Mary's Church, its overgrown ruins now offering sanctuary to the wildlife as well as us. For the more energetic, a rigorous walk up to the Devil's Pulpit offers stunning views back to the abbey over the Wye; the beautiful vistas here truly do, as Wordsworth described it, 'connect the landscape with the quiet of the sky'.

4

LOWER REDBROOK, RIVER WYE

gentle, deep swim under the imposing old
on railway bridge with a great cider pub.

▶ In Lower Redbrook, 2 miles SE of Monmouth
A466, park in pay car park opp NP25 4LP.
ollow path from corner down to old railway
ridge and cross to other side. Swim anywhere
ownstream of tiny Boat Inn (see listing).
mins, 51.7849, -2.6739

THE BIBLINS, RIVER WYE

n a gentle meander of the Wye, this beach
nder an old, wooden suspension bridge
ffers shelving access to deep pools. For
ore spots, follow river downstream on
ther bank.

▶ From A40 interchange for Whitchurch
r just S of it if travelling S) follow signs for
ymonds Yat (West) then Crockers Ash, S on
side of A40, past service station, then turn
onto Sandiway Lane past HR9 6D. Go R at
rk by cream house, then L signed Biblins at
-junction. After ½ mile turn R on hairpin at
oward Campsite (see listing) on signed track
Biblins, park R in lay-by after 150m. Follow
iblins track to river.
0 mins, 51.8266, -2.6553

3 KERNE BRIDGE, RIVER WYE

The ideal start to a 2¼-mile swim, kayak
or float downstream to Lower Lydbrook.
Beautiful countryside, dappled shade and
slow, meandering curves in the river with a
few shallow rapids.

→ On B4234 in Kerne Bridge, 3 miles S of Ross-
on-Wye and 350m after passing B4229 junction
to Monmouth, park in car park R (before HR9
5QX). Follow slipway down to launch.
2 mins, 51.8655, -2.6080

4 SYMONDS YAT, RIVER WYE

Beautiful stretch of the Wye with a small,
sandy bay in a meadow, shelving to a deep
swim. Understandably busy in summer.

→ From A40 interchange for Whitchurch
follow signs to Symonds Yat (West). Follow
road 1.5km into village and bear L down steep
lane past HR9 6BL to Ye Old Ferrie Inn (01600
890232) and car park at end. Walk upstream
100m.
5 mins, 51.8464, -2.6439

5 LORD'S GROVE, RIVER WYE

Another great place to enjoy the Wye, with a
handy little pontoon to dive in from. Walk up
the bank and drift back down the river.

→ Park as for Lower Redbrook (see entry) and
follow footpath upstream to pontoon for ½ mile.
For a longer swim walk to 51.8001, -2.6912.
10 mins, 51.7931, -2.6833

6 LIVOX QUARRY & WYE GORGE

Deep, clear blue waters and white beaches in
dramatic, wild quarry amphitheatre on shore
of the great Wye Gorge. Complicated access.

→ A466 for 2½ miles N of Chepstow, through
St Arvans. Field gate on R opp Livox Cottages
and bus stop (NP16 6HF, 51.6746, -2.6747).
Follow footpath down to woods and pick
up track alongside quarry. Footpath runs
50m south-east of lakeshore, inside quarry
boundary, but has been blocked in places.
Footpath eventually leads on to the Wye Gorge.
Road entrance often has security. Private.
30 mins, 51.6752, -2.6623

7 WOORGREENS NATURE RESERVE

Once open-cast mines, these rewilded
quarries are now a secluded nature reserve
home to abundant birdlife, dragonflies,
newts and lizards. Come in late spring to
hear the delightful call of the cuckoo.

→ From Coleford follow B4226 Speech

House Road dir Cinderford to car park L ⅓ mile past Speech House Hotel (GL16 7EL, 01594 822607). Road to R leads to lake. Shorter walk from smaller parking area L after another ⅓ mile.
15 mins, 51.8135, -2.5388

8 PENTWYN FARM SSSI

A rare example of traditionally managed farmland, with glorious wild flower meadows, barn and orchard, and magnificent views over the Wye Valley. Best in late spring and summer. See Gwent Wildlife for a map of the reserve.
→ Heading N through Penallt, take fork R at Celtic cross to the Inn at Penallt (NP25 4SE, 01600 772765). Park on grass by barn and walk to end of farm track.
5 mins, 51.7810, -2.6927

9 SCULPTURE TRAIL, FOREST OF DEAN

A delightful walk through a range of terrains to find a collection of unique sculptures, commissioned specifically for their sites.
→ Park as for Woorgreens Lake (see entry). Follow footpath W to pick up Sculpture Trail.
5 mins, 51.8057, -2.5605

10 TUFA WATERFALL, SLADE BROOK

A beautiful woodland walk carries you to the longest tufa waterfall in Britain, gently tumbling over the calcified dams. Stunning!
→ Follow footpath sign from entrance to Forest and Wye Valley Camping Site (GL15 6QU, see listing), take path downhill until you meet Slade Brook.
15 mins, 51.7459, -2.6303

11 HUNDRED TREES AVENUE

A majestic row of twisted, ancient trees on the edge of a beautiful woodland.
→ Take A466 NE from Llandogo and park on L at junction signed The Narth Pennarth. Follow road over river (Bigsweir Bridge) and pick up Offa's Dyke footpath to R, follow down through meadow to tree line.
20 mins, 51.7364, -2.6648

12 DINGLE WOOD

A pretty little wood with a carpet of wild garlic undulating over the curious 'scowles' or excavations left from open-cast iron mining.
→ Take B4228 NW from Coleford. Park in lay-by R after 1 mile by entry to sawmill, beyond GL16 8NS. Cross road and follow path to furthest point ahead to find scowles, 51.7991, -2.6402.
15 mins, 51.8008, -2.6358

13 FINDALL CHIMNEY

owering air shaft linked to Findall Mine
tanding proudly above a forested mining
cowle' and cave. Ideal wild camp spot.

→ Park in Upper Soudley near Top Road, GL14
TY. Enter Old Staple-edge wood via pathway
 51.7908, -2.5035, near the T-junction sign.
ollow the path uphill until you reach the
ld mining forest track. Follow this through
wo switchbacks to a crossroads, turn R to
himney.

0 mins, 51.7928, -2.5069 🏕🔦🍴⛰

14 DARKHILL IRONWORKS

ascinating and extensive remains of the
irst ironworks to produce steel railway lines,
 1857. Lovely walks in the wider area.

→ Leave B4228 S of Coleford through Sling
ast GL16 8JJ and on ½ mile to car park L
00m beyond crossroads. Follow path to the
onworks.

0 mins, 51.7766, -2.5957 🚶🏕🍴🚂

5 MIRYSTOCK BRIDGE & TUNNEL

idden in plain sight in an old cutting are the
losed entrance to an elegant oval tunnel
spelled Mierystock) and this bridge from

the disused railway, which you can walk over.
The cutting is wet, boots advisable.

→ Take B4234 S from Lydbrook. Park in lay-by
on L by road signs just before A4136 (GL17
9LT). Turn L onto A4136, after 140m cross
onto footpath to tunnel and bridge.

15 mins, 51.8282, -2.5606 🚶🚉🔦🍴🚂🏕

16 TINTERN QUARRY & RAILWAY

Interesting walk to an old railway tunnel
entrance and lines.

→ On B4228 2½ miles N of Chepstow, pull off
by entrance to Tintern Quarry (NP16 7JW). Follow
lane opp to Offa's Dyke Path, follow S ½ mile and
turn R down to steps near quarry building, follow
old railway line L ½ mile to tunnel.

45 mins, 51.6732, -2.6555 🚉🚶

17 SHAKEMANTLE QUARRY

Intriguing old quarry workings exposing
great ribs of dolomite. Larger quarry popular
with climbers but no climbing Mar–June when
peregrines nest.

→ Park at the end of Tramway Rd, Ruspidge
and continue along footpath into wood, past
larger quarry on L (51.7997, -2.5043). Follow
lower path to R for ½ mile, dolomite ribs on L.

5 mins, 51.7951, -2.5040 🏕🔦🚶🚂🧗

ROCKS AND VISTAS

18 SUCK STONE, HIGH MEADOW WOODS
Weighing in excess of 30,000 tons, the imposing old Suck Stone is the largest detached block of rock in the British Isles. Natural ledges and overhanging trees provide a perfect wild camp spot.

→ From A4136 through Staunton, turn N onto Wellmeadow, then R onto Reddings Lane, GL16 8NZ. Follow ½ mile and park L opp driveway. Walk on ⅓ mile then turn L onto Wysis Way.
15 mins, 51.8229, -2.6657

19 WINTOUR'S LEAP
This dramatic cliff is reputedly where Royalist Sir John Wintour jumped to safety into the Wye astride his horse in the Civil War to escape pursuing Parliamentary forces.

→ Heading S out of Woodcroft on the B4288 pull off L opposite NP16 7QL. Walk back 50m to small gate opposite and follow Offa's Dyke path towards Wye.
5 mins, 51.6628, -2.6639

20 THE BUCK STONE, STAUNTON
Commanding wild views across the Wye valley, the striking Buck Stone used to rock until it was toppled by a rowdy group in the 19th century. After that mishap it was secured in place.

→ On A4136 W out of Staunton, take first L after White Horse Inn. R at triangle and Meend Cottage to GL16 8PD. Bear L at next fork and park in lay-by immediately R. Head back to walk up R fork track for 300m, around curve, to rock on L.
4 mins, 51.8069, -2.6664

21 SYMONDS YAT ROCK
Once the site of an Iron Age hillfort, this rock is now is home to peregrines, goshawks sparrowhawks and buzzards. Spectacular views 150m above the dramatic Wye Valley.

→ Walk up miners' path from The Saracen's Head pub (HR9 6JL, see listing), or head N from Berry Hill on Grove Road through Hillersland and park in pay car park L after GL16 7NZ. Follow trail to rock. 40 mins from pub, 10 mins from car park.
40 mins, 51.8408, -2.6346

22 COPPET HILL
Stunning sunset hilltop in a nature reserve, perfect for kite-flying, picnics and stargazing.

→ Heading S through Goodrich, take L fork signed Courtfield and no through road opposite Post Office over B4229. After ⅓ mile

ark R on triangle at R turn to HR9 6JF. Follow gned footpath up from triangle through oods to summit.
5 mins, 51.8586, -2.6179 🏞️🚶‍♂️✳️

3 DEVIL'S PULPIT, TINTERN
egend has it that the Devil taunted the onks working below at Tintern from this eautiful vantage point high above the Wye.
▶ Park in one of the car parks near abbey in ntern (NP16 6TE). Walk over the footbridge cross the Wye and follow LH fork in path phill to meet Offa's Dyke Path. Follow signs o to pulpit.
5 mins, 51.6925, -2.6630 🏞️🚴🚶‍♂️👥🍴➡️

4 PRISK WOOD RESERVE
enallt produced mill stones from xceptionally hard quartz rock known as udding-stone. Myriad old quarry workings nd mossy millstones are to be found in this ood and around the river.
▶ Take Lone Lane W of Penallt. Pull off L arefully just before Cherry Orchard Farm NP25 4AJ), walk on to footpath R and down to the woods and L to the old loading bay.
mins, 51.7791, -2.6764 🏞️🚵🐾💧

25 GARDEN CLIFF, WESTBURY-ON-SEVERN
Quiet, secluded spot to enjoy views of the Severn Estuary. Rapid erosion makes this one of the finest locations for picking up loose fossils from the shore – no removal from the cliff, as it is an SSSI.
➔ Heading E out of Westbury-on-Severn on A48 turn R onto Rodley Road at crossroads, then R onto Strand Lane down to river. Park at without blocking private road (or park at top of Strand Lane if no space here) then walk through gap. Cliffs on L, far end is best.
3 mins, 51.8172, -2.4145 🚶‍♂️🚵

26 HAROLD STONES & VIRTUOUS WELL
In Trellech village – 'Tre' meaning settlement and 'llech' meaning slab – these standing stones were supposedly erected by the last Saxon King, Harold, but are probably 3,000 years older. Nearby is the Virtuous Well, a place of pilgrimage in the 17th century.
➔ Park in Trellech; The Lion Inn (NP25 4PA, 01600 860322 is a cheery pub) and follow B4293 S to stones on L 160m after fork in road. From same fork, take Llandogo Road 250m for well in field L with small iron gate (NP25 4PZ).
10 mins, 51.7428, -2.7262 ✝️🚵

27 KING ARTHUR'S CAVE

This impressive double-opening cave lies 87m above the Wye, at the base of a rocky outcrop in a woodland clearing. Flint tools and bones, including mammoth, found in its multiple chambers indicate it was occupied during the Upper Palaeolithic. Later claimed occupants, such as the Kings Vortigern or Arthur, left no traces.

→ Park as for swimming at the Biblins (see entry), continue down road 60m and take R footpath.

5 mins, 51.8367, -2.6589

28 ST ANTHONY'S WELL

Wild camp in hammocks strung from trees next to this wonderful stone-lined well and refresh yourself in the famously cold, crystal-clear bath: immersion in its waters was said to benefit those suffering from arthritis.

→ From Mitcheldean take Abenhall Road S signed Flaxley 1¾ miles, turn R on Lower Spout Lane S at GL17 0EA and park on the bend after ¼ mile. Take the well-worn footpath into woods to W and follow stream.

5 mins, 51.8392, -2.4796

29 ST MARY'S CHURCH, TINTERN

Seek out the quietly beautiful St Mary's Church, once a retreat for the monks who lived in the valley below at Tintern. Its overgrown ruins offering sanctuary to the wildlife. A peaceful place.

→ Park in Tintern (e.g. Wireworks car park NP16 6TQ). From junction in front of Royal George Hotel (NP16 6SF, 01291 689205), take unnamed road to L of Forge Road. At top of rise take grassy path R which winds up by the church.

15 mins, 51.6965, -2.6811

30 ST JAMES' CHURCH, LANCAUT

Embraced by a wide coil of the Wye, this picturesque peninsula hides a lost medieval village, and only its church is left to see. The walk takes you through Lancaut Nature Reserve SSSI, with steep, wooded slopes leading down the to the river. Bring walking boots for the steep and rough paths and look out for the old limekilns.

→ Lancaut is signed off B4228 N of Woodcroft, dir NP16 7JB. Turn L and park in lay-by L after ¼ mile. Signed paths to church.

20 mins, 51.6651, -2.6708

SLOW FOOD

31 THE PANTRY, ST BRIAVELS

Mary greets everyone with a smile in her café and deli with wonderful, locally sourced produce. A great place for picnic provisions.
→ East Street, St Briavels, GL15 6TA, 01594 530740.
51.7376, -2.6399 🍴

32 SEVERN & WYE SMOKERY

Top-quality café, restaurant and shop selling a range of smoked fish and meat, complemented by other local produce.
→ Chaxhill, Westbury-on-Severn, GL14 1QW, 01452 760191.
51.8268, -2.3830 🍴

33 SEVERN CIDER

Award-winning, traditionally crafted cider, perry and vinegar from an onsite shop also stocking other local products.
→ The Old Vicarage, Awre, Newnham, GL14 1EL, 01594 510282.
51.7732, -2.4270 🏪

34 KINGSTONE BREWERY

Traditional, award-winning micro-brewery. Regular events, and a range of glamping options in the Hop Garden next door. Open Mon–Fri.
→ Tintern, NP16 7NX, 01291 680111.
51.7051, -2.6736 🏪⛺

35 BROCKWEIR & HEWELSFIELD SHOP

Award-winning community shop and café selling fresh local produce.
→ Mill Hill, Brockweir, Chepstow, NP16 7NW, 01291 689995.
51.7124, -2.6588 🍴🏪

36 THE POTTING SHED, WHITCHURCH

A much-loved, retro-styled café, restaurant and B&B serving good, honest food in a relaxed environment
→ Whitchurch, HR9 6DJ, 01600 892830.
51.8530, -2.6572 🍴

COSY PUBS

37 THE SARACEN'S HEAD INN

A traditional pub, loved for its views over the Wye from the sunny terrace. Take the hand-pulled ferry across the river, or use as a base to head up to Symonds Yat Rock (see entry).
→ Symonds Yat East, HR9 6JL, 01600 890435.
51.8404, -2.6383 🚣🏊🚶🍴

38 THE PENNY FARTHING INN

A recently refurbished 17th-century bar and restaurant with a great garden and reputatio
→ Aston Crews, HR9 7LW, 01989 750366.
51.9066, -2.4773 🏪

39 THE BOAT INN, PENALLT

One of the oldest public houses in the area, serving a range of local ales, ciders and foo A special place with a steep, terraced garde tucked in by the River Wye and a footbridg to Lower Redbrook (see entry).
→ Lone Lane, Penallt, Monmouth NP25 4AJ, 01600 712615.
51.7848, -2.6743 🏪🏪

40 THE OSTRICH INN, NEWLAND

A charming, traditional village pub, known for its eight changing ales and delicious, locally sourced and seasonal food.
→ Newland, Forest of Dean, GL16 8NP, 01594 833260.
51.7832, -2.6486 🏪🏪🍴

41 THE ANCHOR INN, TINTERN

Originally a cider mill and grain store for the monks: parts of the inn date back to the 12th century. Stunning location right by the abbe
→ Chapel Hill, Tintern, NP16 6TE, 01291 689582.
51.6979, -2.6783 🍴🏪

RUSTIC HAVENS

42 THE DONKEY SHED

Vast views over the Wye Valley in this modestly named but beautifully modern little house hidden up a tiny lane.
→ Hillside House, Whitebrook, NP25 4TU, sawdays.co.uk.
51.7540, -2.6724 🏕🎴

43 BROOKBANK FOLLY

Cosy, hand-built timbered cottage for two, full of crooked charm and romance.
→ Mitcheldean, Forest of Dean, sykescottages.co.uk.
51.8494, -2.4856 🏕🐾🎿

CAMP & SLEEP

44 BEECHES FARM CAMPSITE

Sweeping views across the Wye Valley from the hills above Tintern Abbey. Closed in winte
→ The Beeches Farm, Miss Grace's Lane, Tidenham Chase, NP16 7JR, 07791 540016.
51.7020, -2.6550 ⛺🎴

5 FOREST & WYE VALLEY CAMPING SITE

very friendly, family-run campsite with
spotless facilities, a little shop and café, and
glamping pod. Walks to spectacular tufa
waterfall (see listing). Delightful.

→ Bearse Farm, St Briavels, Lydney GL15 6QU,
01594 530777.
51.7436, -2.6237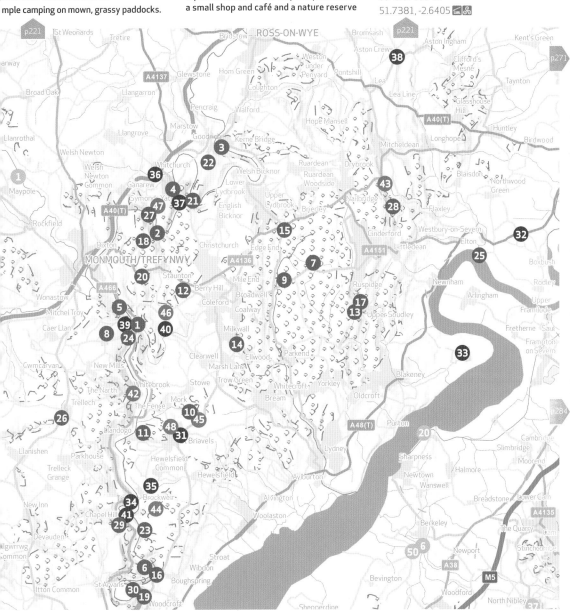

6 CHERRY ORCHARD FARM

Simple camping on mown, grassy paddocks.

The farm borders the road but it's a quiet
village location. Hot showers, no electric hook-
ups but caravans are welcome. B&B available.
The Ostrich Inn is nearby (see listing).

→ Newland, Coleford GL16 8NP,
01594 832212
51.7907, -2.6483

47 DOWARD PARK CAMPSITE

A peaceful, out-of-the-way campsite with
a small shop and café and a nature reserve

next door, above the Symonds Yat gorge and
Biblins (see entry). Closed in winter.

→ Great Doward, HR9 6BP, 01600 890438.
51.8379, -2.6567

48 ST BRIAVELS CASTLE YHA

Characterful youth hostel in an 800-year-old
castle, with a variety of accommodation.

→ Church Street, St Briavels, GL15 6RG,
0345 3719042.
51.7381, -2.6405

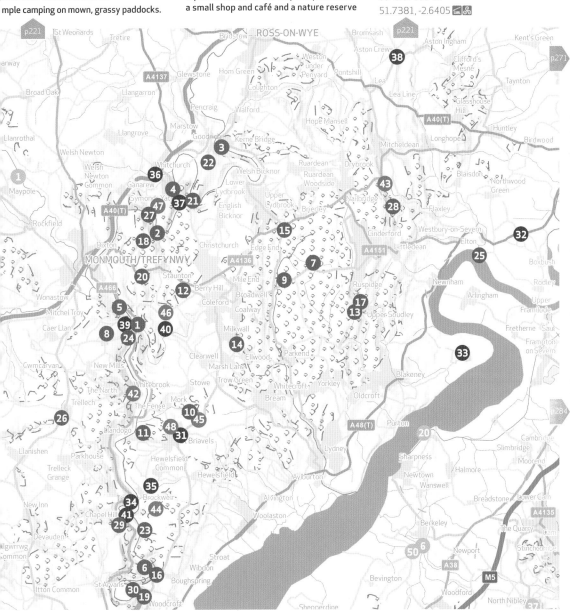

NORTH COTSWOLDS

Our perfect weekend

→ **Swim** below the Boat Inn and marvel at the Tithe Barn roof in Ashleworth, then seek out the quirky Hartpury Bee Shelter.

→ **Explore** Spoonley Wood for the Roman villa remains, slowly being reclaimed by nature.

→ **Ascend** the hill to Cromwell's Stone along the Cotswold Way, before stopping to try the chilli chocolate from Farmcote Herb and Chilli Farm.

→ **Plunge** into Witcombe Waters for a refreshing dip on a hot summer's day.

→ **Treat** yourself to delicious picnic goodies from Primrose Vale Farm Shop and feast among the wild flowers at Crickley Hill.

→ **Clamber** up Leckhampton Hill as the sun sets to marvel at the mysterious Devil's Chimney.

→ **Visit** the legendary Rollright Stones and try to count the King's Men – said to be impossible.

→ **Wonder** at the view and watch the setting sun snuggled in a blanket, waiting to stargaze atop Cleeve Cloud.

→ **Pitch** up inside a Norman moat in Holycombe for a peaceful evening under the stars.

Picture a quintessentially English village and the pretty, honey-coloured stone cottages and open village greens of the Cotswolds begin to drift across your mind. Spanning five counties, the rich farmlands here are criss-crossed by 4,000 miles of picturesque drystone walls – and 3,000 miles of scenic footpaths and bridleways bring thousands flocking to sample their pastoral charms.

The fertile plains and ancient woodlands have attracted settlers for thousands of years. The area is dotted with Neolithic burial chambers like Belas Knap, Bronze and Iron Age hillforts such as Beckbury Camp, and mysterious monuments like the Rollright Stones. The Romans came and conquered, building villas and settlements, paving the Fosse Way for 230 miles from Exeter to Lincoln, much of it now incorporated into modern roads. The medieval wool trade ensured prosperity for the area, seen in the benefaction of many prosperous estates and 'wool churches'.

The second-largest Area of Outstanding Natural Beauty in the United Kingdom is defined by the 'spine of the Cotswolds', a steep escarpment of Jurassic limestone that creates a rich and diverse landscape of rare grassland habitats, wild flower meadows, wooded vales and broad floodplains. Beautiful hilltops like Cleeve Cloud offer stunning views and the perfect spot for kite-flying or a picnic, while woodlands such as those a Foxholes reserve provide meandering paths through spring flowers.

The River Severn offers many opportunities for a swim or kayak as it wend its way from Tewkesbury to Gloucester, past the camping ground of the Lower Lode Inn and the Saxon charm of Odda's Chapel, while the Windrush has secluded spots for discreet skinny-dips and passes romantic ruins.

Great food, elevated by the demanding tastes of weekending Londoners, ensures that the area boasts a generous selection of independent pubs, farm shops, cafés, and fine dining. Local produce adorns the menus of award-winning chefs and the rustic Butchers Arms at Eldersfield and the award-winning Horse and Groom at Bourton-on-the-Hill offer gastro delights with their seasonal dishes.

Despite its popularity, this area still harbours secret destinations, quiet walks along ancient holloways and unspoilt remnants of the history that was so important to its prosperous development. The unique remains of the Roman villa at Spoonley Wood are a worthy reward for those willing to explore, while St Kenelm's Well, nestled in the hillside, is a delightful find with a poignant story. Visitors return time and time again, and it's easy to see why

5

SERENE SEVERN

ASHLEWORTH QUAY, RIVER SEVERN

At the end of a pretty little lane is a delightful swim from a jetty, next to a great unspoilt pub (see listing). The NT Ashleworth tithe barn is a short walk away (see listing).

→ Park at The Boat Inn, Ashleworth (GL19 4HZ, see listing) and walk to jetty.

min, 51.9236, -2.2645

ODDA'S CHAPEL, RIVER SEVERN

A great place to stroke against the current, below the Anglo-Saxon charms of the chapel and adjacent St Mary's church. Lovely walks in both directions.

→ Deerhurst (GL19 4BX) signed off A38, 1½ miles S of Tewkesbury. Pay car park opposite chapel. Walk across to the Severn footpath to find beached area and jetties downstream.

3 mins, 51.9676, -2.1944

LOWER LODE, RIVER SEVERN

The 15th-century riverside pub here runs a small camping and caravan site (open May–end Sept). A short walk upstream: along the footpath are many opportunities for a dip in the River Severn.

→ Lower Lode Inn, Forthampton (GL19 4RE, 01684 293224), is signed from the A38 about 2½ miles W of Tewkesbury.

3 mins, 51.9844, -2.1777

WILD WINDRUSH

4 ST OSWALD'S CHURCH

A secluded meander of the River Windrush with deep pools on the bend for swimming, ideal for a skinny-dip.

→ At crossroads by cricket ground S of Swinbrook (OX18 4DX) take road to Widford and after ½ mile turn R on no through road over river to St Oswald's Church (51.8067, -1.6048). Park by road and walk along bank, or up driveway to church and R down to river at wall.

3 mins, 51.8057, -1.6038

5 BURFORD, RIVER WINDRUSH

A beautifully clear section of the Windrush, featured in Roger Deakin's book 'Waterlog'. Idyllic.

→ Take Swan Lane out of Burford centre and turn R onto Witney St at end. Lay-by on L by stile after ½ mile (past OX18 4DR). Follow footpath to meander by the willow tree.

2 mins, 51.8021, -1.6227

6 MINSTER LOVELL HALL, RIVER WINDRUSH

This pretty Cotswold river runs through the romantic grounds of the ruined hall. Just deep enough to swim, with a deeper section downstream above weir and footbridge in meadows.

→ In Little Minster turn past Old Swan pub (01993 862512, see listing) and OX29 0RN to parking on R at turning. Follow signs down to church, ruins, and river below.

5 mins, 51.7992, -1.5265

7 SHERBORNE PARK, RIVER WINDRUSH

A glorious swim in deep pools, secluded by trees and totally secret.

→ Head S from Clapton-on-the-Hill 1¾ miles to car park opp Northfield Barn (GL54 3DL). Walk S past farm, take track L down to cross river, over bridges then L on footpath upstream 500m through two fields into trees.

35 mins, 51.8409, -1.7283

OTHER RIVERS & LAKES

8 WITCOMBE RESERVOIR

Access to these beautiful lakes is limited to a single footpath, making it secluded for an afternoon picnic. This is a trout fishery and popular with fishermen. 'No Swimming' signs.

→ From St Mary's Church in Great Witcombe (GL3 4TS), walk along lane N 100m to find signed footpath on L through field gate. Footpath continues through field on R and down to the dam by the farm. Footpath continues across dam to all lakes but 'no swimming'.
10 mins, 51.8324, -2.1394 🎠🚶

9 STONESFIELD, RIVER EVENLODE
Several deep swimming spots are to be found on this beautiful, quiet stretch of the river, though it is shallow at the bridge.
→ From S end of village follow footpath at the end of Brook Lane (beyond OX29 8PS). Cross bridge and head R to find deeper sections on bend in middle of field.
10 mins, 51.8438, -1.4311 🏊🚶🎠

SACRED & ANCIENT

10 ROLLRIGHT STONES
Borrow divining rods from the local warden to test the magic when you cross the stone boundary. The main site is the Kings Men, an impressive, fully formed stone circle.
→ Signed Little Rollright from the A3400 S of Long Compton. Park in lay-by on L after ½ mile (before OX7 5QB). The Whispering Knights are down a path back alongside the road, and the King Stone is on the opposite side of the road though sadly these are fenced.
2 mins, 51.9753, -1.5710 🐕🐄🎠✝🎠

11 GREAT WITCOMBE ROMAN VILLA
Once a bustling and thriving community villa with impressively preserved mosaic pavements and great views. Walks along the Cotswold Way. EH Free.
→ Signed on R off Birdlip Road, 300m E of Brockworth, GL3 4TW.
5 mins, 51.8267, -2.1475 🐕🚶🎠🎢

12 OUR LADY'S WELL
The waters from this graceful 14th-century well house overlooking the Severn Valley, dedicated to St Anne, were believed to have medicinal properties. It is now dry.
→ Very limited parking at St Swithun's church in Hempsted (beyond GL2 5LH). Footpath is at bottom of graveyard, through gate and field, past house, then 200m across field to well.
10 mins, 51.8541, -2.2707 🚶🏞✝

13 ASHLEWORTH TITHE BARN
Vast, stone-tiled 15th-century tithe barn with a beautifully beamed interior. The Boat

...n is further down the lane near the river.

Signed from Ashleworth, on road to ...hleworth Quay swimming spot (see entry), ...19 4JA. NT, free dawn to dusk.
...mins, 51.9251, -2.2661 🏊♨️

... BELAS KNAP, CLEEVE HILL

...fantastic example of a Neolithic long
...rrow from 3000 BC, with far-reaching
...ews above Humblebee Wood on the
...tswold Way. The large mound covers
...veral stone chambers which held nearly 40
...eletons, some in sitting positions.

Signed from Winchcombe heading S on
...463s, take Corndean Lane. Layby L after 1
...le at GL54 5AL (51.9345, -1.9718). Follow
...tswold Way through gate opp steeply up to
...rrow and summit. With map, can walk on 2½
...iles to Cleeve Cloud hillfort (see entry).
...0 mins, 51.9272, -1.9708 ✝️♨️👣⊞☘

...5 SPOONLEY WOOD ROMAN VILLA

...he remains of this Roman villa, built around
...courtyard, are hidden deep among the
...ees of Spoonley Wood. Remnants of the
...alls are still standing, flagstones are still
...place, and there is a section of beautiful
...osaic floor protected by a small roof. A
...orthy reward for the persistent explorer.

→ Take Sudeley Hill S from Winchcombe.
1½ miles after Sudeley Castle take R at fork
signed Brockhampton. Park just after gated
bridleway sign to R after 1½ miles (GL54
5AR); verges are wider before crossroads
200m further on. Head along bridleway, past
house on L, then take well-worn track to R
immediately after track to L. Head straight on
to the corner of the field where the track turns
towards the house R and take sharp L into
corner of the wood. Villa 250m.
30 mins, 51.9294, -1.9361 👣⛰️ℹ️⊞☘

16 ST KENELM'S WELL, WINCHCOMBE

Nestled into the hillside, this 19th-century
building covers a spring said to have
appeared where the body of a prince rested
on its funeral journey. It continues to delight
as you lift the latch to venture inside, though
it may be locked. Refresh yourself with the
crystal-clear waters and take a moment to
reflect whilst reading the inscriptions on
the walls.

→ Take Castle St then Sudeley Hill SE out
of Winchcombe. After 1 mile find Sudeley
Hill Farm on L (GL54 5JB) and footpath up
to L through kissing gate. Cross three fields,
ascending as you go.
10 mins, 51.9486, -1.9381 👣🚏☘

WOODS & WILDLIFE

17 FOXHOLES WOOD

Dappled shade aplenty in this delightful little woodland nature reserve, with great oaks, badgers and numerous tracks. Bluebells carpet the floor in spring.

→ Follow Chuch Road/Bruern Road N from Milton-under-Wychwood. After 1½ miles turn L down no-through-road to OX7 6RW, 800m to find car park R at end. Follow track on and turn L at end to Foxholes Copse and other glorious walks beyond.

10 mins, 51.8851, -1.6310

18 COOPER'S HILL

A famous annual cheese-rolling race from the top of this incredibly steep hill is held at the end of May bank holiday, but there are glorious walks along the Cotswold Way around it all year.

→ From E side of Brockworth take Painswick Road S then L onto Cooper's Hill no through road after 1¼ miles. Small car park after ½ mile on R by red postbox and footpath sign. Follow path around and up hill to avoid erosion of main slope.

15 mins, 51.8315, -2.1575 🚴🏃🚶🛍️↩️

RUINS & FOLLIES

19 THE EYECATCHER

Built in 1740 as a sham ruin, this impressive pinnacled wall with empty arches dominates the skyline above the fields. Lovely views.

→ Park by St Peter & St Paul's Church on Fir Lane in Steeple Aston (OX25 4SF). Walk down Cow Lane and take footpath sign to L to view from above, continue on to view from below.

15 mins, 51.9306, -1.2991 🖼️🏃

20 CROMWELL'S STONE, BECKBURY CAMP

Standing in the corner of Beckbury Camp hillfort, affording beautiful views across the valley, this sandstone monument marks the spot where Thomas Cromwell is said to have watched Hailes Abbey burn during the Dissolution.

→ Park at Farmcote Herb and Chilli Farm (GL54 5AU, see listing) and follow bridleway on for 100m. Turn R through gate onto Cotswold Way for ¼ mile to monument in copse as you ascend steep hill. Or approach from Hailes Abbey car park (GL54 5PB), following Cotswold Way for 1¼ miles.

30 mins, 51.9679, -1.9095 🖼️📷🚶🏃

HARTPURY BEE SHELTER

Victorian stone bee house, like a dovecote
for bees. A wonderful piece of unique and
highly decorative architecture, which was
built to protect 28 skeps of coiled straw,
holding up to 840,000 bees, from rain and
too much sun.

→ From Hartpury follow Corsend Road 1¾
miles then take L, dir GL19 3DE, at St Mary
the Virgin Church. The shelter is in the church
graveyard.

mins, 51.9108, -2.3207 ✝

SUNSET HILLTOPS

22 BROADWAY TOWER

Three-storey, three-turreted folly built in 1789
on the crest of the Cotswold escarpment,
with glorious views over a multitude of
neighbouring counties. Tasty food at Morris
and Brown café, and an intriguing nuclear
bunker nearby for added curiosity!

→ Signed from the A44 2¼ miles E of
Broadway roundabout, entrance to country
park after ½ mile, beyond WR12 7LB. Park by
road or at the Morris & Brown café (pay), or
alternatively take energetic 45-minute walk
to Cotswold Way from Broadway.

mins 52.0242, -1.8355 🚶🖼️📷🏞️🎒💷

23 CLEEVE CLOUD CAMP

Stunning views from the highest point in the
Cotswolds across to the Malverns and Wales.
This grassland hillfort, set in the vast, wild
expanses of Cleeve Common, is perfect for a
picnic, kite flying and stargazing.

→ Park to the S at Cleeve Hill Common car
park, by the transmitters (beyond GL54 4EU)
or to N at Cleeve Hill car park beyond golf club
(signs on B4632 just N of GL52 3PW). Walk up
to summit. For a longer walk with map, follow
the Winchcombe and Cotswold Way 2½ miles
to Belas Knap barrow (see entry).

1 min, 51.9276, -2.0234 🚶🏞️📷🌸

24 CRICKLEY HILL

A rich landscape supporting wild flowers and
butterflies. The perfect sunset hilltop for
glorious views across the county, picnics and
stargazing. Popular.

→ Well signed off the A417 E of Gloucester,
or Leckhampton Rd S out of Cheltenham, near
the Air Balloon roundabout (GL4 8JY).

3 mins, 51.8478, -2.1012 🚶🏞️📷🏕️🚲🌸

25 DEVIL'S CHIMNEY, LECKHAMPTON HILL

A famous and dramatic pillar of rock on the
edge of the escarpment. Legend recounts
the Devil sitting atop Leckhampton Hill,

29

26

27

throwing stones at churchgoers. The stones were thrown back and trapped him under ground, where his fiery temper vented through the chimney. In truth it is thought to be a quarrymen's joke.

➜ Head S out of Cheltenham on Leckhampton Rd. After ½ mile turn L onto Daisy Bank Rd no through road, 100m to car park R. Head uphill and turn R to join Cotswold Way past limekilns and various old quarries to chimney on R. 25 mins, 51.8640, -2.0792 🚶📷⛱🚻

SLOW FOOD

26 FARMCOTE HERB & CHILLI FARM

A thriving garden farm offering a wealth of herbs, chilli plants and associated treats such as chilli chocolate and Bhut jolokia sauce from one of the hottest chillies in the world. What Jane and Tom don't know about their plants isn't worth knowing!

➜ Farmcote, GL54 5AU, 01242 603860. 51.9607, -1.9121 🍴

27 OVER FARM SHOP

Outstanding PYO and farm shop offering an array of seasonal fruit and veg, local cheeses, meat and ciders. Tearoom above shop, seasonal events at the farm.

➜ Over Farm, GL2 8DB, 01452 341510. 51.8740, -2.2748 🍴🛶

28 DUNKERTONS CIDER COMPANY

Premium organic cider from a family-run business. Taste, learn to blend, and buy here in their onsite shop.

➜ London Road, Charlton Kings, GL52 6UT, 01242 650145. 51.8772, -2.0280 🍷

29 THE OLD MILL, LOWER SLAUGHTER

Quaint Cotswold café, museum and craft shop, overlooking the river. Delicious food; the cream tea and ploughman's are exquisite.

➜ Mill Lane, Lower Slaughter, GL54 2HX, 01451 820245. 51.9016, -1.7636 🍴

30 PRIMROSE VALE FARM SHOP, BENTHAM

Pick your own fruit all summer long and have an ice cream in the café, or buy local game, cheese, bread, and other produce in the shop all year. Children's playground outside and a Halloween farm trail.

➜ Shurdington Road, Bentham, GL51 4UA, 01452 863359. 51.8510 -2.1401 🍴🚶

HORSE & GROOM, BOURTON-ON-THE-HILL

...arming Georgian gastropub with stylish ...rden and elegant rooms. Locally sourced ...es and produce make for delicious, award-...nning food with great, friendly service. ...oms available.

Bourton-on-the-Hill, GL56 9AQ, ...386 700413.
...9914, -1.7485

THE SWAN INN, SWINBROOK

...gh-quality, seasonal dishes using local ...oduce such as Swinbrook beef and ...tswold cheese, in a stylish inn with ...aditional oak settles, elm beams and ...agstone floors.

Swinbrook, OX18 4DY, 01993 823339.
...8048, -1.5924

THE FOX AT ODDINGTON

...ward-winning pub serving seasonal British ...od in a traditional, ivy-clad stone building. ...alled garden for lazy summer days, roaring ...res for winter, and rooms to stay.

High Street, Lower Oddington, GL56 0UR, ...451 870555.
...9317, -1.6627

34 THE FEATHERED NEST

Cosy bar with log fires, award-winning food, accommodation, and beautiful views over the Evenlode Valley. A 'Times' Top 100 restaurant and Gastropub of the Year.

→ Nether Westcote, OX7 6SD, 01993 833030.
51.8816, -1.6725

35 THE GLOUCESTER OLD SPOT

Typically English country inn focused on serving great meals from fresh local ingredients and offering a variety of well-kept local ales, ciders and wines. Terracotta tiled floors and a well-appointed garden.

→ Piff's Elm, Tewkesbury Road, Cheltenham, GL51 9SY, 01242 680321.
51.9331, -2.1491

36 THE BUTCHERS ARMS, ELDERSFIELD

Friendly, rural pub with outstanding high-end food sourced from local suppliers.

→ Lime Street, Eldersfield, GL19 4NX, 01452 840381.
51.9719, -2.2723

37 THE CHURCHILL ARMS, PAXFORD

Comfy fire and flagstone floors provide the setting to sample local beers and an exquisite

menu prepared by Nick Deverell Smith, who honed his skills under Gordon Ramsay.

→ Paxford, GL55 6XH, 01386 593159.
52.0385, -1.7320

COSY PUBS

38 THE FOX INN, BURFORD
Traditional 17th-century riverside inn. Great food and real ales.

→ Great Barrington, Burford, OX18 4TB, 01451 844385.
51.8162, -1.7046

39 MOUNT INN, STANTON
Spectacular views across the Cotswold countryside, great food, and a warm welcome.

→ Stanton, WR12 7NE, 01386 584316.
52.0063, -1.8968

40 THE KINGS HEAD INN, BLEDINGTON
The quintessential English village pub: roaring log fires in winter, spacious village green in summer, delicious food, and a warm welcome.

→ The Green, Bledington, OX7 6XQ, 01608 658365.
51.9027, -1.6477

41 THE BOAT INN, ASHLEWORTH
Wonderful, characterful pub in a riverside

setting with a quay, ideal for a dip in the Severn (see entry).

→ Ashleworth Quay, Gloucester, GL19 4HZ, 01452 700272.
51.9238, -2.2649

42 THE PLOUGH INN, FORD
Pretty Cotswold stone pub, unspoilt and friendly. Wood-burners and large garden. Real ales and great food.

→ Ford, GL54 5RU, 01386 584215.
51.9630, -1.8725

43 THE PLOUGH, PRESTBURY
Thatched, dog-friendly inn with traditional cider and real ales served straight from the cask via serving hatches. Cosy snug and spacious garden with boules court.

→ Mill Street, Prestbury, GL52 3BG, 01242 361506.
51.9146, -2.0448

44 THE WHEATSHEAF, NORTHLEACH
A friendly, comfortable, and bustling old coaching inn; cosy in the winter with a pretty garden for the summer. Great choice of ales, wine and food. Rooms available.

→ West Road, Northleach, GL54 3EZ, 01451 860244.
51.8309, -1.8381

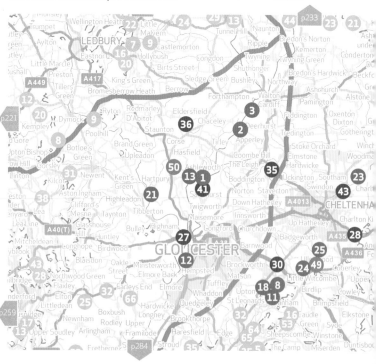

OLD SWAN, MINSTER LOVELL

tstanding traditional inn with beams and
aring fires. Well-prepared, simple menu.
ndy for the Windrush river and Minster
vell ruins (see entry).

Minster Lovell, OX29 0RN, 01993 862512.
..7991, -1.5394

FALKLANDS ARMS, GREAT TEW

aditional 16th-century pub with
commodation serving great food. On
e village green, with inglenook fireplace,
gstone floors and timber beams.

19–21 The Green, Great Tew, OX7 4DB,
.608 683653.
.9605, -1.4249

AMP & SLEEP

MILL COTTAGE, UPPER SWELL

egant accommodation for up to six in a group
listed buildings, overlooking an ornamental
ke in the heart of the Cotswolds.

Upper Swell, stays.co.uk.
.9404, -1.7449

POSY, WILDWOOD BLUEBELL

el at one with nature in this pretty
epherd's hut with a wood-burner, set in a
uebell wood. Camping field with bell tents

available to hire for groups, and a luxury
barn for families.

→ Heath Barn, Donnington, GL56 0XU,
wildwoodbluebell.com
51.9616, -1.7011

49 STAR GLAMPING, ULLENWOOD

Dog-friendly 'hobbit' pods and yurts with
a fire pit and the option to book a table for
breakfast.

→ National Star, Ullenwood Manor Road,
Ullenwood, GL53 9QU, 01242 527631.
51.8500, -2.0856

50 RECTORY FARM, ASHLEWORTH

Fantastic rural campsite on a working farm,
with basic amenities. Farm shop on site,
three pubs and a bakery nearby.

→ Rectory Farm, Lawn Road, Ashleworth,
Gloucestershire, GL19 4JL, 01452 700664.
51.9348, -2.2889

51 COTSWOLDS CAMPING AT HOLYCOMBE

Pitch your tent on the peaceful site of a
Norman castle, surrounded by a water-
filled moat. Airstream and gypsy caravans
are among the glamping options available.
A very quiet site: children over 12 only,
no groups or dogs, and no music, live or
otherwise. Booking online only.

→ Holycombe, Shipston-on-Stour, CV36 5PH,
cotswoldscamping.com.
52.0090, -1.5500

52 COTSWOLD CARP FARM

Small, adults-only campsite with all pitches
set alongside a lake. Dogs welcome, on a lead
onsite.

→ Bourton-on-the-Water, GL54 2FH,
01451 821795.
51.8820, -1.7461

53 HAYLES FARM SHOP & CAMPSITE

Tranquil campsite set on family-run fruit
farm with café and shop, right by Hayles
Abbey ruins. Delicious, home-made food,
cider and apple juice, with fire pits and wood
sales onsite.

→ Winchcombe, GL54 5PB, 01242 602123.
51.9664, -1.9232

54 DENFURLONG FARM, CHEDWORTH

A great little campsite with farm shop
and café. Fantastic breakfast served each
morning. Informal pitches and minimal
lighting, bring a torch and enjoy the stars.

→ Denfurlong Farm, Fields Road, Chedworth,
GL54 4NQ, 01285 720265.
51.7938, -1.9051

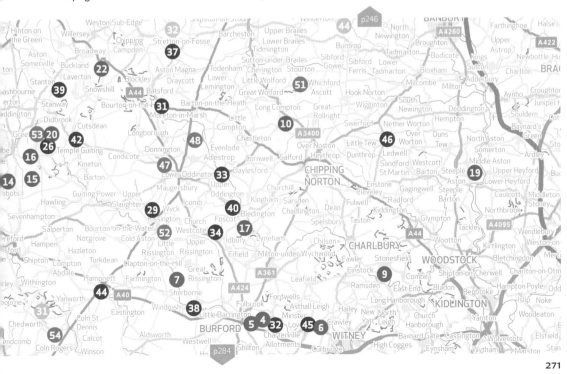

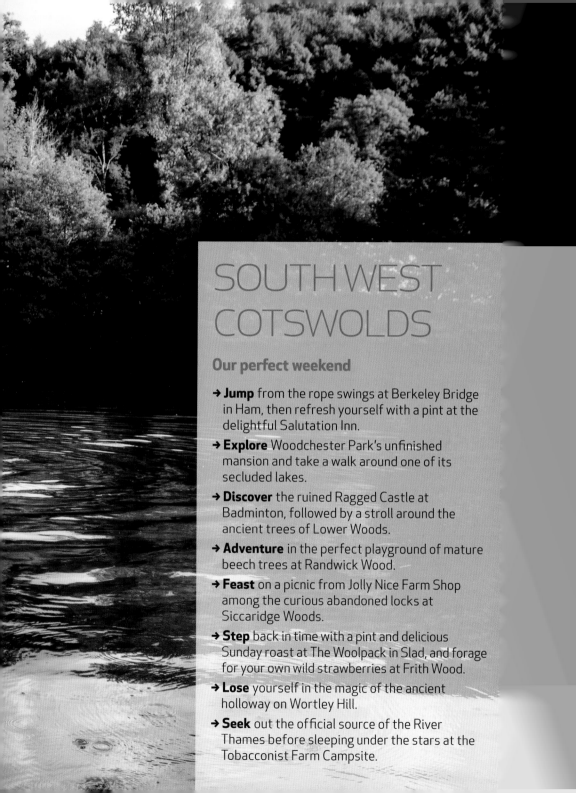

SOUTH WEST COTSWOLDS

Our perfect weekend

→ **Jump** from the rope swings at Berkeley Bridge in Ham, then refresh yourself with a pint at the delightful Salutation Inn.

→ **Explore** Woodchester Park's unfinished mansion and take a walk around one of its secluded lakes.

→ **Discover** the ruined Ragged Castle at Badminton, followed by a stroll around the ancient trees of Lower Woods.

→ **Adventure** in the perfect playground of mature beech trees at Randwick Wood.

→ **Feast** on a picnic from Jolly Nice Farm Shop among the curious abandoned locks at Siccaridge Woods.

→ **Step** back in time with a pint and delicious Sunday roast at The Woolpack in Slad, and forage for your own wild strawberries at Frith Wood.

→ **Lose** yourself in the magic of the ancient holloway on Wortley Hill.

→ **Seek** out the official source of the River Thames before sleeping under the stars at the Tobacconist Farm Campsite.

There is an honest authenticity in the South West Cotswolds that is quite palpable to those who visit. The locals are friendly and welcoming, sharing their genuine hospitality in vibrant, convivial pubs such as The Woolpack in the picturesque village of Slad, and The Salutation Inn in Ham, where you enter as a visitor and leave as a friend.

This part of the Cotswolds differs from its more polished northern counterpart in that it offers an intriguing glimpse into an alternative way life – one largely forgotten in our fast-paced, technological world. Tourism although still an important economic driver, does not feel a burden here, with many more quiet, off-the-beaten-track wonders hiding amongst the peaceful villages, rolling wolds and rural farmland.

There is a strong literary and cultural heritage to the Cotswolds. William Morris, father to the Arts and Crafts movement, lived at Kelmscott, and many villages hold annual festivals of food, drink, music and literature. The Slad Valley, immortalised by local Laurie Lee in *Cider with Rosie*, boasts sunset hilltops at Swift's Hill, bubbling streams, refreshing dips in Slad Brook and forest bathing under the ancient beeches at Frith Wood.

The 102-mile Cotswold Way winds across glorious landscape from Chipping Campden in the north to Bath Abbey in the south. Along its path, walkers will find ancient holloways such as Wortley Hill, babbling streams and rivers such as the Little Avon, perfect for a dip on a hot summer's day. A destination for all seasons, its beauty never dulls but changes throughout the year, from vibrant, fresh spring through to warm, earthy autumn.

The lush Frome Valley, named the Golden Valley by Queen Victoria, sees a nod to the area's industrial past. The disused and now rewilded Cotswold Canal runs beside the River Frome, and at the exquisitely restored portal of the Sapperton Tunnel sits the Tunnel Inn, complete with roaring log fire in winter and a delightful garden for sunny days. Not far from here is the stunning Siccaridge Wood, where curious, abandoned locks are dotted along the footpath through an ancient forest abundant with wild garlic and spring flowers.

And as evening falls, there are many opportunities and vistas perfect for stargazing in this Dark Sky area. Climb Haresfield or Painswick Beacons, or seek out the Neolithic Hetty Pegler's Tump for kite-flying opportunities stunning sunset views or a romantic moonlit night walk.

5

RIVER & LAKES

LECHLADE-ON-THAMES

There are many places to dip into the young Thames around Lechlade, but this is the perfect stretch for longer immersion: walk upstream to the pool and drift down, or kayak down to a pub.

→ Head S over Ha'penny Bridge on A361 past GL7 3AG), car park R after 450m. Pool ¼ mile upstream, above footbridge, near the Round House at junction with River Coln. Downstream is The Trout Inn at St John's Bridge (GL7 3HA, see listing).

5 mins, 51.6885, -1.7042 🏊🚶🏕🅿

CHEESE WHARF, RIVER THAMES

A delightful little roadside picnic area with river swing, this was once an old cheese-loading wharf.

→ Head E and S from Lechlade on A417, dir Buscot, past The Trout Inn (GL7 3HA, see listing), continue for ½ mile to parking on L.

min, 51.6839, -1.6765 🏊🚶🏕🅿

BUSCOT WEIR, RIVER THAMES

A wonderfully large, deep weir pool with trees, rope swings and lawns in the pretty NT hamlet.

→ Continue S from Cheese Wharf (see entry) and turn L in Buscot to find car park R (opp SN7 8DA) after 150m.

2 mins, 51.6804, -1.6683 🏊🚶🏕🅿

4 KELMSCOTT, RIVER THAMES

Wild, open stretch of Thames downstream from William Morris's famous home. You could walk all the way to the weir pool and car park at Grafton Lock (51.6920, -1.6079), or Radcot Bridge (51.6930, -1.5884, see Ye Olde Swan campsite listing).

→ From The Plough Inn, Kelmscott (GL7 3HG, see listing) follow road R past manor onto trackway, parking at end. Follow river downstream through fields with many access points. Stately home closed for restoration during 2020.

20 mins, 51.6857, -1.6309 🏊🚶🏕🅿🏔

5 SLAD BROOK

Hidden away in the trees of Longridge Wood lies this tranquil body of water, where the brook pools to form a pond. Part of the Laurie Lee Way.

→ Take B4070 NE from Stroud dir GL6 7QT. After 3 miles park in lay-by R at double junction. Head to N end to follow sign for the Laurie Lee Way down to the brook at the

bottom of the glade.

15 mins, 51.7775, -2.1673 🏊🚶🅿

6 BERKELEY BRIDGE, HAM

The popular Little Avon River, running past historic Berkeley Castle, provides a cooling paddle on a hot day and is sought out by young and old. Rope swings and jumps dependent on water level.

→ Park near castle gatehouse in Berkeley (GL13 9BQ). Walk S and take footpath through field on L 50m after white iron bridge.

15 mins, 51.6851, -2.4577 🏊🅿

7 LITTLE SOMERFORD, RIVER AVON

Idyllic, deep pools in orchard and meadow upstream of mill. Many more riverside areas in field upstream. On footpath but near private garden so be respectful.

→ 3 miles E of Malmesbury. Take Mill Lane by railway bridge. Park in lay-by on L and continue on footpath ½ mile, around side of Kingsmead Mill, over bridge and into woods. More swimming locations downstream in Great Somerford accessed from path at 51.5446, -2.0598. Recommended pub the Volunteer Inn, (01249 720316).

15 mins, 51.5597, -2.0686 🏊❓🏕🅿

8 PARKMILL POND, WOODCHESTER PARK

A series of five sheltered lakes in the grounds of an unfinished Victorian mansion. Beautiful woodland walks and intriguing boathouse. No Swimming signs.

→ Woodchester Park is signed off B4066 between Dursley and Stroud (GL10 3TS); car park is NT (pay). The last and lowest lake (Parkmill) is the most secluded. Be discreet.
30 mins, 51.7065, -2.2479

9 LAKE 104, FAIRFORD

Crystal-clear water in a beautifully rural location, Lake 104 forms part of an extensive range of old gravel pits, now returned to nature.

→ Park in Fairford and follow footpath down Waterloo Lane (GL7 4BW), turn L across bridge and continue with river to R, bearing L to Lake 104, with smaller lakes to R.
30 mins, 51.7033, -1.7663

10 COTSWOLD COUNTRY PARK BEACH

A popular and safe place with café and facilities to introduce children to the delights of open-water swimming and other sports. Best to book ahead.

→ Signed from B4696 just E of Somerford

Keynes, GL7 6DF; marked as Keynes Country Park on OS maps. Open 10am–7pm, Apr–Oct
1 min, 51.6622, -1.9604

11 CLEVELAND LAKES

Walk along the Thames path and marvel at the crystal-clear waters of the surrounding lakes in this lush, green nature reserve, important to migrating and wintering birds

→ Park at Waterhay car park SE of Ashton Keynes (51.6387, -1.9149) and follow Thames Path E to lakes. Fishing and water sports lake
15 mins, 51.6458, -1.9029

SACRED & ANCIENT

12 AMPNEY CRUCIS CROSS

A 14th-century medieval cross shaft with unique carvings, discovered in the rood tower of the church in 1860. Lovely walks around the village, including footpath E to the stump of a partner cross at 51.7157, -1.9053.

→ In Ampney Crucis (GL7 5RY, off A417 E of Cirencester) turn at war memorial for Church of the Holy Rood. Cross in churchyard.
1 min, 51.7157, -1.9070

13 FROCESTER TITHE BARN

One of the best-preserved and most important tithe barns in the country, built in the late-13th century and still in use.

→ In Frocester, GL10 3TN, head SE down Court Road from junction at centre of village. Barn at end of lane on R; park carefully.

1 min, 51.7249, -2.3105 🐾

14 HETTY PEGLER'S TUMP

Does a Neolithic barrow that you can crawl into take your fancy? With chambers? Uley Long Barrow (nicknamed after Hester Pegler, who owned it in the 17th century) gives you all this. Bring a torch!

→ Follow the B4066 from Dursley towards Stroud through Uley, past GL11 5BH and after a mile park in lay-by R (51.6977, -2.3024). Walk on 200m to signed path L up to barrow.

5 mins, 51.6985, -2.3056 🐾🕇🐾

15 CIRENCESTER ROMAN AMPHITHEATRE

With a capacity for over 8,000 spectators, this is one of Britain's largest Roman amphitheatres. Built outside the town walls of Corinium (Cirencester) in the early 2nd century, this oval gem is tucked unobtrusively away and awaits discovery.

→ Follow A429 from Cirencester Waitrose roundabout SW just under ½ mile, take L onto Chesterton Lane, then L onto Cotswold Avenue after ½ mile. Follow ¼ mile to car park L just after entrance to amphitheatre (GL7 1TN).

3 mins, 51.7114, -1.9720 🐾🐾🛝🐾

16 CLIMPER WELL

Nestled in a tranquil glade lies one of the sources of the River Frome. The stream bubbles over the path, which is lined with wild garlic in spring. Enchanting circular walk with two bowl barrows in field opposite farm.

→ From Birdlip take B4070 S for 1½ miles. Turn L, past Climperwell Farm (GL4 8LQ) and park L near footpath sign after 200m. Follow path S and take R fork to well 20m on L. Follow path round to L for circular walk. Alternatively, walk in on footpath behind Fosters Ash Inn (see listing).

2 mins, 51.8059, -2.1189 🚶🐾🛝🐾🐾🐾

17 WINDMILL TUMP

The delightfully named Windmill Tump is in fact a chambered long barrow holding secrets from the Neolithic. Constructed before 3500 BC, it served as a final resting place for two centuries, with traces of sacrificial offerings found in the forecourt.

→ On A433 S from Cirencester turn for Rodmarton. At crossroads take L signed Hazelton (dir GL7 6PU) ½ mile and park in lay-by at sign for barrow. Follow path.
5 mins, 51.6744, -2.0990 🚶🏕🌲♿✝

18 THE LONG STONE, MINCHINHAMPTON

Possibly a burial chamber closing stone, the naturally holed Long Stone sits regally in its own grassy ring at the side of the road.
→ Follow Tetbury Street SE out of Minchinhampton, past GL6 9JH. Keep R at fork and park on R after ¼ mile (51.6973, -2.1698). Cross road back 70m to gate in wall.
1 min, 51.6978, -2.1699 ✝♿

19 THAMES HEAD, TREWSBURY MEAD

Marked by an unassuming stone block under an ash tree is the official point where the River Thames starts its journey. Seven Springs stakes a less picturesque rival claim (51.8506, -2.0507) – close enough to visit both.
→ Take A433 SW from Cirencester. After 2⅓ miles, past GL7 6NZ, park L in lay-by just before brow of hill and low bridge (signs). Walk back 150m (fast traffic) to footpath marker R, and follow Wysis Way N across field to stone marker.
15 mins, 51.6944, -2.0298 🚶

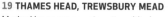

RUINS & REMNANTS

20 PURTON HULKS

A unique collection of abandoned boats and ships, purposely beached since the early 1900s to help stop erosion of the riverbank. The largest ships' graveyard in Britain.
→ On A38 2½ miles S of Slimbridge roundabout, turn R through Breadstone. A mile past Breadstone take R on bend for Purton. After 1½ miles turn R into Purton car park (GL13 9HP). Cross river and walk L ½ mile on Severn Way.
10 mins, 51.7371, -2.4558 🚶🚣

21 SICCARIDGE WOOD

Coppiced, ancient woodland reserve full of lily-of-the-valley, wild garlic, bluebells, primroses and purple orchids. At dusk you may see deer or hear nightingales. Explore the derelict locks along the old canal towpath.
→ From crossroads at Sapperton follow road for Edgeworth ½ mile to gravelled pull-off just before Daneway Inn (GL7 6LN, see campsite listing). Walk on 100m, over bridge to footpath L into woods.
3 mins, 51.7285, -2.0925 🚶🏕🍺🚗♿

22 SAPPERTON TUNNEL & ROUNDHOUSE

[Th]e magnificently restored portal of Britain's [th]ird-longest canal tunnel (sadly blocked [by] collapses) on the now-disused Thames [an]d Severn Canal. Follow the towpath to the [in]triguing Coates Roundhouse built as a tied [co]ttage for canal workers.

→ Leave A419 W of Cirencester through [g]ates. At T-junction turn R then L signed [Ca]rlton and canal tunnel, then R after ¾ [m]ile to park at Tunnel House Inn (GL7 6PW, [se]e listing). Entrance to tunnel is to L of pub [dr]iveway. Walk S along towpath to derelict [ro]undhouse.

[1]0 mins, 51.7040, -2.0503 🚶📷🅿️🎫🚌

23 THE RAGGED CASTLE, BADMINTON

[Hi]dden away amongst the trees, this [fo]rgotten, little 1750s folly is an almost [fo]rgotten remnant of a frivolous era.

→ Take A433 from Didmarton dir Dunkirk. [Af]ter 1½ miles, past GL9 1AH, take L between [st]one pillars to Badminton (unsigned). Park on [R] after ½ mile, just before tree-lined avenue. [Fo]lly in woods opposite junction.

[5] min, 51.5733, -2.2827 📷🎫

TREES & MEADOWS

24 TORTWORTH CHESTNUT

Reputedly from a nut planted during the reign of King Egbert in AD 800, certainly recorded from 1200, this fantastical-looking chestnut stands next to the local church where cream teas are often served on summer Sundays.

→ From the B4509 just E of J14 on the M5, turn N signed Damery and follow ⅓ mile to St Leonard's Church in Tortworth (GL12 8HF). Park next to church and walk to R in graveyard.

1 min, 51.6373, -2.4285 🎫🍴

25 FRITH WOOD, SLAD

An alluring ancient wood with soaring beeches, swathes of bluebells, wild garlic and wild strawberries; if foraging, keep an eye out for a glimpse of the very small and rare pointy-shelled Ena montana snail.

→ Park as for Slad Brook swim (see entry). Follow footpath at SW of junction (51.7761, -2.1804) into wood.

2 mins, 51.7752, -2.1834 🚶🚻🎫🚌⛺♿

26 LOWER WOODS, WICKWAR

The wetland nature of this secluded ancient wood means it has been untouched by

farming and humans for centuries, allowing birdsong and wild flowers to flourish in the dappled shade.

→ From N end of Station Rd through Wickwar take Chase Lane E, signed Inglestone Common. Keep R at fork (GL12 8JY) and ¾ mile further turn R opposite big farmhouse onto gravel road. Park at end of road. Various paths into wood.

1 min, 51.5908, -2.3677

27 PASQUE FLOWER MEADOW, BARNSLEY

A secluded stretch of hillside on open access land, adorned with swathes of the rare and glorious, purple pasque flower each May. Walk, picnic, photograph.

→ Head N on A429 from Cirencester for 2¾ miles, park in layby R shortly past GL7 5EU. Hop over fence, turn L and follow curving path downhill away from road.

2 mins, 51.7597, -1.9232

28 RACK ISLE, BIBURY

A boggy meadow resplendent with wild flowers in early summer, and home to water voles, kingfishers, grass snakes and dragonflies. Next to Arlington Row, once home to weavers who dried prized cloth on racks here. William Morris called Bibury the

prettiest village in England, and this is its most beautiful spot.

→ Parking along A4425 in Bibury, near GL7 5NN. Rack Isle is over river; cross little stone bridge to Arlington Row. NT, free.

5 mins, 51.7588, -1.8346

29 RANDWICK WOOD

Magnificent, mature beeches with winding paths, dips and hollows create the perfect playground in this wood for all seasons. Take your mountain bike, play on the rope swings or absorb the stunning autumnal colours.

→ From Stroud centre take Cashes Green Road 1 mile, then just before Randwick turn L onto Ash Lane (GL6 6EX) and park in NT car park at top of hill after ½ mile.

1 min, 51.7601, -2.2580

30 MIDGER WOOD

An almost ethereal dell, offering peaceful walks through the mossy oaks, bluebells and wild garlic, and a babbling brook of tiny, calcified tufa waterfalls.

→ Follow A46 from Dunkirk N for 2⅓ miles and turn L after GL12 7EH. Park in layby L after ⅓ mile; wood to R.

1 min, 51.6033, -2.2936

CHEDWORTH WOODS

peaceful walk through Chedworth Nature
eserve along the old railway line brings
ou to this bubbling tufa spring, where the
ne-rich water deposits calcite to create a
urious waterfall formation. Perfect for a
mantic proposal!

→ Take A429 S from Northleach, after ½
ile turn R signed Roman Villa and Yanworth.
ollow signs to park at NT Chedworth Villa
eyond GL54 3LJ). Follow footpath sign
ast visitor's centre, take L fork up to railway,
nd follow L about 400m. A locked tunnel is
eyond.

0 mins, 51.8149, -1.9232 🚶🏊💧👤📖

CRACKING CLIMBS

2 PAINSWICK BEACON

lso known as Kimsbury Camp, this hillfort
the perfect spot for an afternoon stroll
hrough wild flowers, kite-flying or stargazing
he best dark skies in the area. Shares the hill
ith a 19th-century golf course.

→ Signed off A46 at fork, 1¼ miles N of
ainswick, dir GL6 6SU. Painswick Beacon car
ark is lay-by R. Several paths to top, including
lysis and Cotswold Ways.

0 mins, 51.8073, -2.1925 🏕️📷🏊🚶⛺🌟

33 BRACKENBURY CAMP

Climb the sublime sunken path to the
summit, explore the surviving hillfort banks,
and adventure in the woods at the top.

→ Take B4060 NW out of Wotton-under-Edge,
dir GL12 7PB. Park in lay-by L at summit of
hill (51.6497, -2.3699). Walk back 300m to
footpath sign and cross road to follow to top.

15 mins, 51.6523, -2.3670 🏊🚶👤🚴🌟

34 SWIFT'S HILL, SLAD

Immortalised in the prose of Laurie Lee's
Cider with Rosie, this double-bump hilltop
offers the perfect place for a picnic among
orchids, stargazing or wild camping.

→ From Stroud, take B4070 NE dir Slad.
About ¾ mile from edge of town, turn R
signed The Vatch (dir GL6 7LA) and follow
½ mile to park in lay-by after cattle grid
(51.7590, -2.1817). Follow path to top of hill.

5 mins, 51.7589, -2.1799 🚶🏊⛺🌟📷🌟

35 HARESFIELD BEACON

Stunning views across the Gloucestershire
countryside and over the Severn Estuary.
Walk up to the bronze 'topograph' viewpoint
and roll back down, or take a picnic and a
blanket and wait for the stars to appear.

38 BIBURY TROUT FARM

One of England's oldest working trout farm in a picture-perfect Cotswold village. Farm open daily, café open daily, Mar–Oct. Catch your own trout weekends, Mar–Oct. The Swan Hotel over the bridge also offers good food (01285 740695). Busy in summer.

→ Bibury, GL7 5NL, 01285 740215.
51.7604, -1.8363 🍴 🏠

39 THE ORGANIC FARM SHOP, CIRENCESTER

Set in the stunning Cotswold countryside, this 160-acre farm offers all things organic: a well-stocked shop, café offering delicious food inspired by the vegetable garden, woodland walks, camping, glamping, and cookery and textile courses.

→ Burford Road, Cirencester, GL7 5HF, 01285 640441. (Sat nav may dangerously mislead, entrance on Burford Road/B4425.)
51.7318, -1.9394 🍴 🥗 ⛺ 📷

40 JOLLY NICE FARM SHOP & KITCHEN

Once a petrol station, now a handsome hotchpotch of wooden buildings, locally crafted yurts and a picnic meadow, where a few rare-breed sheep and cattle quietly graze. With café and butcher, definitely a destination for the discerning foodie to fill up.

→ Frampton Mansell, GL6 8HZ, 01285 760868
51.7146, -2.1140 🍴

41 THE KING'S ARMS, DIDMARTON

Cosy 17th-century coaching inn serving top-quality food from home-grown and local produce. Dog-friendly accommodation.

→ The Street, Didmarton, GL9 1DT, 01454 238245.
51.5856, -2.2636 🍴 🍴 📷

42 THE POTTING SHED, CRUDWELL

A beautiful country pub with bare stone walls, timbered ceilings and a roaring log fire. High-quality, local and seasonal food.

→ The Street, Crudwell, SN16 9EW, 01666 577833.
51.6346, -2.0672 🍴 🍴

43 LAVENDER BAKEHOUSE, CHALFORD

Charming and popular café serving generous portions of home-made fare. Gift shop.

→ 20 London Road, Chalford, GL6 8NW, 01453 889239.
51.7210, -2.1522 🍴

→ In Stroud take Farmhill Rd by GL5 4AS and follow N out of town 2 miles. Turn L signed Haresfield and park at Shortwood NT or Standish Wood car parks (GL6 6PP). Cotswold Way passes through.
20 mins, 51.7783, -2.2618 📷 🏊 🚶 🐾 🌳

36 WORTLEY HILL HOLLOWAY

Part of the Cotswold Way, this mysterious, sunken holloway path feels like the setting for myths and legends.

→ Heading S out of Wortley take L at red postbox after GL12 7QP. Continue 170m to park on R just after 'The Barns'. Follow footpath opposite up hill.
5 mins, 51.6248, -2.3346 📷 🏊 🚶

37 TYNDALE MONUMENT

Built in 1866 in memory of local man, William Tyndale, executed in 1536 for translating the New Testament into English. Stunning views over River Severn.

→ Take B4060 S out of North Nibley and park on R next to graveyard, near GL11 6DS. Walk back 50–100m and follow footpath opposite.
15 mins, 51.6588, -2.3725 🚶 📷

WOTTON FARM SHOP

eat little farm shop, café and plant
ntre. Quirky potting sheds in which to eat
guettes and rolls followed by a great slab
home-made cake.

Bradley Road, Wotton-under-Edge,
12 7DT, 01453 521546.
.6450, -2.3623 🍴

THE VILLAGE PUB, BARNSLEY

varm welcome and a great atmosphere
ait at this convivial pub serving posh pub
ıb with fantastic service.

Barnsley, GL7 5EE, 01285 740000.
.7446, -1.8905 🍴🛏🛶

THE BELL, SAPPERTON

elaxed, well-styled village pub with a
rden and roaring fires offering delicious
al and seasonal food. Usually closed
ondays in winter.

Sapperton, GL7 6LE, 01285 760298.
.7279, -2.0761 🛏🍴

THE TUNNEL HOUSE INN, COATES

dden in a hollow by Sapperton Tunnel (see
try), totally off the beaten track – at the
d of its own bumpy canalside track, in fact.
ell worth the journey for roaring log fires
winter, beautiful summer gardens, real ale
d hearty food.

Tarlton Road, Coates, GL7 6PW,
.285 770280.
..7041, -2.0512 🛏🍴

KINGS HEAD, FRANCE LYNCH

ucked away at the end of a narrow lane,
is charming rural pub has been serving the
cals for over 300 years.

France Lynch, GL6 8LT, 01453 882225.
.7310, -2.1402 🛏

NEW INN, NORTH NIBLEY

rmer cider house nestled in its own lush
tural amphitheatre of vines, trees and
rdsong. Forget the world for a while,
tting on the veranda in the sunshine at any
me of year.

Waterley Bottoms, North Nibley, GL11 6EF,
1453 543659.
.6652, -2.3507 🛏🍴

THE SALUTATION INN, HAM

delightful free house offering real ciders,
ff-sales' hatch, heritage games, its own
icro-brewery beers and regular events,

---

including the notorious 'Sally Singalong'.

→ Ham, Berkeley, GL13 9QH, 01453 810284.
51.6833, -2.4639 🛏🍴

51 OLD BADGER INN, EASTINGTON

Great, friendly and welcoming village pub
that doesn't rest on its laurels. Real ciders,
local ales, and honest pub food.

→ Alkerton Road, Eastington, GL10 3AT,
01453 822892.
51.7462, -2.3242 🛏🍴

52 THE WOOLPACK, SLAD

Loved by visitors and locals alike, this
truly independent inn retains all the old-
world Cotswold charm that won the famed
patronage of local author Laurie Lee.

→ Slad Road, Slad, GL6 7QA, 01452 813429.
51.7642, -2.1869 🛏🍴

53 FOSTON'S ASH INN

With a great reputation for food, a glorious
rural setting, and a welcome for hikers and
their dogs.

→ The Camp, near Stroud, GL6 7ES,
01452 863262.
51.8014, -2.1252 🛏🍴

54 BATHURST ARMS, NORTH CERNEY

A friendly pub offering good-quality food, a
range of local ales, and accommodation. In
summer enjoy their pretty Cotswold garden
next to the babbling stream.

→ North Cerney, GL7 7BZ, 01285 832150.
51.7701, -1.9732 🛏🛶🍴

55 STROUD BREWERY TAP

Fantastic, friendly bar in the brewery itself,
with organic beer, wood-fired pizzas, and live
music. Opening times vary, check website.

→ Kingfisher Business Park, London Road,
Thrupp, GL5 2BY, 01453 887122.
51.7238, -2.2005 🛏

56 BLACK HORSE, AMBERLEY

Amazing views across the valley from this
400-year-old pub serving local ales and food.
Children and dogs welcome, rooms available.

→ Littleworth, Amberley, GL5 5AL,
01453 872556.
51.7128, -2.2201 🛏🍴

57 THE TROUT INN, LECHLADE

An inn since 1472, with a beer garden and
camping field for the summer and log fires in
winter. Home-cooked food, regular jazz and
folk evenings, and its own theatre company.

→ St Johns Bridge, Farringdon Road, GL7 3HA, 01367 252 313.
51.6901, -1.6783 ▮

58 THE PLOUGH INN, KELMSCOTT

Dog-friendly local with craft beers, real fires, two restaurants showcasing local produce, and rooms with king-size beds.

→ Kelmscott, GL7 3HG, 01367 253543.
51.6899, -1.6410 ▮▮▮▮▮

WILDER CAMPING

59 THISTLEDOWN FARM CAMPING

Tranquil camping on an organic farm with oodles of space, splendid views, super-clean facilities and wood-fired pizza oven.

→ Tinkley Lane, Nympsfield, GL10 3UH, 01453 860420.
51.7057, -2.2707 ▮▮▮

60 TOBACCONIST FARM CAMPSITE

Family-run campsite with modern facilities and beautiful Cotswold outlook.

→ Tobacconist Road, Minchinhampton, GL6 9JJ, 07854 750473.
51.7036, -2.1816 ▮▮

61 DANEWAY INN CAMPING

A quiet, secluded, back-to-basics pub camping field near Siccaridge Wood (see entry).

→ Dane Lane, Sapperton, GL7 6LN, 01285 760297.
51.7295, -2.0899 ▮▮▮▮▮

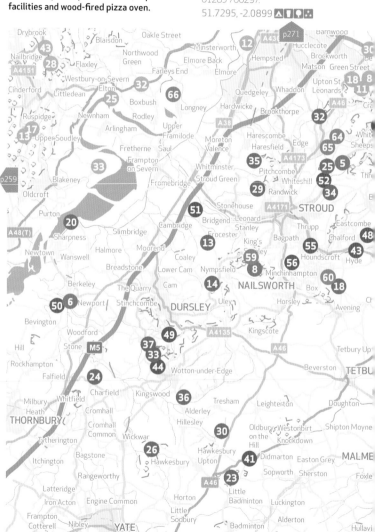

ABBEY HOME FARM

w-intensity camping, as close to wild as
u can get on a campsite, at Cirencester's
mous Organic Farm Shop (see listing).
rking farm, quite strict rules about
iving before evening!

Abbey Home Farm, GL7 5HF,
eorganicfarmshop.co.uk
.7318, -1.9392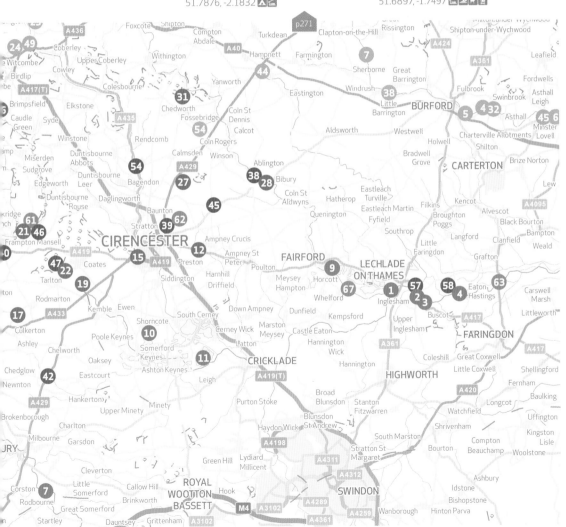

YE OLDE SWAN CAMPING & GLAMPING

mpsite and furnished tipis on a grassy
nd in the Thames, just across the water
om the pub.

Radcot, OX18 2SX, 01367 810220.
.693, -1.5884

p271

RUSTIC HAVENS

64 UNDER THE WALNUT TREE, PAINSWICK

A pretty shepherds' hut tucked away in the
grounds of Painswick Lodge, with access to
heated outdoor pool.

→ Painswick Lodge, GL6 6UB,
canopyandstars.co.uk
51.7945, -2.1733

65 PAINSWICK GLAMPING

Quiet site offering a pod, shepherds' hut, and
in summer a small, well-kept camping area
around a mill pool. No under-12s.

→ Beech Farm, Beech Lane, Stroud, GL6 6SH,
07866 520636.
51.7876, -2.1832

66 THE GLAMPING ORCHARD, LONGNEY

Choice of glamping retreats. Stay in 'Warwick
Knight' a wonderfully converted 1950s
caravan with rooftop garden, or a bell tent.

→ Peglass Cottage, Longney, GL2 3SW,
07974 174534.
51.8205, -2.3493

67 GREAT FARM, WHELFORD

Choices include an old railway carriage, a
gypsy caravan or a shepherds' hut, and also
two cottages in the area. A delightful spot
next to the River Coln, with deep pools below
the footbridge, perfect for a gentle swim
against the current.

→ Great Farm, Whelford. canopyandstars.co.uk
51.6897, -1.7497

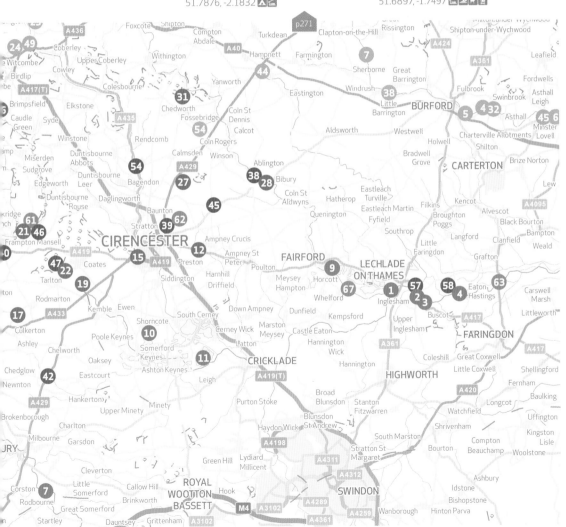

Ordnance Survey National Grid References

1 High Peak
1. SE 086 092
2. SK 168 953
3. SK 074 886
4. SK 082 889
5. SK 127 887
6. SK 080 979
7. SK 109 899
8. SE 055 087
9. SE 038 047
10. SK 116 990
11. SK 169 924
12. SK 056 984
13. SK 209 996
14. SK 257 926
15. SK 173 892
16. SK 088 861
17. SK 077 860
18. SJ 999 853
19. SK 230 899
20. SK 141 914
21. SE 031 108
22. SK 091 869
23. SK 195 892
24. SE 036 048
25. SK 091 958
26. SE 016 134
27. SK 282 953
28. SK 222 906
29. SE 147 056
30. SE 003 075
31. SK 269 922
32. SE 217 065
33. SK 262 918
34. SK 204 865
35. SE 049 116
36. SK 037 932
37. SD 974 106
38. SK 288 906
39. SE 007 063
40. SK 268 924
41. SK 048 851
42. SK 038 961
43. SK 163 854
44. SE 162 067
45. SE 251 045
46. SE 260 037
47. SK 124 856
48. SD 976 113
49. SE 199 040
50. SK 102 853

2 South West Peak
1. SK 009 685
2. SJ 965 652
3. SJ 982 685
4. SK 012 732
5. SJ 948 719
6. SJ 993 595
7. SK 005 624
8. SK 020 623
9. SJ 995 782
10. SK 069 672
11. SK 075 675
12. SJ 939 771
13. SK 008 747
14. SK 054 717
15. SK 077 725
16. SK 001 759
17. SJ 952 673
18. SJ 987 656
19. SJ 973 812
20. SK 038 820
21. SJ 964 651
22. SJ 990 607
23. SJ 975 675
24. SJ 988 798
25. SJ 981 685
26. SJ 952 715
27. SK 112 598
28. SK 073 564
29. SJ 959 671
30. SK 070 639
31. SK 006 621

3 White Peak
1. SK 171 728
2. SK 177 714
3. SK 120 727
4. SK 088 769
5. SK 128 588
6. SK 151 514
7. SK 123 710
8. SK 114 638
9. SK 160 635
10. SK 110 525
11. SK 098 549
12. SK 141 531
13. SK 136 583
14. SK 131 583
15. SK 145 525
16. SK 128 837
17. SK 173 752
18. SK 153 609
19. SK 178 695
20. SK 140 731
21. SK 150 729
22. SK 133 834
23. SK 188 714
24. SK 158 779
25. SK 194 658
26. SK 172 681
27. SK 134 826
28. SK 132 505
29. SK 149 824
30. SK 095 560
31. SK 175 522
32. SK 127 604
33. SK 131 555
34. SK 152 757
35. SK 174 818
36. SK 150 665
37. SK 190 717
38. SK 090 669
39. SK 180 756
40. SK 180 756
41. SK 175 500
42. SK 188 543
43. SK 100 651
44. SK 123 523
45. SK 195 721
46. SK 151 733
47. SK 131 506
48. SK 176 660
49. SK 125 568
50. SK 126 659
51. SK 177 808
52. SK 106 591

4 Dark Peak
1. SK 269 859
2. SK 255 795
3. SK 211 640
4. SK 205 695
5. SK 336 724
6. SK 244 753
7. SK 259 692
8. SK 204 833
9. SK 199 770
10. SK 313 606
11. SK 204 749
12. SK 241 721
13. SK 246 773
14. SK 292 565
15. SK 322 524
16. SK 207 849
17. SK 260 814
18. SK 260 806
19. SK 262 738
20. SK 224 622
21. SK 243 627
22. SK 279 729
23. SK 297 587
24. SK 239 771
25. SK 374 547
26. SK 215 762
27. SK 228 763
28. SK 227 623
29. SK 235 621
30. SK 249 634
31. SK 358 593
32. SK 209 572
33. SK 300 571
34. SK 257 618
35. SK 269 565
36. SK 311 560
37. SK 222 822
38. SK 259 721
39. SK 246 778
40. SK 240 710
41. SK 220 764
42. SK 242 708
43. SK 255 657
44. SK 294 569
45. SK 332 669
46. SK 337 753
47. SK 231 815
48. SK 240 643
49. SK 299 608
50. SK 275 580
51. SK 229 542
52. SK 208 836
53. SK 200 779
54. SK 191 767
55. SK 221 609
56. SK 219 769
57. SK 294 606
58. SK 321 518
59. SK 235 831
60. SK 287 542
61. SK 293 659

5 Nottinghamshire
1. SK 537 538
2. SK 591 722
3. SK 434 868
4. SK 718 478
5. SK 447 318
6. SK 639 400
7. SK 828 832
8. SK 709 780
9. SK 517 229
10. SK 649 435
11. SK 451 313
12. SK 508 235
13. SK 824 826
14. SK 535 742
15. SK 748 779
16. SK 695 338
17. SK 438 384
18. SK 433 499
19. SK 634 531
20. SK 703 895
21. SK 759 651
22. SK 503 523
23. SK 691 729
24. SK 637 753
25. SK 593 666
26. SK 645 647
27. SK 612 624
28. SK 520 341
29. SK 761 799
30. SK 558 476
31. SK 567 350
32. SK 435 449
33. SK 675 602
34. SK 441 688
35. SK 603 647
36. SK 548 741
37. SK 677 468
38. SK 701 253
39. SK 682 354
40. SK 688 227
41. SK 694 572
42. SK 698 331
43. SK 671 238
44. SK 771 342
45. SK 707 499
46. SK 492 489
47. SK 838 341
48. SK 805 762
49. SK 710 607
50. SK 706 543
51. SK 629 516
52. SK 472 515
53. SK 829 834
54. SK 541 537
55. SK 543 732
56. SK 719 797
57. SK 723 344
58. SK 751 386
59. SK 681 329
60. SK 767 343
61. SK 607 658

6 Lincolnshire Wolds
1. TF 015 965
2. TF 104 700
3. SE 973 189
4. TA 340 019
5. SK 940 684
6. TA 321 007
7. TF 229 824
8. TF 547 775
9. TF 564 580
10. TF 485 893
11. TF 089 735
12. TF 144 681
13. TF 113 705
14. TA 115 189
15. TF 435 899
16. TF 189 616
17. SE 880 217
18. TF 349 650
19. TF 389 756
20. TF 280 929
21. TF 157 742
22. TF 133 874
23. TF 421 998
24. TF 265 806
25. TF 217 595
26. TF 421 762
27. TF 210 830
28. SK 985 709
29. SE 975 211
30. TF 196 634
31. TF 194 631
32. TF 260 695
33. TF 330 874
34. TF 308 960
35. TF 328 873
36. SK 685 717
37. TF 495 586
38. SK 946 835
39. TF 156 905
40. TF 219 594
41. TA 236 032
42. TF 214 640
43. TF 253 790
44. TF 183 727
45. TF 499 539

7 North Shropshire
1. SJ 143 113
2. SJ 156 129
3. SJ 351 173
4. SJ 393 154
5. SJ 328 158
6. SJ 435 329
7. SJ 453 391
8. SJ 548 396
9. SJ 332 165
10. SJ 287 372
11. SV 000 000
12. SJ 293 309
13. SJ 205 258
14. SJ 280 363
15. SJ 325 311
16. SJ 541 151
17. SJ 560 231
18. SJ 525 237
19. SJ 385 199
20. SJ 295 144
21. SJ 320 374
22. SJ 580 404
23. SJ 272 236
24. SJ 268 212
25. SJ 647 329
26. SJ 286 247
27. SJ 514 175
28. SJ 336 150
29. SJ 220 107
30. SJ 446 326
31. SJ 444 135
32. SJ 556 124
33. SJ 313 250
34. SJ 572 396
35. SJ 266 339
36. SJ 162 128
37. SJ 448 306
38. SJ 332 328
39. SJ 322 244
40. SJ 298 170
41. SJ 309 249

8 Central Staffordshire
1. SJ 889 555
2. SJ 984 227
3. SK 014 161
4. SJ 969 186
5. SK 056 246
6. SJ 995 225
7. SK 119 423
8. SK 143 437
9. SJ 999 493
10. SJ 795 305
11. SJ 707 377
12. SJ 898 555
13. SK 131 431
14. SK 114 340
15. SK 065 396
16. SJ 986 215
17. SJ 857 572
18. SJ 788 244
19. SJ 818 451
20. SK 034 442
21. SK 112 470
22. SJ 899 370
23. SJ 772 201
24. SK 019 170
25. SJ 797 308
26. SK 101 408
27. SJ 851 355
28. SK 026 476
29. SJ 995 231
30. SK 117 432
31. SJ 958 277
32. SJ 753 473
33. SK 000 491
34. SK 076 492
35. SJ 979 229
36. SJ 070 426
37. SK 132 438
38. SK 064 490
39. SK 094 411
40. SK 106 425
41. SJ 946 592
42. SK 127 291
43. SK 020 173

9 South Derbyshire
1. SK 163 481
2. SK 203 293
3. SK 369 285
4. SK 280 260
5. SK 339 272
6. SK 347 436
7. SK 322 400
8. SK 335 238
9. SK 377 225
10. SK 409 330
11. SK 380 491
12. SK 338 459
13. SK 375 432
14. SK 360 239
15. SK 162 327
16. SK 342 259
17. SK 303 271
18. SK 208 527
19. SK 303 515
20. SK 374 216
21. SK 249 380
22. SK 287 439
23. SK 306 265
24. SK 406 228
25. SK 322 494
26. SK 218 415
27. SK 179 466
28. SK 329 431
29. SK 303 360
30. SK 422 358
31. SK 345 451
32. SK 351 446
33. SK 266 501
34. SK 344 433
35. SK 264 371
36. SK 387 261
37. SK 374 286
38. SK 382 211
39. SK 146 469
40. SK 334 279
41. SK 232 517
42. SK 324 298
43. SK 357 291

10 South Lincolnshire & Rutland
1. TF 189 235
2. SP 837 909
3. TF 026 064
4. SP 928 984
5. SP 936 080
6. SK 932 062
7. SK 948 121
8. SK 864 136
9. SK 990 094
10. TF 241 103
11. SK 980 169
12. SK 937 156
13. SK 785 038
14. TF 397 423
15. SK 984 432
16. TF 079 203
17. SK 921 112
18. SK 948 387
19. SP 913 970
20. SK 924 111
21. SK 970 161
22. SK 880 363
23. SK 949 0
24. SK 913
25. SK 850
26. TF 113
27. SK 999
28. SK 812
29. SK 880
30. TF 145
31. SK 892
32. SK 922
33. TF 025
34. SK 833
35. SK 949
36. SK 993
37. SK 851
38. SK 929
39. TF 033
40. SK 939
41. TF 074
42. SK 916
43. SK 967

11 Shropshire Hills
1. SJ 540 0
2. SJ 186 0
3. SO 208 9
4. SJ 594 0
5. SO 297 8
6. SO 599 8
7. SO 436 9
8. SO 586 9
9. SO 336 8
10. SJ 533 0
11. SO 225 9
12. SJ 374 0
13. SO 367 9
14. SO 593 8
15. SO 351 9
16. SO 308 8
17. SO 328 8
18. SO 477 9
19. SO 415 9
20. SJ 390 0
21. SJ 383 0
22. SO 339 8
23. SO 481 8
24. SO 450 9
25. SO 304 9
26. SO 557 8
27. SO 567 8
28. SO 221 9
29. SO 247 9
30. SO 193 9
31. SO 521 8
32. SO 324 8
33. SO 506 9
34. SO 393 9
35. SJ 286 0
36. SO 222 9
37. SJ 342 0
38. SO 543 8
39. SO 289 9
40. SO 348 8
41. SJ 563 0
42. SJ 454 0
43. SJ 524 0
44. SO 348 8

O 297 882
O 323 897
O 609 994

**outh
ordshire**
O 774 785
O 746 865
672 033
O 765 801
O 724 954
O 748 893
O 820 852
O 935 918
O 933 803
U 737 141
U 826 075
U 624 000
U 643 043
O 873 911
O 900 929
O 852 847
O 827 821
O 767 992
O 933 869
U 643 095
O 915 734
O 751 764
U 694 025
O 954 883
O 762 765
U 728 003
O 732 997
U 701 020
O 637 876
O 765 801
O 887 768
O 778 886
U 954 037
O 808 958
O 897 908
O 923 796
O 715 925
U 630 063
O 803 787
O 644 780
U 696 024
U 769 123
U 662 045

**orth
ickshire**
P 207 961
K 331 141
K 033 081
P 023 918
K 031 043
K 253 047
K 304 173
P 215 957
K 213 186
P 091 820
P 209 928
P 194 983
P 053 987
K 067 131
P 317 943
P 296 754
K 044 127
P 312 893
K 259 075
P 092 964

21 SK 097 065
22 SP 323 879
23 SK 075 060
24 SK 216 181
25 SP 197 788
26 SK 262 073
27 SK 136 253
28 SK 294 008
29 SK 177 037
30 SK 378 065
31 SK 249 130
32 SK 084 135
33 SP 311 894
34 SK 342 000
35 SK 281 156
36 SK 102 105
37 SK 080 093
38 SK 128 292

14 Leicestershire
1 SK 569 176
2 SK 539 220
3 SK 579 153
4 SP 493 940
5 SK 539 121
6 SP 534 797
7 SK 556 148
8 SK 474 077
9 SK 463 170
10 SP 652 811
11 SK 605 102
12 SP 615 759
13 SP 547 978
14 SK 516 159
15 SP 799 862
16 SK 495 063
17 SK 494 133
18 SK 510 147
19 SK 460 148
20 SP 510 966
21 SP 438 795
22 SK 525 112
23 SK 523 046
24 SP 592 793
25 SP 737 831
26 SK 435 183
27 SK 354 059
28 SK 538 131
29 SP 455 813
30 SP 736 836
31 SK 751 192
32 SP 364 996
33 SK 764 011
34 SP 551 781
35 SP 544 844
36 SP 725 863
37 SK 570 009
38 SK 622 129
39 SK 412 176
40 SP 545 844
41 SK 552 129
42 SP 790 967
43 SP 798 929
44 SK 647 159
45 SK 368 092
46 SK 414 055
47 SK 354 064
48 SK 721 137
49 SP 699 903
50 SP 665 832
51 SK 581 040

15 North Herefordshire
1 SO 428 634
2 SO 526 507
3 SO 530 415
4 SO 438 736
5 SO 403 738
6 SO 506 744
7 SO 336 447
8 SO 473 393
9 SO 458 656
10 SO 390 584
11 SO 360 602
12 SO 359 717
13 SO 588 740
14 SO 400 632
15 SO 252 787
16 SO 408 692
17 SO 366 779
18 SO 482 702
19 SO 355 623
20 SO 454 440
21 SO 299 496
22 SO 335 475
23 SO 324 594
24 SO 592 776
25 SO 479 723
26 SO 483 770
27 SO 508 539
28 SO 329 597
29 SO 454 575
30 SO 425 654
31 SO 419 586
32 SO 394 564
33 SO 507 744
34 SO 517 610
35 SO 591 727
36 SO 556 636
37 SO 405 738
38 SO 543 512
39 SO 249 536
40 SO 302 568
41 SO 250 591
42 SO 468 649
43 SO 414 690
44 SO 390 581
45 SO 508 736
46 SO 403 688
47 SO 255 480
48 SO 627 565
49 SO 259 457
50 SO 400 425
51 SO 420 629

16 South Herefordshire
1 SO 477 172
2 SO 457 203
3 SO 395 265
4 SO 587 268
5 SO 566 279
6 SO 569 375
7 SO 561 384
8 SO 688 288
9 SO 723 308
10 SO 591 367
11 SO 580 354
12 SO 657 327
13 SO 344 385
14 SO 444 304
15 SO 320 291
16 SO 322 403
17 SO 405 244
18 SO 511 313
19 SO 627 303
20 SO 669 312
21 SO 319 431
22 SO 272 376
23 SO 368 294
24 SO 436 250
25 SO 331 348
26 SO 377 340
27 SO 357 329
28 SO 389 269
29 SO 375 271
30 SO 578 344
31 SO 699 256
32 SO 326 274
33 SO 318 340
34 SO 611 357
35 SO 340 249
36 SO 563 310
37 SO 541 299
38 SO 329 267
39 SO 363 406
40 SO 326 283
41 SO 376 425
42 SO 548 291
43 SO 568 347

17 The Malverns & Worcestershire
1 SO 744 603
2 SO 796 532
3 SO 714 658
4 SO 922 422
5 SO 952 451
6 SO 792 740
7 SO 762 380
8 SO 769 680
9 SO 778 382
10 SO 750 521
11 SO 670 558
12 SO 929 588
13 SO 860 404
14 SO 690 667
15 SO 885 428
16 SO 749 372
17 SO 668 570
18 SO 783 534
19 SO 662 584
20 SO 755 362
21 SO 979 402
22 SO 759 400
23 SO 956 402
24 SO 811 402
25 SO 748 531
26 SO 772 457
27 SO 797 526
28 SO 812 535
29 SO 841 407
30 SO 754 483
31 SO 804 674
32 SO 700 568
33 SO 838 419
34 SO 904 425
35 SO 851 587
36 SO 700 548
37 SO 776 469
38 SO 662 524
39 SO 750 519
40 SO 783 623
41 SO 751 412
42 SO 835 591
43 SO 787 749
44 SO 916 404

18 South Warwickshire
1 SP 260 574
2 SP 210 556
3 SP 143 523
4 SP 099 517
5 SP 237 565
6 SP 092 505
7 SO 997 459
8 SP 305 521
9 SP 080 636
10 SP 694 594
11 SP 079 470
12 SP 398 514
13 SP 410 618
14 SP 764 656
15 SP 285 723
16 SP 030 457
17 SP 202 568
18 SP 289 675
19 SP 767 660
20 SP 254 600
21 SP 210 713
22 SP 200 603
23 SP 592 548
24 SP 378 614
25 SP 386 598
26 SP 348 593
27 SP 331 427
28 SP 365 473
29 SP 439 651
30 SP 049 490
31 SP 359 658
32 SP 184 399
33 SP 241 471
34 SP 376 671
35 SP 300 446
36 SP 180 711
37 SP 138 599
38 SP 434 497
39 SP 093 437
40 SP 224 700
41 SP 373 685
42 SP 213 436
43 SP 373 474
44 SP 353 402
45 SP 015 572
46 SP 223 770
47 SP 567 681
48 SP 666 648
49 SP 389 660
50 SP 465 556
51 SP 616 606
52 SP 290 527
53 SP 218 696
54 SP 107 512
55 SP 529 653
56 SP 409 651
57 SP 375 671

19 The Wye Valley
1 SO 536 097
2 SO 549 144
3 SO 582 187
4 SO 557 166
5 SO 529 107
6 ST 543 975
7 SO 629 129
8 SO 523 093
9 SO 614 120
10 SO 565 054
11 SO 541 043
12 SO 562 115
13 SO 651 105
14 SO 589 088
15 SO 614 145
16 ST 547 973
17 SO 653 108
18 SO 542 140
19 ST 541 962
20 SO 541 122
21 SO 563 159
22 SO 575 179
23 ST 542 995
24 SO 534 091
25 SO 715 132
26 SO 499 051
27 SO 546 155
28 SO 670 157
29 ST 530 999
30 ST 537 964
31 SO 559 045
32 SO 737 143
33 SO 706 083
34 SO 535 009
35 SO 545 017
36 SO 548 173
37 SO 561 159
38 SO 672 232
39 SO 535 097
40 SO 553 095
41 SO 532 001
42 SO 536 063
43 SO 666 168
44 SO 548 005
45 SO 570 051
46 SO 553 104
47 SO 548 156
48 SO 558 045

20 North Cotswolds
1 SO 819 250
2 SO 867 299
3 SO 878 317
4 SP 274 119
5 SP 261 115
6 SP 327 112
7 SP 188 158
8 SO 904 148
9 SP 392 162
10 SP 295 308
11 SO 899 142
12 SO 814 173
13 SO 817 252
14 SP 021 254
15 SP 044 256
16 SP 043 277
17 SP 254 207
18 SO 892 147
19 SP 482 260
20 SP 063 299
21 SO 780 236
22 SP 113 362
23 SO 984 254
24 SO 931 165
25 SO 946 183
26 SP 061 291
27 SO 811 195
28 SO 981 198
29 SP 163 225
30 SO 904 169
31 SP 173 325
32 SP 282 118
33 SP 232 259
34 SP 226 203
35 SO 898 260
36 SO 813 304
37 SP 184 378
38 SP 204 131
39 SP 071 342
40 SP 243 227
41 SO 818 250
42 SP 088 293
43 SO 970 240
44 SP 112 147
45 SP 318 112
46 SP 396 292
47 SP 176 269
48 SP 206 292
49 SO 942 168
50 SO 802 262
51 SP 309 346
52 SP 175 204
53 SP 053 297
54 SP 066 105

21 South West Cotswolds
1 SU 205 989
2 SU 224 983
3 SU 230 980
4 SU 256 986
5 SO 885 087
6 ST 684 985
7 ST 953 845
8 SO 821 013
9 SP 162 005
10 SU 028 959
11 SU 068 941
12 SP 065 018
13 SO 786 029
14 SO 789 000
15 SP 020 014
16 SO 918 119
17 ST 932 972
18 ST 883 999
19 ST 980 995
20 SO 686 043
21 SO 937 033
22 SO 966 005
23 ST 805 860
24 ST 704 932
25 SO 874 085
26 ST 746 880
27 SP 053 067
28 SP 115 066
29 SO 822 068
30 ST 797 894
31 SP 053 129
32 SO 868 120
33 ST 747 948
34 SO 876 067
35 SO 820 088
36 ST 769 918
37 ST 743 956
38 SP 113 068
39 SP 042 036
40 SO 922 017
41 ST 818 874
42 ST 954 928
43 SO 895 024
44 ST 750 940
45 SP 076 051
46 SO 948 032
47 SO 965 005
48 SO 904 035
49 ST 758 963
50 ST 680 983
51 SO 777 053
52 SO 871 072
53 SO 914 114
54 SP 019 079
55 SO 862 028
56 SO 848 015
57 SU 223 990
58 SU 249 990
59 SO 813 008
60 SO 875 005
61 SO 938 034
62 SP 042 036
63 SU 285 994
64 SO 881 106
65 SO 874 098
66 SO 760 135
67 SU 173 990

Converting decimal degrees to minutes and seconds.

The whole number of degrees will remain the same (i.e. 50.1355° still starts with 50°). Then multiply the whole decimal by 60 (i.e. 0.1355 x 60 = 8.13). The whole first number becomes the minutes (8′). Take the remaining decimal digits and multiply by 60 again. (i.e. 13 x 60 = 7.8). The resulting number becomes the seconds (7.8″).

**Wild Guide
Central England**

Words:
Nikki Squires, Richard
Clifford & John Webster

Photos:
Nikki Squires, Richard
Clifford & John Webster
and those credited

Editing:
Candida Frith-Macdonald

Proofreading:
ProofProfessor

Design:
Oliver Mann
Marcus Freeman

Distribution:
Central Books Ltd
50, Freshwater Road
Dagenham, RM8 1RX
020 8525 8800
orders@centralbooks.com

Published by:
Wild Things Publishing Ltd.
Freshford, Bath, BA2 7WG

hello@
wildthingspublishing.com

the award-winning, best-
selling adventure travel
series, also available as
iPhone and Android apps.

Author acknowledgements:
In memory of our friend, Lee Fairclough, the real reason why we live each day as if it's our last. Your untimely exit from life led to a series of adventures which ultimately culminated in this book. This is for you.
Thank you to Daniel and Tania whose books and adventures initially inspired us to write our own edition of the Wild Guide. To The Hobbit Hut at Brookhouse Woods which gave us the perfect space to turn our book idea into a reality. To Stuart for walking up Kinder Scout on the hottest day of the year, for always giving support and showing a genuine interest in the progress of the book, and to Hailey for putting up with Stuart. Barry, Lucy and The Webblets to melted shoes, river swims and nettle rash. To Jon (plus Charlotte and the rabbits) for selflessly visiting pubs to provide extra photos. To Simon Mellor for dragging his family around a windswept country park, only for the entry to be culled during editing. Thank you to Candida Frith-McDonald for your meticulous fact checking and editing prowess. To Steve and Ian for Friday evenings.
To our families who continue to support our crazy adventures: Rachel, Ethan and Clarissa; Meg, Caitlin and Izzy for enduring walks up those hill forts in the rain; Val and Mark for scouting out Lincolnshire in one of the hottest summers on record, providing photography support, research and hot dinners; Ash and Bernadette for your support, advice and shelves; Janet and Graham, Michael and Arlo for aiding our research.
And finally, to all the people we met along the way who, often without knowing it, have made the contents of this book so rich and varied: your passion and enthusiasm for everything you do has truly inspired us, we hope we have represented you well.

Other books from Wild Things Publishing